PENGUIN BOOKS

Tears of the Moon

Tears
of
the
Moon

Guo Sheng

PENGUIN BOOKS

PENGUIN BOOKS

Penguin Books (NZ) Ltd, cnr Airborne and Rosedale Roads, Albany, Auckland 1310, New Zealand
Penguin Books Ltd, 80 Strand, London, WC2R 0RL, England
Penguin Putnam Inc, 375 Hudson Street, New York, NY 10014, United States
Penguin Books Australia Ltd, 250 Camberwell Road, Camberwell, Victoria 3124, Australia
Penguin Books Canada Ltd, 10 Alcorn Avenue, Toronto, Ontario, Canada M4V 3B2
Penguin Books (South Africa) (Pty) Ltd, 24 Sturdee Avenue, Rosebank, Johannesburg 2196, South Africa
Penguin Books India (P) Ltd, 11, Community Centre, Panchsheel Park, New Delhi 110 017, India
Penguin Books Ltd, Registered Offices: 80 Strand, London, WC2R 0RL, England

First published by Penguin Books (NZ) Ltd, 2003

1 3 5 7 9 10 8 6 4 2

Copyright © Guo Sheng 2003

Designed by Mary Egan
Typeset by Egan-Reid
Printed in Australia by McPherson's Printing Group

A catalogue record for this book is available from the National Library of New Zealand.

ISBN 0 14 301872 8

www.penguin.co.nz

Contents

Remember?
Remember . . .
This piece of bloodcurdling,
brokenhearted memory is
forever with me, us
&
I,
We
Remember it all . . .

To my family members
who did not live to see this book

Preface

Reader, the day after I moved into my Parnell apartment, I promised some old friends of mine, John and his wife Alice, that I would bake them New Zealand's finest scones for morning tea, at my new dwelling, the following weekend.

As all my good friends know, I am a hopeless hostess – one you must have a great deal of patience to tolerate! The promised day arrived and I was still crawling, just like an ant, on top of the hot stove in great despair – 'Come on! *Edmonds Cookery Book*! Where are you?' – with my guests' feet already on my doorstep.

'No rush! We just had our breakfast,' soothed Alice.

And so I made the scones, while Alice chatted to me and John stood at the big lounge window, gazing out at tranquil Parnell. Suddenly, he turned and asked, 'Do you know very much about Parnell – this tiny slice of Auckland?'

'This tiny slice of Auckland?' I repeated. 'Well, I know that in the early days they used to call it "Poor and Proud Parnell" – don't ask me why! It also used to be known as "Official Bay", because most of the government officials lived here. The Maori name is really Wai-ariki – which I'm pretty sure means "Waters of the Head Chief". That could be talking about the way the little bay is protected by Hobson Bay, or maybe there was a sacred spring nearby – right?'

I watched John's face as I reeled off this information, pleased by his surprised expression. It made me feel bold and full of knowledge. I continued, 'You know, in fact, in this tiny slice of Auckland a number of well-known names crop up again and again in the early stories.'

'Such as?' he interjected.

'Like Jean Batten, Goldie's brother, Sir John Logan Campbell, and –'

Not waiting till I finished, John asked most seriously, 'And who are Jean Batten and Goldie?' But as I went to answer him, he laughed, 'Yes, yes, alright! That's not too bad for such a tiny Chinese woman – living in one of Auckland's proudest suburbs; working in New Zealand's largest bank; baking New Zealand's finest scones for her guests; chatting about the famous citizens of the Queen City and one-time capital of New Zealand! Are you trying to show us Kiwis up?'

'What's that supposed to mean?' I replied, immediately angry and defensive. 'Since when are you a Kiwi and not me?'

'Take no notice of him! He's just trying to wind you up,' laughed Alice. She turned to her husband and said, 'Here are your scones dear; keep quiet and you can have as many as you wish. But if you keep winding her up you'll wear out your welcome and you'll have to bake your own hot-buttered scones!'

John chuckled at his success in needling me. He picked his scone up, took a big bite, then continued with his mouth full, 'Gee, not too bad eh! This scone is delicious. I just can't believe it's made by such a tiny Chinese woman. Oops, sorry, tiny Kiwi-Chinese woman!' Again he chuckled.

I went red. I turned to Alice and tried to retrieve the atmosphere by adding, 'In fact, I shouldn't really force your husband to say that. But sometimes, you know, with my unbalanced heart, I just can't help it.'

An awkward pause ensued so I continued, 'Do you know what my grandfather used to call me? "A little Oliver Twist!" He thought I was the one who would always demand something more. And now, when I look back, I realise he was perfectly right. You see, the day I left my homeland I vowed inwardly that I would never return. After I arrived in New Zealand I was determined to stay, and dreamed of becoming a New Zealander. Now I am one. And, indeed, straight away I longed for something more – I greatly regretted that my ancestors didn't plant me in New Zealand in the first place!'

'Why?' asked John and Alice simultaneously, with shocked expressions.

I could make no reply. Another long silence fell. It was John who made an effort to break it this time.

'Yes, why?' he repeated. 'We have known each other for many years now. Alice and I have always been curious about you. Why did you come to New Zealand? What made you abandon your career, family, life and everything over there, and later, even your citizenship? When you came to New Zealand you had absolutely nothing – no money, no family and not even a word of English. We saw you struggle; we saw you fight; we saw you diligently make your way, turning New Zealand into your second homeland. And now we listen to your desire to be "planted" in New Zealand. Why here? New Zealand is such a far-flung corner of the earth, thousands of miles away from the rest of the world. Sometimes we really don't have a clue about what's going on elsewhere. We pride ourselves on being hard-working, innovative, do-it-yourselfers with a real desire to succeed and so do your people. But why aren't your country-men as proud of their motherland as we are of ours?'

'Yes, why? Tell us why,' echoed Alice . . .

Why?

It's a long tale,
It's an unforgettable tale,
It's a bloodcurdling, brokenhearted tale and

It's hidden inside of me,
It's hidden inside of my family,
It's hidden inside of our people, our nation for many years

As I, we, found it
Far too hard to face,
Far too sad to recall,
Far, far, far too dreadful to pour out from my, our heart's core . . .

Prologue

The Guos

From the time I became old enough to understand, I knew that my family name was Guo and our native place was Ku-Shan province, lying in midland east China. But in fact our real family name is Kong and Ku-Shan isn't our native place. Our grandfather's grandfather was a poor lumberman, from Mohe, in Hei-Long-Qang province, a very cold forest belt right at the top of north China, by the border of Russia covered with snow all year round. The average temperature there is around minus five degrees Celsius but during the winter the icy wind lowers it dramatically to minus 20 to 30 degrees.

Because of the harsh climate with its poor living conditions, my grandfather's grandmother developed very severe rheumatic arthritis, so, in their early middle age, they decided to move away from this frigid zone and down south to their maternal native place Fei-Yn – a very poor village, lying between the branches of the Chang-Jiang and Huai rivers in Ku-Shan province.

The family settled happily in the south with its more temperate climate. My grandfather's grandfather soon found himself a job as a monorail steam-truck driver in a local coal mine, and his wife found herself expecting their seventh child. At that time, their fourth child, and the only son of the family, my grandfather's father Xing-Yun, had just turned nine. As the family was far too poor to send him to school, every day he had to go to work with his father and help with the steam furnace fire which, in turn, helped the family earn their living.

Spring went by, summer arrived and another new life – a son – arrived. The family was joyous, as my grandfather's grandparents longed for sons to fulfil their glorious dream – to build up the Kongs!

One night shift at the coalmine, a tumult of screams suddenly burst forth from the village below, followed by a cry – 'A mountain torrent has burst forth in our village!'

At this, hundreds of the local miners poured out of the mine and ran towards their homes. My grandfather's grandfather grabbed Xing-Yun, commanding him: 'Listen son! Don't move! Stay here and wait till my return!' With that, he swiftly closed the steam furnace door, locked his son inside the truck and raced after the others.

Another outburst of heart-rending screams swelled from the doomed village . . . then a dead silence . . .

The next thing Xing-Yun could remember, he was woken by a deep voice saying, 'Child! Wake up! Child, you are the only survivor of your village!'

When he opened his eyes, a black-faced miner cried and hugged him tightly. They marched, together with hundreds of other weeping miners, towards the village, which had become a vast expanse of water – covered by thousands and thousands of dead bodies. Some of them still had their cloth wrappings on their arms; some of the eldest children still held their younger siblings' hands in their own; some of the women still carried their babies on their backs; some of the men still clasped their elderly on their shoulders; some of them were facing down towards the earth, appealing for redress of grievance; some were facing up towards the heavens – their mouths, eyes and hands opened wide and pleading for mercy . . .

The miner gently put Xing-Yun down and they stood in silent tribute for a while, until the miners broke out with a tragic cry – 'Heaven, where are you? Heaven, can you hear us? Heaven, please have mercy on us! Please help us! Please bless us all . . .'

> *The flesh-and-blood mountains*
> *emitted a plaintive cry;*
>
> *The inferior village*
> *rued its powerlessness in a dead silence;*
>
> *The vast expanse of water*
> *repented its atrocious invasion and annexation;*
>
> *This homeless nine-year-old survivor's heart*
> *was broken:*
>
> *'Tell me heaven!*
> *Where is my home?*
>
> *Tell me heaven!*
> *Where is my family?'*
>
> *Child,*
> *Bear it!*

Child,
Live!

The monorail steam-truck
is now your home;

The miners
are now your family!

Two years later a diamond mine was discovered in India. One day the owner of the coalmine returned from a visit there, bringing a huge diamond; his companions carried a large box of wine and together they jumped onto their truck. They sat down, put the diamond beside them and began to drink heavily to celebrate their success. They carried on and on late into the evening, until everybody was dead drunk and had fallen higgledy-piggledy into a deep sleep. Their treasure was left completely unguarded. Suddenly, several brigands, menacing-looking strangers, crept onto the truck, stealthily looking around. Xing-Yun quickly took off his ragged winter jacket, covered the diamond, lay his body on top, and pretended to be asleep. And so tired was he, after such hard physical work all day long, that the profound quietness sent him into a heavy sleep.

Next thing he knew, he was being woken up by the owner's kicking and shouting – 'Bloody bastard! Get up! Where is my diamond? Tell me where my diamond is!'

'Diamond? I don't know,' answered Xing-Yun, still half asleep.

'Bloody bastard! Who said you were allowed to go to sleep? Bloody get up!' The owner carried on kicking and shouting and woke Xing-Yun completely.

Xing-Yun then jumped up, pulled away his jacket and

pointed to the diamond, saying, 'Here! Here is your diamond!'

When the owner saw his diamond was under Xing-Yun's body and covered by his jacket, he burst out in anger, like thunder, 'How dare you! I keep you for pity, bloody heartless bastard! Now you steal my diamond! Oh no! No! How could I be so blind as to give shelter to a thief! You stole my diamond and hid it under your jacket!' His blows and kicks rained down on Xing-Yun like a storm of shots and shells.

'Don't beat me! Let me explain. I didn't steal your diamond. I was helping you to hide it!' cried Xing-Yun, shielding his head and screaming with pain.

The words – 'I was helping you' – finally caught the owner's attention and stopped him short. After Xing-Yun had explained what had actually happened the owner burst into tears, and enfolding him, said, 'Oh, no! Sorry son. I am terribly sorry son. You are my hero! You are my honour! You've saved my lifeblood – my diamond!'

In reward, the owner of the mine arranged for Xing-Yun to work in his office as his teaboy. Later, Xing-Yun was told – 'I want you to be my shadow and follow me around everywhere. Wherever I go, you must go. I want you to learn, to acquire the knowledge of mining skills from me.'

Xing-Yun did remarkably well, learned extremely quickly, and grew surprisingly fast. At the age of 19, the owner took him as a son-in-law, married to his only daughter, to bear their family name – the Guos. And he gave Xing-Yun a new first name – Zhong-Chen. Zhong means sincerity and loyalty, Chen means honesty and unselfishness. The owner believed strongly that his protégé was a remarkably Zhong-Chen young man!

And so, this was where our Guo family name came from, and where we Guos physically began.

Soon, this young and vigorous family had five children, all sons.

Another three years later, the family was completed by the birth of their sixth child, another son, my grandfather. They provided their children with the best quality of education. Eventually, their eldest two sons inherited their father's business and they became mining experts. Another two of the sons were interested in the press and they became journalists. Another, who was drawn to politics, later became an official of Chiang Kai-shek's government. Their baby son, our grandfather, was really fond of the management of trade and enterprise and he became a successful businessman.

Sadly however, none of their children died from natural causes – their lives were all cut short by force. One son died during the Civil War in 1940; two died during the Land Reform Movement in 1950; another two died in a forced labour camp, during the Anti-Right campaign of 1957. And their baby son – my grandfather – died during the Cultural Revolution in 1966. Twenty-four years after the death of their baby son, in 1991, their baby son's only son, my father, also died suddenly and unexpectedly. His death was said to be from cancer.

But I do not wish to anticipate my tale. Once I have related my family's story you will be able to make your own judgement on whether my father really died from cancer, or suicide, or murder, or manslaughter – at the hand of his own flesh and blood, the one he used to love so dearly . . .

One

生日宴會

The Birthday Party

Saturday, 4 June 1983. Today was Yee Bing's birthday, and I had been invited to his birthday party at the White Swan Hotel. It was one of the largest and most prestigious hotels in Guanchou.

So I finished work early and rushed home. I had a quick shower, slipped into my mother's bedroom, sat in front of her dressing table and helped myself to her extensive selection of cosmetics. She was so lucky – the wife of a highly respected man, she had hardly ever been employed in her life; she belonged to no party, no society. What an unfettered existence! Absolutely carefree and able to enjoy herself. The nail polish, make-up and French perfume all there for her to take pleasure from.

Summer had just arrived, so I put on a milky cream hand-embroidered silk blouse and a pair of navy blue fine woollen trousers, very Western in their cut, and a pair of French-style black high-heeled summer shoes – clothes Chinese women hardly ever wore in public places since the Cultural

Revolution, so as to avoid being conspicuous.

'Where are you going?' asked Mum.

'A birthday party,' I replied.

'You look so beautiful today,' she said, with her proudest smile.

'Of course! Of course! My daughter is always beautiful!' chimed in Dad. 'Smell – the perfume is beautiful too. Very subtle. I can smell you, dear,' he added with a tiny hint of challenge, glancing at Mum. 'Look, why don't you sit down – I would like to take a photo of you,' said Dad, opening his camera.

Chu-zhi, chu-zhi, the light flashed twice.

'Thanks Dad!' I stood up, ready to go.

'What time is the party?' asked Mum.

'Seven o'clock,' I answered.

'Well, time for you to go, my dear daughter. And, listen, do not forget to find yourself a nice, suitable, handsome husband.' Now Mum's expression was serious.

'As we shall not be able to keep you for ever,' added Dad, serious too.

I was rather embarrassed and annoyed by such remarks. Especially my mother's – what exactly did she mean by 'a nice, suitable husband'? I simply said nothing and left for the party.

Yee Bing . . . Yee was his family name, Bing was his Christian name – meaning 'army'. For the Chinese, it was a very 'Red' name – a very 'Revolution' name. Not surprisingly, he came from a so-called 'Red Proletariat Revolution' family. Both his parents were members of the Communist Party and had been with Mao on the Long March when they were teenagers. After the Cultural Revolution Yee Bing's father became the chief commander of the Xuei-Chen military army. His mother became chief of the Communist Party Committee at the army's military hospital. They dwelt in a large mansion right in the middle of Guanchou city. This property used to belong to a famous businessman's family, a so-called 'Capitalist Class' family. During the Proletariat Cultural Revolution in China thousands of the Red Guards burst into these supposed Counter-Revolutionary, Capitalist private properties, forcing the occupants to leave at once. Many of them were evicted empty-handed – without even a scrap of paper to their name. They were forced to labour in their native town, or to live in a slum area, or in someone else's garret or garage. These brutal dispossessions were known as 'Sao Di Chu Men', meaning 'sweep away from home'. Then the Party's Cultural Revolution Committee reallocated these properties to the Committee high-ranking officials, like Yee Bing's parents.

Yee Bing was an only child. When the Cultural Revolution was launched he was aged just 15. Because of his family's background, one might even say his genetic inheritance, he eventually became a very radical Red Guard. He pledged loyalty to the Great Leader Chairman Mao, the Great Proletariat Cultural Revolution, the Nation and the Country. At the age of 22 he followed both his parents' footsteps and became a fully-fledged member of the Communist Party. Thus began his manhood.

I met Yee Bing after the Cultural Revolution. When the country finally awoke from its nightmare, education once again became vital. Both of us were studying at Guanchou University, receiving our long-delayed education. He was doing economics and management and I was doing accounting. Very often, we were at the same lectures and each question time Yee Bing had some smart challenge for the professor – who was not always able to answer it. This was, perhaps, the reason why he caught my eye.

To my surprise, when I arrived at Yee Bing's party he was waiting just inside the front door of the hotel. Instead of his customary army uniform, he wore a white short-sleeved summer shirt with an open collar, tan trousers and a pair of dark brown leather shoes. It was a somewhat unadorned and plain outfit but he looked extremely smart and handsome. This was indeed the first time I had seen him wear normal clothes. For Chinese people, wearing an army uniform was still very much in vogue – and even considered fashionable as well as revolutionary.

'Happy birthday!' I said, and handed him a present. It was a book of poems by Li Bei, a very famous Chinese classical poet.

'Oh, thank you! It's so kind of you. Poetry! Poetry! Just what I wanted. How did you know?' he said with great excitement. He put his arm around my shoulder and we walked together towards the reception desk.

'Where are all the other guests?' I asked.

'Right here!' he answered, then touched my face gently and added softly, 'You! You are the only one in this world I am dying to be with!'

His fascinating smile and glittering eyes fixed upon me and he reached my heart with his eyes . . .

After our two-person dinner party Yee Bing suggested that we go for a walk then go to his home for supper, and I agreed. We strolled through the park, next-door to the hotel. He steered us towards the bush-walk, which he knew was my favourite spot. When we reached it he took my hand gently, bent down and kissed me tenderly.

'I love you,' he said. Then quietly, 'Could we go home now?'

'Home? I thought the evening had just started!' I said, surprised.

'Yes . . . I . . . I mean . . . I mean my home,' he whispered nervously.

24

And, I don't know why, but I was suddenly like a helpless little girl, and I did exactly as I had been asked.

Yee Bing had a very powerful personality. He was extremely charming and charismatic, but also a bit wild. He would talk proudly about his time as a 'Great Hero' – a Red Guard – recounting how he had been an eye-witness to the cruelty of other guards and their severe punishment and torture of the alleged Counter-Revolutionaries and Capitalists.

One of these awful tortures was called 'Xiong Kie Xiong Lien', meaning 'inlay necklace'. They would force the accused Counter-Revolutionaries to parade through the streets in public disgrace with a very heavy wooden board hung from their necks with a thin wire. The board was covered with white paper, printed with phrases such as 'Down with Counter-Revolutionary XXX!' After a few hours, the wire would cut into their necks, their blood would start dripping all over the place, and many of them collapsed under the torment.

Another punishment was called 'Kao Ren Gan', which meant, 'roast or dry human body'. The Counter-Revolutionaries would be forced to stand under the strong summer sun, in front of Mao's image, to admit their errors and beg for punishment – from sunrise to sunset. They were not allowed to drink or eat, or to go to the toilet. If they survived the day, they then had to carry on into the next day, and on and on. Most of them fainted after a few hours, and some of them never regained consciousness.

Another was called 'Zhuang Go Dong', or 'through the dog kennel'. About 10 or 20 Red Guards stood in a circle with their legs apart. They forced those people to crawl through their legs. Some of the Red Guards used thick belts to beat the people's buttocks – forcing them to accelerate and crawl faster. One of the university's woman professors could not bear it, and she went back home and hung herself. Then she became 'Wei Shui Zi Sha', meaning, 'commit suicide to escape punishment'.

Then there was the most dreadful one called 'Zi Wao Chen Fa', which meant, 'self punish'. These innocent people were forced to slap their own faces until they swelled up. At the same time, they were made to call out loud – 'Wao Yu Zhu, Wao Ga Shi!' – meaning 'I am guilty, I deserve to die'. If they slapped their faces too softly they were made to butt their heads against a concrete wall. One well-known university professor refused to do so. They beat him up and threw him against the concrete wall and his blood and brains jetted out and he died instantly.

When Yee Bing vividly described these dreadful events in front of our classmates, some of the younger ones, who had come from working-class families with no experience of the Great Proletariat Cultural Revolution whatsoever, started screaming. They thought that he was exaggerating and making these horror stories up to frighten them. But to me, they were not foreign. I knew he wasn't exaggerating, nor was he making these stories up. The cruelty he so vividly eyewitnessed was true. This kind of inhuman torture had been experienced by myself and my family, together with millions of other innocent victims, for 10 long years.

Nevertheless, since Yee Bing had tried to make friends with me, I found he had changed a lot and was much softer and gentler. He even started to feel ashamed of mentioning the Cultural Revolution in front of me. One day he admitted to me, 'The more I mature, the more I realise that the Cultural Revolution has been cruel, barbaric and senseless. It really should be called the Cruel Revolution! I wish that one day the Party would make a formal apology to all the victims in public.' I was deeply touched by his comment. It couldn't have been easy for him to say so. Especially as he was a second generation member of a Loyal Proletariat Revolutionary Family and a Loyal Member of the Party.

Even more to my amazement, Yee Bing started becoming fond of the so-called Decadent, Dissolute Capitalist Class Lifestyle, and worshipped my parents! He frequently visited them, eager for my father to give him extra tuition in his economic studies. And from my mother he desired lectures on such classics as Chinese history, poetry and so on. Sometimes he would have long chats with my father – obviously on economics, not politics. In time, my father started to grow fond of him too, once calling Yee Bing 'a young charming'!

In my belief, love changes everything. And I believed that Yee Bing was truly changed. I did not want to listen to or question too much what he had done in the past – whether he was simply an eyewitness or really a participant; to me, it was all quite comprehensible and intelligible. During those years he was young and naive, and one could argue that he was one of the victims too. As for his family, well, unfortunately nobody can choose their family. Yee Bing's charming, charismatic nature and strong personality were most attractive, and that seduced me to forgive, to forget and to fall in love.

Upon our arrival at Yee Bing's house a uniformed soldier greeted us, then opened the gate. We walked down the long path towards the house, and when we reached the front door we saw Wu-Ma (their housekeeper) waiting there.

'Hey! Xiao Bing! ('Little Army', his pet name). Where have you been? It's nine-thirty! We all waited for your birthday dinner until eight-thirty, but your Mum and Dad had to go to an important meeting at eight o'clock.' She sounded a bit upset.

'Oh, sorry Wu-Ma. I forgot to tell you this morning that we'd planned to have my birthday dinner out.'

'We? You mean your Mum and Dad forgot?'

'Oh, no, no, I mean Sheng and I,' he said casually and strolled into his room. I followed him in. He closed the door, leant against it and began to laugh. 'Oh, goodness me! Eight o'clock's important meeting – waiting till eight-thirty!'

Someone knocked on the door. 'Yes?' Yee Bing called.

'Here's some tea and snacks for you. Can I come in?' asked Wu-Ma.

Yee Bing swiftly opened the door. He looked at the tea-tray with a huge smile. 'Wow!' he said with great excitement. 'How did you know? This afternoon I thought it would be very nice if you could make this for our supper tonight and you did. You just did! Thank you! You're the best. You're number one.' he said, putting his thumbs up.

It was a kind of sweet made with sugar, walnuts, sesame, peanuts and golden syrup. We Chinese make it for the Chinese New Year. It wishes happiness and good luck for the coming year. And I like it too, it's not too sweet but very tasty.

'Of course, you little rascal. I knew, I knew exactly what you wanted.' Wu-Ma said with a big smile, and then walked out closing the door behind her.

The truth was, Yee Bing had been brought up by Wu-Ma, like a half-mother. Because both of his parents were very radical revolutionaries and loyal Party members who devoted their whole lives to serving the military, the Revolution and the Party, Wu-Ma was sent by the Party to serve Yee Bing's family when he was born. So, in her mind, Yee Bing was always a little baby and had never grown up. What he wanted, he got. He had been so spoiled by her. That made him rather self-willed, quick to anger and uncontrollable at times. People could easily read both his happiness or sadness. Luckily, his charming, adorable nature balanced him a lot. Somehow, that made him even more attractive and popular with me, our friends, and our society.

'Now, this is all ours!' said Yee Bing, reaching for my wrist. 'Come, come sit here.' He pointed to his knee.

Again he started to kiss me, saying, 'I love you, I love you, I want you to be mine! Will you marry me?'

'Marry?' I was dumbfounded. The thought had never crossed my mind. I stared at him, not knowing what to say.

Suddenly he stood up. He sat me in the armchair and knelt on the floor in front of me. He put both of his arms on top of my knees, pushed his face very near to mine, and whispered softly, 'Please marry me . . . Please say yes . . . Please . . .' Then he cupped my jaw in his hands, held my face up gently and asked, 'Do you love me? Please say yes! Please answer me! Please!' He kept asking, again and again, and I could see tears welling up in his eyes.

'Yes. I love you.' The words were finally out.

'Will you marry me? Will you be my wife?' he pressed.

'Yes. I will,' I answered helplessly.

He was just like a dolphin, jumping up from the floor. 'Yes! You are mine!' he exulted. 'Yes! You are mine!' He kissed me and we embraced.

My heart was pounding, my blood was boiling. I loved him! I loved him dearly! If he was willing, I wanted to give myself away right then.

'You are mine! You are mine!' he kept repeating with great excitement, embracing me even tighter. I could hardly breathe.

'No, no, I am not going to touch you,' he cried and kissed me softly, then whispered right into my ear, 'I would like you to be the most proud bride in this world!' (According to ancient Chinese custom, the most proud bride in this world is a virgin bride.)

Then Yee Bing took a pad and pen and walked towards me, looking like a Most Sincere and Powerful General!

'Let us formulate a plan,' he announced solemnly. 'First of

all, the date. Ninth of the ninth? I like nine, it's a very lucky number, and means – "forever"! It's my favourite number too. And, it's your birthday too! Our birthdays are really special, aren't they? Look, today is my birthday and you became mine.' Then he put down his pen, placed both his hands on top of mine and asked, with his proudest smile, 'Ninth of the ninth, okay?'

'Yes,' I agreed immediately, then added, 'Nine is my favourite number as well –'

But not even waiting until I finished, Yee Bing interrupted, 'Will it be too long? Oh, no, I can't wait that long! Look, today is only the fourth of June, we have to wait for exactly three months and five days.'

He then added, after a pause, 'But, but, we must have plenty of time to get ready, mustn't we? Second. "Permission". Now –' He stopped and looked at his watch, then announced, 'It's 12: 45. Too late. Tomorrow morning early, you and I are going to get permission from our parents.' Suddenly he stopped. 'But . . . rather an announcement than a permission, I think.' He crossed out the word 'Permission', changed it to 'Announcement' and looked perfectly confident.

'What a great general!' I looked at him admiringly and laughed inwardly.

'Will you do that for me tomorrow morning first thing?' he asked.

'Yes. I will.'

'Promise?'

'Yes. I promise.'

'Now, third. The wedding arrangements. Oh, God! What a headache! Well –'

Here I interrupted him. 'Oh, no! It's nearly one o'clock in the morning! I've got to go. Mum will be terribly worried.' He looked at me, then at his watch. He seemed extremely disappointed. Finally he stood up and said, 'I will take you home.'

Before we said goodbye he held me tightly, then gently touched my nose and said, 'Remember your promise?' I nodded. 'I'll ring you tomorrow,' he added calmly and stood under the moonlight to watch me run upstairs.

The next thing I knew, Dad was gently shaking me awake. It was only seven in the morning but the sun was already high. 'Phone for you,' said Dad, passing the phone to me.

'Who is it?' I asked, half-awake.

'It's me, Yee Bing. Still in bed? Listen, I'm going to my parents' room now and I'll ring you straight back afterwards.'

Throwing the phone down, I jumped out of bed, still in my pyjamas and bare feet, hurried into my parent's room and saw that Dad was still sitting in bed reading the morning paper. Mum was in her dressing gown, carrying in some ginseng tea. I jumped onto their bed, gathered up my feet and sat cross-legged, like a Turk, and yawned.

'You were rather late last night,' said Dad, then teased, 'Did you find yourself a handsome husband like me?'

'Yes!' I answered excitedly.

'You did?' said Mum and Dad simultaneously.

I nodded, and smiled a bit nervously. 'I have got an announcement.'

'Are you going to be married?' asked Dad, shocked.

'To Yee Bing?' Mum interrupted anxiously.

'Yes. We are going to be married on my birthday, this year,' I answered very quickly with my heart pounding and my face burning.

There was a deathly silence. Then I raised my head and saw Mum standing there transfixed, staring at me in horror. 'Poun-Loooooooooooung!' A terrible noise. To my dismay, Mum dropped the tea-tray on the wooden floor. The cups and saucers

31

shattered. Mum's face had turned white as a sheet and her body was trembling. Dad was stunned too.

I pulled a chair towards her and helped her sit down. 'What's wrong Mum? Are you okay Mum?' I asked. Tears were streaming down her face.

'What's the matter? What's the matter with Yee Bing?' I kept asking repeatedly.

'How could you? How could both of your bloods mix together?' she eventually answered. 'Can't you remember the Cultural Revolution? Can't you remember what we went through? Can't you remember how we survived? Can't you remember the death of your grandparents? Can't you remember your sister's marriage? Can't you remember why we are now living here? Can't you remember who wrested our home, our house, our property from us? Can't you remember the ten years' humiliation, the bullying, the beating? Can't you remember the torture and the cruelties? Can't you remember? No, you can't! No, you've forgotten everything!' Mum's shaking voice finally ran out of breath.

I burst into tears and ran to my room. I slammed the door shut, swept all my vases, pictures, books and clothes onto the floor, then jumped into the bed and sobbed.

The telephone rang loudly but nobody picked it up. About an hour later there was a knock on the door, but nobody answered that either.

Between Mum and Dad's bedroom and my own was a glass door, so I could hear Dad berating her. 'How could you? How could you say that to her? She is no longer a little baby girl. She is a mature woman. She should be able to choose her own love. It hurts her! It will hurt her for her whole life. Especially as it is her first love.'

'I know that, but as a mother I have to!' I heard Mum reply. Do you forget that she's our flesh and blood? Don't you remember the political campaigns that convulsed our country? Who knows what will happen tomorrow? Another Cultural Revolution? Can you bear to see your flesh and blood suffer again?'

'Yes, I know. But, but, she's 30!' pleaded Dad.

'True indeed, but the Cultural Revolution stole 10 years from us. Think of her as 20! She is still young, there are plenty of opportunities and a bright future waiting for her. Why should she risk being involved with such a family?'

'It's all my fault! It's all my fault! I should have stopped her earlier.' Dad blamed himself again and again.

'How could we know? So many young people in and out, all the young men flattering her – how were we to know which was which?' soothed Mum.

'But do you realise how powerful his family are? Now everything done can't be undone. It will be a worse nightmare for her to refuse this marriage! Especially if she gives the real reason, the consequences will be serious. We could end up in jail. Do you realise?' Dad's voice was trembling.

'For my children, for this family, I am prepared to face whatever will be. But if she decides to go I shall have nothing more to do with her!' Mum declared adamantly.

I listened and listened, and my heart was broken.

Mum or Yee Bing? Yee Bing or Mum? I loved them both! How could I choose?

Two

真相

The Truth

The phone kept ringing all day but nobody would pick it up. I knew it must be Yee Bing. He was the kind of person who refused to give up. Until finally, at 10.45 pm, it rang again, and I took a deep breath and picked it up.

'It's me, Yee Bing. Where have you been? I've been ringing you all day and I've been to your home as well, but nobody was there. I was terribly worried. Why didn't you call me? What's going on?'

'Oh, I'm sorry,' I lied calmly. 'I had no time to ring you. Both my parents had food poisoning and I was at the hospital with them all day.'

'Oh, no!' said Yee Bing. 'How are they now? Still in hospital? Is there anything I can do to help?'

'No, thanks. They're okay now, at home, but very tired.'

'I'm so sorry to hear about it. There must have been no chance for you to talk to them?'

'No.'

'Well, don't worry about it, leave it till tomorrow,' he tried to comfort me, then rushed on, 'But I have great news to tell you – this morning I talked to *my* parents and they were so pleased to hear our announcement! They really appreciate your obvious intelligence, bright personality and your many qualities. They said as long as we are happy, they will be happy too. I am sure that will be your parents' answer as well.'

'Oh, thank you! How marvellous!' I tried to sound joyful to conceal my true feelings but I could not keep it up. 'I must go,' I pleaded, 'I'm exhausted!'

Still buoyed by his great excitement, Yee Bing blew a kiss down the phone to me and hung up. When I put the phone down, I saw Dad sitting there with tears in his eyes, watching me. He looked so sombre. Then he simply stood up, said nothing and walked away. It was the first time in my life I had seen my father cry.

Early the next morning Yee Bing called in unannounced. I quickly closed my parents' bedroom door, rushed into the bathroom, washed my face with cold water, tried to put a smile on my face and then opened the door to greet him.

'Are you okay? You look rather pale,' he said quickly and walked in.

'Oh, yes. I'm okay now. But I was very worried yesterday,' I replied.

'How are your parents now?' he enquired with concern.

'Fine. They just need to catch up on some sleep.' This way I hoped to stop him greeting them.

'Oh, you had me so worried all day yesterday!' he said, and hurried towards me. Then he held me tightly and added, 'Promise! Next time something like that happens, you must ring me so I can come and help.' He looked quite upset, and repeated, 'Will you promise?'

I nodded an apology, 'I'm sorry.'

Yee Bing and I agreed that I needed more time to recover from my exhaustion of the day before, so we went out. With the great disappointment and anxiety of trying to cover up my problems, I tried chattering to him as he led us towards the park that he'd taken me to on the night of his proposal. Suddenly I felt dizzy and the world turned black.

Next thing I knew, Yee Bing was holding my hand and calling my name. There were doctors and nurses all around me and I realised I was in a hospital emergency room.

'Yes, her blood pressure is rather low, and she's quite pale. Is there any chance she could be pregnant?' the doctor enquired.

'No, doctor. We're not married,' Yee Bing replied.

'Are there any emotional problems involved?'

'No – oh, yes. Her parents had food poisoning yesterday and she was in the hospital all day looking after them. She's probably worried and overtired.'

'How are you feeling now?' the doctor asked me.

'Fine, doctor. I might be overtired – I haven't eaten since the day before yesterday.' Which was true.

'Why not?' The doctor asked, rather confused.

'I forgot,' I answered calmly, then added, 'My parents were ill.' And I used this opportunity to let my tears out a bit, and decided the wisest course was to leave the hospital as soon as possible.

We went to the nearest café. Yee Bing bought me three cups of hot chocolate with lots of sugar, and he forced me to drink it all. It was rather crazy, but I felt much better.

'You gave me such a fright!' he said. Then he drew in his breath and added, 'I wish the ninth of the ninth was today – then I could take total care of you at once. I'll never allow anything like this to happen to you again! How come you forgot to eat for over 40 hours?' He looked at his watch in puzzlement and shook his head. I didn't answer him.

'Well, I will take you home now,' he said. 'Remember to have something to eat first, then have a rest. Ring me afterwards. I will be at home waiting.' He kissed me softly. 'I love you!' he said with a sad-looking smile, gazing at me.

It was the first time that I felt Yee Bing was not just smart and charming, he was also very thoughtful, caring and responsible. It gave me a wonderful feeling of security and safety.

Even though the Cultural Revolution was over, the legacy for our nation was a complete lack of trust. Through all the years of unpleasant harshness we had experienced, the strongest lesson we had learnt was that no one could be trusted except your own flesh and blood – and sometimes there were even doubts about them.

Yee Bing and I really did come from totally different family backgrounds. Under Mao, the Red Proletariat Revolution Class could never mix with the Counter-Revolution Class. Like fire and water, we were Life and Death Struggling Class Enemies, which made our love a very intricate and complex matter. Therefore, while I loved Yee Bing dearly, I lacked the confidence to be completely open with him, or to discuss everything with him.

We could discuss a book, a film, music, art or a classical Chinese poem over the phone for hours and hours, but as soon as he mentioned politics or his family background I would become a very quiet listener and wait for him to change the subject naturally. As for his curiosity about my own family history, I would simply say nothing then change the subject. The Cultural Revolution was far too recent, much too dangerous for me to discuss with him. I believed strongly that on this particular issue there could be no common ground between us.

When I arrived home I saw that Li-Yee (our housekeeper) was in the kitchen. She came Monday to Saturday to help my mother with the general housework.

'You are all home today?' she greeted me.

'Yes, we are having a long weekend, Li-Yee,' I replied.

Then I saw the shovel full of the broken vases, pictures and flowers. The mop stood inside the bucket with the duster nearby, all in front of my bedroom door. The door was closed, and when I opened it I saw that Dad had just finished tidying up the mess I had made yesterday. I knew my father, he didn't want Li-Yee to see it.

'Oh, sorry! Do you want to use your room? I'm finished now,' Dad said quietly. I felt a bit guilty. 'No, no, Dad, it's alright,' I said.

After my father left, I went straight to bed. About 15 minutes later, he came back with a bowl of hot noodle soup and said, 'Listen, you haven't eaten since yesterday. You must finish this off for me!' He stood there frowning at me for a while, and then walked away.

My mind was fully occupied by the problem of how I was to answer Yee Bing. I had absolutely no time to feel sorry for myself, but I knew very clearly that it was a thorny dilemma, that Mum was not a person to easily change her mind, and nor was Yee Bing a person to easily give up. What was I to do?

About five o'clock that afternoon, Yee Bing rang and asked whether I would like to have dinner with his family. I politely declined and we agreed to meet afterwards.

'How are you feeling now?' he asked, when we met, putting one of his arms round my shoulders and planting a huge kiss on my forehead. 'You are a worry! But how are your parents?'

'They are much better now, thank you.'

'Have you talked to them?' he pressed.

'Not yet . . .'

'Why not?' He sounded impatient.

'Before I make my announcement, I would like to have a discussion with you first,' I answered a bit nervously.

'What about?' He looked rather puzzled.

'Well, I've been thinking,' I began. 'To be married on my birthday this year seems much too rushed. Look, you have one more year to go to complete your Masters degree and I have another two years to go to complete my studies too. As you know, I also have a full-time job. It's not as easy as you think, being a full-time student. After we've got married, our parents will expect us to have a child, and no doubt our studies would be badly disrupted. To ensure we both complete our postponed education is the most important thing for our future careers. So, I believe it is wisest to put the completion of our education before our marriage,' I concluded. I thought this was the only diplomatic way for me to cool him down a bit, and also buy some breathing space for myself.

Yee Bing was totally stunned by my speech, and a long silence fell between us.

Finally, he cried with his sharp eyes fixed upon me, 'Is there any pressure on you to change your mind?' He moved both his hands on top of mine and held them tightly. 'Please tell me the truth! I want the truth!' His hands were like blocks of ice.

I was shocked by his extraordinary perception and his penetrating stare. I drew in my breath, and said as calmly as I could, 'I'm sorry, I don't mean to upset you. Please don't misinterpret it. It's the truth. I purely think of our future and our career paths.'

There was another deathly silence. Then he stood up and said, 'I will take you home.'

Two days later I received a letter from him:

Dearest Sheng,

With much respect for our true love, I have to accept what you suggested yesterday. I do not want you to be disappointed in either our love life or our career ambitions. I'll wait and love you forever!

However, despite my acceptance I must be very honest with you that I really do not want this. But I have to tell you everything from my heart, as I promised you before. Since I saw you early yesterday morning I have had a strong feeling that you have been hiding something from me, that there must be some pressure on you, and that you have found it too difficult to discuss it with me. I know you very well, Sheng!

In my heartfelt wish that our tragic history does not revisit this innocent generation, I want to shout:

'Please have mercy and let us dream!'

Please understand how much I love you! Please remember how much we love each other! Please treasure how much we would, could, should offer each other!

I love you for ever!

Yours, Bing

When I put the letter down, my tears were flowing.

Later, the door opened gently. It was my mother. She was carrying a cup of soup. When she saw I was crying, she put the soup on my little tea table near the armchair and sat beside me on my bed. She dried my eyes with her handkerchief, moved my head onto her shoulder, and then said softly, 'Sorry, Mum does not mean to hurt you, you should understand how much Mum loves you. But we have suffered enough, and Mum can't bear to let you, her own flesh and blood, live through another nightmare. Mum dreams of seeing you happy in a safe stable life, as Mum won't be with you forever. You are a young woman with romantic dreams, and that's understandable. But you have to realise that life is not like an illusion, filled with poetry and beautiful scenery. Especially in this society, where we have had to face the ruthless reality, the merciless history!'

'Mum, please stop!' I cried.

Mum burst into tears, walked out, and closed the door behind her . . .

Three

涙海

Tears of the Moon

Now, with my personal life falling to pieces ever since Yee Bing's birthday, I was terribly discontented and distracted. Furthermore, the time was close to end-of-year examinations. Therefore, I endeavoured to put everything behind me and get my life back to normal, as I needed time to cope with my heavy load of studies, my extremely demanding job, as well as to work out exactly what I should do afterwards.

However, one morning I received an unexpected phone call at my office. It was Yee Bing. He said that he wanted to see me very urgently. I asked him what it was about, but he said he preferred to discuss it with me in person. By the way he was talking, I could tell there must be something very wrong. I made a quick apology to my colleagues and rushed out.

When we met, I received neither kisses nor cuddles. Yee Bing looked dreadful, as though he had just been in a fight. His hair was terribly messy, his shirt collar was half in and half out, and he had no socks on.

'Tell me! Tell me what happened with your grandfather!'

he demanded at once.

I was shocked. 'My grandfather? He passed away a long time ago – it's been almost two decades.' I felt as though I was in the middle of a nightmare.

When Yee Bing did not respond, I yelled out, full of anger, 'What? Is this the really urgent question you had to ask me in person? Couldn't it have waited until I finished work? What's my grandfather got to do with you? Tell me!'

He was stunned. He just stared at me in a dead silence.

'Sheng, calm down!' he eventually whispered. 'Please understand, this is a really important thing for me to find out. I am the only child of my family, and our marriage is extremely crucial to them. It will directly affect both of my parents' political lives!'

'What? What's my grandfather got to do with your parents' "political lives"? Alright! If you really want to know about my grandfather, I'll tell you! He was persecuted to death by your ugly, dirty, cold-blooded Party! And your brutal Red Guards!' My tears were gushing out.

'Please don't cry,' begged Yee Bing. 'Tell me what happened. Tell me, please,' he urged once again.

After I had told him everything that had happened to my grandfather and my family he shook his head and looked at me with tears in his eyes. Then he hugged me tightly, kissed me and said, 'I am so terribly sorry. Remember I love you – forever!' I could tell the word 'sorry' was spoken from his heart.

Then he said, 'Yes, I know what your father is like. He is a very nice man, well-educated with a high standard of morality. He is very kind, warm, sophisticated and so easy to approach. How could his father be like that? He must have been innocent! I had a big row with my parents early this morning as I just couldn't believe –'

'What? My grandfather *like what*?' I interrupted. 'What was the row over? What don't you believe? Tell me!'

'After my parents agreed to our marriage,' explained Yee Bing, 'they had to give an account of it to the Party authority to obtain a political investigation of you and your family. They found out through your personal dossier that your grandfather was a long-term secret Japanese war criminal, a Japanese collaborator, and a secret Japanese spy with heavy blood debts. This had been uncovered in 1966, during the Cultural Revolution.' He described the accusations in detail.

From Yee Bing's description of the charges, I could tell that this so-called 'personal dossier' had been trumped up by the Human Resource Manager and Deputy Chairman of the Communist Party Committee of my company, a vindictive individual who was little better than a cold-blooded reptile. This man was grasping at power, deliberately attempting to destroy our career paths – especially of those employees who came from the same kind of family background as I did. We were struggling to obtain our promotional and educational opportunities – and now even our personal lives were at stake! What could I do? I felt utterly powerless. Suddenly his ugly face appeared in my mind . . .

'My break is almost over,' I told Yee Bing. 'I've got to get back to work.' I stood up, leaving him without even saying goodbye. I felt dreadful, as if things couldn't possibly be any worse. My poor grandfather truly was innocent!

Before the Japanese invaded China, my grandfather had been quite a successful businessman who owned three large factories and who had also been invited by the Guanchou local mayor's office to be a financial advisor. After the Japanese occupied the country, they wanted to build a large ordnance factory with railways in it in a slum area near Grandfather's factories in Cantu. If the deal was done, thousands would be homeless. The old and young; women and men; the incense and candles; the tears and kowtows – thousands of poor people knelt on the ground around Grandfather's house, imploring his help.

During that time, China, like other places in the world, was going through an economic crisis. Three of Grandfather's businesses were badly affected. Now, one way or the other, he had to decide whether to endeavour to maintain the family's fortune or to face bankruptcy but save the thousands. Grandfather chose the latter. He sold all his businesses and bought the land from the Japanese and the thousands were saved. He became a god of the poor!

However, after that, the only inheritance he had left for the family was a house and an uncertain future.

Then, during the 1950 Land Reform Movement, because of the large piece of land that my grandfather owned, he became the first major target in Cantu. Nevertheless, he, in turn, was saved by those poor thousands he had saved. They presented a big petition, marching to the local governor's house with pages and pages of signatures and thumbprints. Streamers were hung across the local streets all around.

'Please stop suppressing our proletarians' Saviour!'
'The land he bought was for us poor, not for himself!'
'Please purify the historical records; the land belongs to us!'
'Guo Ci-Xiang is not a landlord, he is a hero of the poor!'
'Please discriminate between "Mercy" and "Evil"!'
'Please discriminate between the "Saviour" and the "Criminal"!'
'Guo Ci-Xiang should be rewarded not punished!'

My grandfather was acknowledged as a most respectable hero of the poor of Cantu.

However, when the Cultural Revolution broke out, all

historical facts were swept away – no differentiation was made between black and white; no distinction was made between fact and distortion. My grandfather was questioned: 'How is it that those thousands of locals could not save themselves from the Japanese, but you could?' And suddenly he became a long-term secret Japanese war criminal, 'a Japanese collaborator and a secret Japanese spy with heavy blood debts'!

This all happened about the middle of May 1966 when I was 13. One Saturday after school, our gardener Hua Yei-Yei (Hua means flower, Yei-Yei means grandfather) opened the gate and I got very excited. Usually on Saturday after school we didn't have to do our homework straight away. Our grandfather was always waiting for us in the garden to take us out to afternoon tea – our prize for being good all week.

'Hey, Hua Yei-Yei! Where's my dearest Yei-Yei? Has he forgotten that today's Saturday?' I asked very loudly.

'Shhhhh!' Hua Yei-Yei put a finger to his lips then whispered, 'Be quiet! Your Yei-Yei has got some people with him.'

I was terribly disappointed. Then, when I was nearly at the door of the house, I saw a policeman from the area where we lived accompanied by a few very cold-looking men walking out of our house. I heard one of the men say to my Grandfather, 'I believe you have got our message today. We want you to have a good think during the weekend and we will be back next Monday morning at eight o'clock.' My Grandfather nodded as they brandished their swords and marched out.

'Who were those men Yei-Yei?' I asked anxiously.

'No! No questions at all,' Yei-Yei answered quietly and we walked into the house. Yei-Yei walked upstairs towards his room and Nana followed him. About half an hour later, Nana came down and told us that Grandfather was too tired today, that he needed some rest and could not possibly take us out this afternoon. We were told to keep quiet and make sure not to disturb him.

'Nana, what's happening?' I asked. I was mature enough to realise that there must be something wrong. But, to my grand-parents, I was their most beloved darling little granddaughter and always the baby.

'No! No questions darling. Please!' answered Nana, exactly the same as Yei-Yei.

That weekend I found myself suddenly much older and more mature. I helped Nana by keeping my Di-Di (younger brother) company, so Nana could have time to be with Yei-Yei.

During the night I had a dreadful nightmare. I dreamt that those cold-looking men were beating Grandfather with very thick whips. My grandfather had a rope wound around his body and I was screaming, 'Yei-Yei! Yei-Yei!' Next thing I knew, Yei-Yei was sitting on the edge of my bed, shaking me with both hands and calling, 'Sheng, wake up! – Yei-Yei is here with you.'

The weekend went very quickly, and soon Monday morning arrived. I got out of bed even earlier than Nana and walked into Yei-Yei's bedroom and asked whether I was allowed to stay home to be with him. Yei-Yei shook his head with a smile and said, 'No! You go to school. Make Yei-Yei proud. Don't worry. Yei-Yei is fine. There is just a little misunderstanding. It will be cleared up very soon.'

As I saw that Yei-Yei's smile had come back, I believed that I must have been overanxious. I gave Yei-Yei the hugest hug that I had ever given him in my life. 'I love you Yei-Yei!' I told him, and walked downstairs ready for school.

Before I left home, Nana held my hand and whispered, 'Remember! Do not tell anybody else in the class.' And I nodded to her in promise.

But after that Saturday the tranquillity of our vital, happy home was totally shattered. The adults stopped smiling, and they started disappearing from the dinner table as well. We hardly saw them each day. My grandfather and my mother stayed in my mother's study all day and all night. My grandmother always closed her bedroom door and sat beside the radio listening to the news intently. After work, the first thing Dad would do was close the dining-room door, with the *People's Daily* (Beijing's daily Communist Party newspaper) and the local newspapers spread out on the table. He read the articles very carefully, highlighted parts, then disappeared into my mother's study with them. Later, I understood that the press was a great power of political propaganda. In those days, all the political articles were written by the Party activists, who were ordered to write them by the Party's high-ranking officials. Those articles yielded vital hints as to the purposes of the political movement and its potential victims.

A week or two later, at school, our teacher told us that everybody had to attend an important assembly in the school hall. The headmaster marched in and announced that on behalf of the Great, Glorious, Right Communist Party of China, the Great Proletariat Cultural Revolution was officially launched, and that the school's end-of-year examinations had now been cancelled. All normal classes were suspended too, as everyone had to take part in this political movement – to make a revolution.

After that assembly, we were given paper, pen, ink and some newspapers to copy, and spent all day making Big Character Posters for the Great Proletariat Cultural Revolution. We were told that the more Big Character Posters you had drawn, the more revolutionary enthusiasm you showed!

Day after day during our last year of primary school we drew posters. We did not even understand what the Great

Proletariat Cultural Revolution really meant or what the Big Character Posters were for. We all got bored.

Then one day after school, on our way back home, my classmate and best friend – Xiao Ling-Tong (his nickname meant 'small well-informed sources') – asked me, 'Do you like Cao Lao-Shi (Teacher Cao)?'

'Why, don't you like him?' I cautiously questioned him back.

'He's so boring!' complained Xiao Ling-Tong. 'He makes me sick! I really don't see why we must write those Big Character Posters every day. What's it all for? He can't even explain what this Great Proletariat Cultural Revolution is all about. I tell you, he's a real idiot! He should let me teach the class. I could teach it far better than he does!' he said, with his proudest expression.

'Oh, come on, Xiao Ling-Tong!' I said. 'Don't be so opinionated and supercilious. He's our teacher – be respectful.' I had great sympathy for Cao Lao-Shi, he looked exactly like my father – so worried, so anxious. And, with his knitted brows, he looked like an old man.

'No, I'm not.' Xiao Ling-Tong looked a bit upset. 'I tell you very honestly – I really do know far more than him! And I can explain it far better than he does.'

'Well then, tell me. What?' I challenged.

'First you have to promise me that you'll never, ever tell anyone in our class.'

'What do you mean? About what? What are you going on about, Xiao Ling-Tong?'

'No! First, you promise – just as I have promised Mama and Papa that I shall never, ever tell anyone in the class.' His face was very serious and he held up both hands.

I raised mine up and clapped them against his. 'Okay! I promise.'

'Cross your heart?'

'Of course. I'd double-cross my heart if I had two.'

'Well, one night I heard Mama and Papa whispering in the kitchen. They said that in the middle of March, Chairman Mao convened an extraordinary meeting of the Politburo Standing Committee in Shanghai, and singled out four men for particular rebuke. One was playwright Wu Han, the author of the increasingly controversial book *Hai Rui Dismissed from Office*. The others were Beijing history professor Jian Bozan, and the vice-mayor of Beijing, Deng Tuo. He also named the director of the United Front Work Department of Beijing municipality, Liao Mosha. And Chairman Mao proposed launching a Cultural Revolution in literature, history, law and economics, and called upon the Politburo Standing Committee to criticise leading bourgeois intellectuals.' Xiao Ling-Tong delivered all this in a rush, almost running out of breath.

'Really?' I yelped with fright.

'Shhhhh! Be quiet!' He put his finger to his lips, looking around in horror.

Then he continued in a whisper, 'But listen to the worst part! Another day, I heard Papa whisper to Mama that Chairman Mao wrote his own Big Character Poster, entitled "Bombard the Headquarters!" In fact, this was Chairman Mao's defiance against the Party leadership and was a signal that the battle is about to begin. Papa said that Chairman Mao's ultimate targets were Chairman Liu Shaoqi and Deng Xiaoping – as they disapprove of this Great Proletariat Cultural Revolution. They say that they are old revolutionaries facing new problems and they do not yet understand how to carry out this revolution. But Chairman Mao said that they were not old revolutionaries facing new problems, but instead were old counter-revolutionaries against the Great Proletariat Cultural Revolution! Papa also said that, in fact, it really is an inner-circle power struggle within the Party. I don't really understand what Papa means by "power struggle". Anyway, he said that Chairman Mao said, "Wo Xi

Huan Tian Xia Da Luan." ("I love great upheavals"). And that recently Chairman Mao wrote a letter to a group of rebel university students, called the Red Guards, in which he praised them and told them – "To Rebel is Justified!" So, you wait and see – Tian Xia Ke Yao Da Luan La! (There will be great upheavals!) But –' Here he suddenly stopped and his eyes watered.

'But what?' I urged. Then I saw his sad expression. 'Are you okay, Xiao Ling-Tong?'

He nodded and sighed. Then he continued, 'But you must keep your promise not to tell anybody in the class! Otherwise my Papa will be like those four poor men and fall on evil days! When Mama and Papa found out that I knew everything they had discussed, they cursed me for eavesdropping on adults' conversations and punished me by making me stay in my bedroom all day without food. They forced me to examine myself and to write a self-criticism, and to promise not to tell anybody in the class. And so I did. But I am no longer a little boy – I am a man, an adult too – I had my first –' He suddenly stopped and went extremely red.

I knew why he went so red, and I had had a very similar experience at home to his. Mum, Dad, Yei-Yei, Nana, they always thought of me as a little girl who would never grow up. In fact, I was no longer a little girl. As a confirmation, I had had my period; I was a woman, an adult too. Then I remembered the day I had my first period, how I cried and thought I might die soon, as I had such severe bleeding. Nana smiled and held my hand and said calmly, 'Don't cry! It's not illness. It's the human body's evolution. It means that your body has matured and you should be congratulated that you are now a big girl! Besides, remember – it's a girl's secret, you should never discuss it with boys, as boys have their own maturing.'

So I said instead, 'I'm so sorry, Xiao Ling-Tong! Your Mama

51

and Papa are far too hard on you. Unjust! You are an adult too! Why shouldn't you be totally trusted and share the confidence of adults? Unjust!' I repeated with great sympathy.

We stood there silently for a while, and I then asked, 'Are you okay?'

He nodded, and then we raised our hands up simultaneously and clapped them together. We made a secret pact and went our separate ways back home.

I believed what Xiao Ling-Tong had told me. I had once heard my mother say that his father was one of the high-ranking officials of the Propaganda Department of the Chinese Communist Party – so news from him was always true and accurate. Xiao Ling-Tong could be a bit opinionated and arrogant, but he never lied.

So, now I knew what was going on. I now understood why my mother was staying in her study all day and night. It seemed that Mum was in similar trouble to the playwright Wu Han. As a voluntary civilisation propagandist of the Neighbourhood Committee, Mum often wrote articles in the local newspapers and magazines on their behalf. 'She is a knowledgeable intellectual,' my teacher had once said in front of the class. Perhaps Mum had been criticised already, like Wu Han. Only, somehow, I didn't think Mum was as important as Wu Han.

After my teacher spoke of Mum in class, I had told Yei-Yei about it. Yei-Yei said that Mum wasn't a knowledgeable intellectual, that she was a fledgling civilisation propagandist – an amateur. He said that she was just like us, she had so much still to learn. Now I hoped that Yei-Yei was right and that Mum was not like this poor Wu Han. Nevertheless, I began to worry about my mother.

But I still couldn't understand or work out what was happening with my grandfather. He was neither an intellectual, nor a politician. 'He has absolutely no interest in politics whatsoever,' I heard Nana say once in front of guests. Yei-Yei was a clever businessman with a big heart – I knew that for sure! Yet he would never do anything against the People's Government – I could say that without doubt. So, why? Why was Yei-Yei now staying in Mum's study all day and night? What had this Cultural Revolution to do with him?

On Sunday morning, the seventh of August, Hua Yei-Yei's grandson Lao-Er, our pedicab driver, got bored, as for the last couple of months we had hardly been out. He came to my room and asked whether I would like to play table tennis with him and I agreed. Di-Di followed us down. The table was set up next-door to the garage. When we got there, Di-Di saw his bicycle, hopped on it and disappeared into the garden. Lao-Er and I started playing.

Suddenly, we heard the dreadful sound of a police jeep's siren. We stopped playing instantly, and listened until it stopped. Then our doorbell rang very loudly. I saw Hua Yei-Yei rush to the gate, look through the small hole at the top, then turn towards Lao-Er and whisper urgently, 'Police jeep! Policemen! Go and take Di-Di to his room, he's in the back of the garden.' He turned to me and said, 'Go and tell Nana and Yei-Yei!' Hua Yei-Yei's face had turned white.

I rushed into the house and ran upstairs. I saw Yei-Yei and Mum coming out of the study and towards the stairs. I blurted out, 'Yei-Yei, there is a police jeep and policemen outside!'

'Go to your room!' Mum ordered.

Lao-Er rushed up carrying Di-Di on his shoulders, then put him down and said to me, 'Come here and watch Di-Di. I'll get your sisters!' He flew out and closed my bedroom door behind him.

My window was just above the front door of the house facing

the gate. So we stood there, watching and waiting, to find out what was going on. We waited about 15 minutes. Then I saw my grandfather, handcuffed, walking out from the house, with the policemen behind him. I started shuddering.

'Oh, no! No! Yei-Yei!' Di-Di cried out and opened the door and ran downstairs. He clutched desperately at Yei-Yei's leg, wailing, 'No! My Yei-Yei! No! My Yei-Yei! No! –'

'Get lost! Bloody fuckin' bastard!' one of the big, strongly-built demon-looking policemen yelled out. Then he reached out a large fat hand, grabbed Di-Di's shirt collar and threw him about six or seven metres to the ground below. Di-Di immediately stopped crying. Yei-Yei cried, 'No!' and tried to run over to Di-Di but the evil man stopped him. Then Hua Yei-Yei rushed across and picked Di-Di up. He shook him, trying to revive him, but without success. Mum rushed over too. Lao-Er quickly pulled his pedicab out of the garage, and Mum carried Di-Di to it and they raced off to the local hospital.

Hua Yei-Yei then ran towards this evil man, seized his collar, and punched him in the head, shouting, 'You! You bloody bastard! He's just a little child! You've killed him, and now I'll kill you!'

They fought each other. With the other two policemen assisting this evil man, they grasped both of Hua Yei-Yei's arms and pulled them down behind him, then handcuffed him very tightly. Then they shouted, 'Fuckin' bastard! Fuckin' bastard!'

Hua Yei-Yei kept screaming, 'You bastards! You have handcuffed a third generation of the Proletariat! You have handcuffed a saviour of our poor! I have been with his family all my life! I know exactly how he and his family saved the poor!'

'Shut up! Fuckin' bastard! Shut up!' one of the policemen shouted, then they pushed Yei-Yei and Hua Yei-Yei into the jeep and the siren started its dreadful sound. They took our Yei-Yei and Hua Yei-Yei away . . .

I was shocked and trembling, and felt absolutely powerless to help. Suddenly, I remembered that A-Yee Nana (our house-keeper, a typical old-fashioned loyal Chinese Buddhist) had a small Kan (a little pavilion specially built for setting Buddha's images) set up behind our kitchen. I ran downstairs, and when I reached it A-Yee Nana was already there. She was kneeling on top of a thick red velvet cushion in front of an image of the 'Thousands Hands Buddha'. Her eyes were closed, tears were streaming down her face, and both her hands were folded in prayer.

'Thousands Hands Buddha', A-Yee Nana once told me, was a most powerful and kind Buddha, who had thousands of hands and was always willing to help people. Those hands helped thousands, millions, billions and zillions who were in despair.

'A-Yee Nana,' I called very quietly, 'I am not a Buddhist, but could I pray for Yei-Yei, Di-Di and Hua Yei-Yei to return home safely?' She opened her eyes, then merely nodded and continued her prayer. I moved another cushion near to her, imitated her, and invoked the blessing of Buddha in a special prayer . . .

We waited and waited. Finally, later that evening Lao-Er returned, with Mum and Di-Di in the back of his pedicab. But there was no Yei-Yei and Hua Yei-Yei. As we saw them come back, we all ran downstairs. When Di-Di walked in, Nana ran towards him and held him tightly, then she cried out and we all joined in. Di-Di started screaming again, 'Yei-Yei! Where's my Yei-Yei?' Mum reassured him, 'Yei-Yei will be back very soon.' And she sent him to bed straight away. About midnight, I was woken by Di-Di's screaming – 'Yei-Yei! Yei-Yei! Yei-Yei!' He had run downstairs to the front door and was trying to open it. Dad rushed down after him then gently picked him up and said softly, 'Di-Di, wake up! Dad is here with you. Yei-Yei will be back very soon.' But even after Di-Di awoke, he still cried loudly and continued to call, 'Yei-Yei! Yei-Yei!'

I have always believed, ever since that day, that Di-Di was saved purely by the Buddha, even though I am not a follower of that religion. On one side of our gateway was a concrete floor with the garage and our children's playhouse, and on the other side was a grass lawn. When Di-Di was desperately clutching one of Yei-Yei's legs, he was on the grass side. That evil man walked towards Di-Di and his right arm was by the grass side as well, and then he threw him out just like a piece of screwed-up paper! If Di-Di had held Yei-Yei's other leg, which was by the concrete floor, I have no doubt he wouldn't be living in this world any more.

Next morning was Monday. Despite Sunday's nightmare, Dad still had to go to work. Before he left, he gently woke me up, then said to me, 'Don't forget to keep Di-Di company today.' Dad knew very well, even though Di-Di and I had a four-and-a-half year gap between us, that we always got on very well. Di-Di liked to follow me around and play with me. After Dad left, I rushed into Yei-Yei's room. To my dismay, his room was tidy and empty – he had not come back home during the night. I quickly went upstairs to Hua Yei-Yei's room, and he wasn't there either. I had to find out what had happened to them. I ran into Nana's room and saw her on her bed, with her tearful eyes fixed upon the ceiling in a frozen stare. 'Nana, are you okay? Nana, don't cry! I love you Nana! Yei-Yei will be back today,' I soothed. As I tried to comfort Nana, I finally comprehended that Yei-Yei must be in very great trouble.

About four o'clock that afternoon Hua Yei-Yei returned home, but still no Yei-Yei. Hua Yei-Yei had a black, bleeding eye – half-closed – and bruises covering his face, neck and arms, and even his hands. We were shocked. When he saw Di-Di was there, his bloody tears streamed down and he held him tightly.

'Oh, thank Buddha! You came back! You came back from death! Owww –' He put Di-Di down instantly, and held one of his eyes as he walked upstairs towards his room. Nana, A-Yee Nana, Mum and Lao-Er all followed him up. About five minutes later, Lao-Er quickly pulled out his pedicab and Mum held one of Hua Yei-Yei's arms and helped him to sit in it. They rushed off to the local hospital.

Mum did not return until next morning. We found out that Hua Yei-Yei had had a five-hour operation, and that Mum had stayed with him until he woke from the anaesthetic. About a week later he returned home, with a thick bandage around his head and covering his left eye. Later, Dad took him back to the hospital, but the news was shocking – Hua Yei-Yei's optic nerve was badly damaged and his left eyesight was permanently lost.

During the time of Hua Yei-Yei's recuperation we waited for our Yei-Yei to return but, sadly, nothing happened. Our house was under siege and we were seized with terror. Outside, our garden wall, which was about three metres high, was covered with Big Character Posters and slogans containing vehement denunciations, with violent language against Yei-Yei and Mum, and, soon after, about Nana and Dad as well. That made us extremely fearful. Every day people banged on our gate, ordering Mum, Dad and Nana to read those posters and slogans.

At that very time, on the eighteenth of August, Mao stood atop Beijing Tiananmen to review the Red Guards and he told a young woman named Shog Bin-Bin (Bin-Bin means genteel) 'Yao-wu-ma!' (Be violent!) – and the young woman took his words for blessing, changed her name to 'Song Violence', and transformed from a woman who once would panic at a dead cockroach, into a so-called 'revolutionary' – who would beat people to death without even a blink. The news spread all over the country. One of Mao's quotations, highlighted and carried on the front pages of the newspapers, read – 'A revolution is not a dinner party, or writing an essay, or painting a picture, or doing embroidery; it cannot be so leisurely and gentle, so temperate, kind, courteous, restrained and magnanimous. A revolution is an insurrection, an act of violence by which one class overthrows another.'

The Cultural Revolution was no longer leisurely and gentle.

Everything Xiao Ling-Tong had told me was coming to pass. Mum was now also under attack. All her articles in the local newspapers and magazines over the past years were now criticised as 'Poisonous Weeds'. They called them Anti-Communist Party, Anti-Socialism, Anti-Revolution. Mum had now became a First Class Counter-Revolutionary and we were all members of a First Class Counter-Revolutionary family. Xiao Ling-Tong had predicted there would be great upheavals, and now, indeed, there were.

One night I saw Nana, Dad, Mum, A-Yee Nana, Hua Yei-Yei and Lao-Er sitting in the living room. I could hear Dad saying very clearly, 'We are terribly sorry about what has happened to you Da-Su (Da means big, Su means uncle – Mum and Dad both called Hua Yei-Yei this name). Obviously you understand very well that our house is now under attack. My mother, wife and I have had a discussion and we would like to suggest that you all go to your own safe homes or relatives for a while, until this Revolution has ended. Certainly, all of your financial matters will be our responsibility. We know you will be badly missed by us all, especially our children. But it's for your safety. We couldn't bear to see you suffer any more violence.'

'No, you shouldn't say "Sorry" to me. It is they – the Party who owe me this blood debt!' Hua Yei-Yei replied in a very aggrieved tone, then added, 'Your father is our three genera- tions' saviour. He has helped me all my life and saved us all.

Without your father's mercy we would have no happy family life. He has done so much for us and for so many years. This is the only time and opportunity for us to do something for your family in return. We must stay and protect you!'

And Lao-Er agreed, 'Yes, Yei-Yei is right. We must stay to protect you all. I am young and strong!'

And A-Yee Nana cried out, 'No! No! It's my home! How could I leave you all while you are under attack? I am not going to leave you while you are in difficulties.'

Then I heard Mum say, 'We very much appreciate your kindness, but you have to understand the situation. Nobody knows what will happen next. It's for your safety. You have supported us for many, many years. You don't owe us anything at all. Now it is time for you to protect yourselves. We must not be selfish and keep you here. You must leave without delay.'

'Yes, she is right. It's for your safety. But you will still be very welcome back here, when it's safe to return,' Nana added.

One day later, very early in the morning, the doorbell began to ring incessantly. Di-Di ran into my bedroom and over towards the window. He gave a shout of excitement – 'Yei-Yei! My Yei-Yei is coming home! My dearest Yei-Yei is coming home!' But the way the doorbell rang it didn't sound like our Yei-Yei. Despite my pessimistic feelings, I went on hoping to invoke our Yei-Yei's safe return and rushed towards the window too. To my horror, it was the local policeman and another five of the cold-looking men.

Di-Di was terrified and started screaming, 'No! No! No –'

Dad rushed in and held him tightly. 'Di-Di, no crying! Dad is here, you are safe. You must stay with your sister. Dad will be back very soon.' Then he went into his room and changed his clothes and, together with Mum, walked downstairs. Hua Yei-Yei came down, calling for Di-Di, and took him into his room.

About half an hour later I saw A-Yee Nana holding one of Nana's arms. They were standing in front of the house. Nana looked absolutely numbed and could hardly move, her eyes vacant, as Mum and Dad walked out together with those men. Lao-Er simply closed the gate then ran towards Nana and, taking her other arm, helped her inside.

After that day, Nana had no tears, no speech, no food, no sleep and the whole house turned into a silent tomb. But, outside, the Big Character Posters excited the violent mob at night. Very often they wore army uniforms and hats, with their faces covered by large gauze masks. They would climb over our garden wall and burst into the house. Brandishing army belts and knives, they demanded everything of value, such as money, jewellery, watches, even food (rice) coupons. We were living in complete terror! Hua Yei-Yei and A-Yee Nana then took over our grandparents' position in the house. They arranged for A-Yee Nana to move into Nana's room, where she sat with her all day and night. Di-Di moved up to Hua Yei-Yei's room. Lao-Er moved down to the living room. My sisters and I all moved into our parents' room, next-door to Nana's.

Then a week or two later, on the third of September, around eight o'clock in the morning, we heard slogans being shouted and a dreadful sound coming closer and closer to our house. We all ran into my bedroom and peered through the windows. To our horror, there was a long procession and our parents were in the middle at the front. Mum was wearing a tall dunce cap made of cardboard with 'Down With The First Class Counter-Revolutionary!' written on it. Around her neck was a big heavy board covered with white paper and the words 'Down With Counter-Revolutionary Ling Yuxin.' (Mum's name) written on it with a big red cross. Dad was kitted out the same. On his dunce cap was written 'Down With The Anti-Revolution Capitalist Class!', and on his white board was written 'Down With The Anti-Revolution Capitalist Class Guo Jinren' (Dad's name), also with a big red cross. The mob wore red armbands with the yellow words 'Red Guard' on their left arms. In their right hands they held the Little Red Book with its red plastic cover. It contained the quotations of Mao's thoughts. The crowd were shouting the slogans and marching towards our house.

Leniency to those who confess their atrocities!
Severity to those who refuse!
Disobedience is a road to death!
Down with Ling Yuxin!
Down with the First Class Counter-Revolutionary Ling Yuxin!
Down with Guo Jinren!
Down with the Anti-Revolution Capitalist Class Guo Jinren!
Down with the cow's demon and snake spirit!
Long live the Great Proletariat Cultural Revolution!
Long live Great Leader Chairman Mao!
Long live Great, Glorious, Right Communist Party of China!
Swear to die in defending the Great Proletariat Cultural Revolution!
Swear to defend the Great Proletariat Cultural Revolution to the
    last!

Suddenly they halted and started banging on our gate. One of the Red Guards shouted in a heavy Beijing accent, 'Open the gate! Open the gate, fuckin' bitch!' (In those days, the Red Guards from Beijing were the most violent Red Guards in China.)

But not waiting for the gate to be unlocked, the Red Guards simply pushed it open and more then a hundred of them came bursting in towards the house.

After they entered, they started shouting and barking orders immediately. 'Where are the bitches? All come here immediately! Can you hear? All come here, fuckin' bitches!' Then they charged upstairs. When they saw Di-Di one of the Red Guards shouted, 'Are you deaf? Fuckin' bastard! What are you up here for? Get down now!' Then I heard Hua Yei-Yei defending him very loudly – 'I am a third-generation proletarian. He is my grandson.'

'No! It can't be! How could your grandson look like a capitalist, wear such nice clothes and leather shoes?' one of the Red Guards yelled at him.

'Don't insult our proletarians! We should wear even better clothes than they do, shouldn't we?' Hua Yei-Yei said, firmly closing the bedroom door.

Then they went to order Nana to come down. A-Yee Nana walked out of Nana's room to the hallway, also protecting her very loudly – 'I am a third-generation proletarian. She is my blood sister. She is now very ill, it's my duty to keep her in bed.' Then she returned to Nana's room, shutting the door as well.

'What? What's the illness? Feigning death? No! She must come down! And now!' the local policeman yelled out.

After they forced Nana down, the local policeman made his announcement:

'Anti-Revolution Capitalist Class Lee Li (Nana's name) and all the Worthy Progenies! Here are our Chairman Mao's Fellow Red Guards, they have come from our Red Capital to fulfil our Great Leader Chairman Mao's mission to question you and search for evidence of your antipathy towards our Socialism, our Red Revolution, our Great, Glorious, Right Communist Party, our Great Proletariat Cultural Revolution, and to get rid of the Four Olds! (Old culture, old customs, old habits and old ways of thinking.) To rebel, to take revolutionary action against you all!'

At this the Red Guards chanted:

Rebellion is justified!
Get rid of the Four Olds!
Establish the Four News!
Without destruction, we cannot establish!
Support whatever the enemy opposes!
Oppose whatever the enemy supports!
Leniency to those who confess their atrocities!
Severity to those who refuse to!
Disobedience is a road to death!
Long live the Great Proletariat Cultural Revolution!
Long live Great Leader Chairman Mao!
Long live Great, Glorious, Right Communist Party of China!

Then the policeman continued:

'First of all, you must all abide by our Fellow Red Guards' stipulation – to hand over all your evidence of Anti-Revolutionary crimes! Such as all the weapons that you have concealed for so long!

'Second. You must all abide by our fellow Red Guards' stipulation, to hand over all your cruel exploiting crimes! Such as all your household keys, bank safety box keys, bank accounts, cash, jewellery, and any other valuable articles.

'Third. You must all confess, criticise your atrocities and expose each other!

'Fourth. You must all be very earnest and tell the truth! This is our Party's policy.'

The Red Guards chanted:

Leniency to those who confess their atrocities;
Severity to those who refuse;
Disobedience is a road to death!

'If you continually play your old hand of trickery and deception, the consequences will be very serious!' He then turned to the Red Guards and said, 'Fellow Red Guards, our Great Leader Chairman Mao is earnestly instructing us:

'When the enemies with guns are annihilated, the enemies without guns still remain. We must not underestimate these enemies.

'After the enemies with guns have been wiped out, there will still be enemies without guns; they are bound to struggle desperately against us, and we must never regard these enemies lightly. If we do not now raise and understand the problem in this way, we shall commit the gravest mistakes.

'The enemy will not perish of himself. Neither the Chinese reactionaries nor the aggressive forces of US imperialism in China will step down from the stage of history of their own accord.'

Again, the Red Guards chanted:

Down with the First-Class Counter-Revolutionary!
Down with the Anti-Revolution Capitalist Class!
Down with the cow's demon and snake spirit!
Enemy must surrender, or be doomed to perish!
Swear to die in defending the Great Proletariat Cultural Revolution!

*Swear to defend the Great Proletariat Cultural Revolution to the
    last!*

The policeman continued: 'My Young Fellows! My Fellow Red
Guards! We must remember our Great Leader Chairman Mao's
earnest instruction – "A revolution is not a dinner party, it's an
insurrection, an act of violence by which one class overthrows
another." Our Great Leader Chairman Mao now personally
guides us to take part in this Great Proletariat Cultural
Revolution. He now gives us the power and the mission.
Are we to be unworthy of this untiring and sincere teaching
and earnest instruction? Are we to fall short of his expectations
of us?'

'No! Of course not! A thousands times not!' the Red Guards
chorused in unison. 'A millions times not! A billion times not!'
they shouted.

'Well done, my Young Fellows! Well done, my Fellow Red
Guards!' he praised them. 'What should we do now?'

And again the Red Guards shouted as one:

Revolution is justified!
Rebellion is justified!
Without destroying, cannot establish!

With that, they were like a pack of mad dogs. They started
shouting, howling, smashing, banging, burning, and beating.

One of the Red Guards seized Nana's hair and slapped her
face. 'Why do you have such shining permed hair and wear
outlandish Western clothes?' he snarled. 'Look, you bitch!
Your trousers fit and are so tight! Look at your leather shoes –
sharp-pointed! Look, fuckin' bitch! Full of the Four Olds!'
Then another briskly handed him a pair of scissors and a razor.
They cut off half of Nana's hair just like the Nazis barbered the

hair of the Jews, and the other half they simply shaved. The legs of her trousers were torn open and they forced her to take off her shoes.

Then the other Red Guards yelled out: 'And those other fuckin' bitches – those Worthy Progenies!' and pointed at us. 'Why do you all wear your hair in long braids and dress in those outlandish Western clothes? Look! Your dress is so short! Look! Leather shoes! Look! Such little bitches, all wearing necklaces and watches! Look! They all look like Yang Run! (Western people). Look! Fuckin' bitches! Full of the Four Olds!' The shouting came from all directions. Rough hands were immediately laid upon us and our hair was hacked off on the spot. Then they cut our dresses and forced us to remove our necklaces, watches and shoes.

One of my sisters was terrified and started screaming out, and they kicked her until she collapsed onto the ground. Then they jumped on her back, and shouted: 'Bloody fuckin' bitches! Bloody fuckin' Worthy Progenies, you fuckin' bitches!' My sister was howling in pain. We all tried to pull her up, to save her. Then they seized each of us by the neck, pinned our arms back and dragged us separately into different rooms.

Meanwhile, all the chairs, furniture, pictures, vases, clothes, shoes, bed linen, books, photo albums, records and toys rained like shells upon the ground beneath the windows. A massive bonfire was lit in our garden as they started to destroy everything, everything and everything, as though it was all Four Olds!

About six or seven of the Red Guards now burst into my room. They banged their thick army belts on top of my small desk loudly and then one of them shouted, 'Listen! Bloody bitch! Bloody fuckin' Worthy Progenies! Now it's time for you to draw a clear line of demarcation from your Anti-Communist Party, Anti-Socialism, Anti-Revolution Counter-Revolution grandparents and parents. You must confess, accuse, expose and criticise their atrocities. You must be in earnest. If you adopt your parents' cunning ways the consequences will be very serious!' One of the Red Guards suddenly shouted the slogans:

Leniency to those who confess their atrocities!
Severity to those who refuse!
Disobedience is a road to death!

My hackles rose, and I was trembling as I stared at them. I had utterly no idea what they were talking about. What did they really want? What ought to be my response? I decided the best way for me was to keep silent.

Another Red Guard banged his thick belt on my bedhead with a loud crack. 'Talk! Talk, bitch! If you do not talk we will beat you to death!' he roared.

I then quickly said, 'My grandparents and parents always taught us to be obedient to our Great Leader Chairman Mao's earnest instruction – "Study well, make progress every day".' This was a quotation of Mao that I had learned at school.

'Fuckin' bitch, you're trying to protect that pack of fuckin' Counter-Revolutionaries!' yelled one of the Guards.

Another Guard seized my hair, slapped my face and threw me onto the floor. 'Fuckin' bitch!' he screamed. Then belts, punches and kicks showered upon me.

'It's true!' I screamed with pain. 'Don't beat me!'

A Guard shouted, 'Yes! It's true! Fuckin' bitch! You tell lies! You lie!' as he hauled me up by the hair, slapped my face hard and kicked me viciously in the groin. I reeled in agony, lost my balance and fell. The back of my head dashed on the corner of my desk, and blood started pouring from my head and nose.

'Don't beat me! Don't beat me!' I kept screaming and begging.

Suddenly the door opened, and Lao-Er came bursting in and grabbed me. We ran downstairs towards the garage and he said to me, 'Quick! Get in.' I climbed into the pedicab, but as he tried to pull it out, the Red Guards were right behind and shouted at us, 'Stop! Stop! Stop!' They pulled me down from the pedicab, upended it and, using their boots and rocks from the garden, began to smash it up.

Undeterred, Lao-Er took his shirt and singlet off and passing his singlet to me, said, 'Come on! Hold your nose with this!' Then he used his shirt to cover the back of my head to stop the bleeding and hustled me quickly out of the gate.

The street outside was packed with people, including a pedicab driver standing on his cab watching the mob inside. 'Hop in,' Lao-Er said to me, and to the driver, 'Go! Hospital!' The Red Guards chased after us shouting, 'Stop! Stop! Stop!' but the pedicab driver exerted every ounce of his energy to start his vehicle and responded loudly, 'Only a kid!' and ran to the local hospital.

When the doctor saw me, she looked very uneasy and asked Lao-Er what was happening. After Lao-Er had described the attack to her she said, 'Come with me,' and we followed her into the operating room. She cut more of my hair off, used disinfectant to wash my head and applied some local anaesthetic before she put the stitches in. Then she dressed the wound. Afterwards she gave me an anti-tetanus injection and told me, 'Now you are safe.' When she saw the bruises which covered my body, I saw tears leak from her eyes. She sent me to the X-ray room, to check my bones, and found that one of my arms was fractured. She then sent me to another room and my right arm was wrapped in a plaster bandage.

When we returned to her, Lao-Er asked if I could stay in hospital for a couple of days, until the Red Guards had gone. She shook her head and said, 'No. Do you think here is a safe place for her? Maybe even worse! It's much better for her to go back home with you.' She frowned at my tears, which were pouring down my face, and added, 'But I could put some extra bandages on her arm and head, just in case she gets another beating.' She then gave Lao-Er lots of extra bandages, disinfectant and some antibiotics, and said to him, 'Actually, the thick dressing is not good for her head wound, it should be a thin dressing, to let it get some air to dry quickly – especially during this hot summer. But you must make sure the wound is washed twice daily and the dressing is changed each time as well. Those antibiotics must be taken four times daily and should be started as soon as possible. Here are some painkillers, for after a while she will certainly need them. Remember, once the Red Guards have gone, take the outside head bandages off at once. The most important thing to remember is that she must be back here for a check within three days.

And by the way, she has lost a lot of blood, so you had better give her some milk with some light food before you take her home. It will give her some energy. Yes, and also start her first antibiotics,' the doctor added as Lao-Er thanked her and we left the emergency room. Only then did he realise that he had no top on! He quickly went back to the emergency room, dug his shirt and singlet out of the rubbish bin, although they were covered in bloodstains, then found the nearest toilet and pointed to a chair beside the door. 'You hold your medicine and sit here, I've got to go inside and rinse these before I put them on.'

Just as I sat down, I heard a terrible shouting from the ward above the emergency room: 'Bloody fuckin' Counter-Revolutionary!' I looked up in time to see a middle-aged woman jump out from a seventh-floor window. With an horrific bang, her head struck the concrete ground only a couple of metres from where I was sitting. The white brains and blood jetted all over the floor like a fire engine's pump, covering my whole body – even my face and head! I screamed in horror. Lao-Er rushed out from the toilet and used his body to shield my face. Then he held me and said, 'Don't cry. I am here, you are safe.' My whole body was shaking, both of my legs were like soft sticks, and I could hardly walk. Lao-Er used his hand to rub her blood and brains off my face and hair as best as he could, and then he quickly put me on his back and ran towards the front gate of the hospital.

When we reached the gate, three of the Red Guards who were involved in my beating were waiting there. When they saw us, one of them shouted again, 'Bloody fuckin' bitch! Where are your legs?'

Lao-Er then set me down on a chair by the gate, and said softly, 'Come on, she is very ill now. Look, those are her medicines. Be kind, she is just a kid. We are all lucky, born into a right family! Aren't we?'

One of the Red Guards looked at him, looked at me, and shouted, 'Feign death! Bitch!' Then added, 'We want you back at the house as soon as possible!'

'Of course, of course,' Lao-Er answered very quickly, and they marched away.

Lao-Er carefully watched them disappear up the street before he took me across to a food store. He bought me some milk and small lemon cakes, saying, 'The doctor said you have lost a lot of blood. You must eat them now. It will give you energy. But I really don't understand why they ordered you back home as soon as possible. What's happening over there now?' he wondered.

When I had finished the milk, Lao-Er gave me the antibiotics, but I couldn't eat any of the cakes as I felt so dreadful. While we were there, a group of people clustered around us, staring at me. Some of them asked Lao-Er what had happened to me. And then I realised that our clothes were covered with bloodstains, my head and arm were all covered in bandages, my face was covered with bruises and bloodstains, the bottom of my dress was cut very unevenly and the left side was ripped open right up to my waist.

'No worries, she just had an accident, fell over on the floor,' Lao-Er told the crowd. Then he quickly finished off all the cakes and asked, 'Are you okay now? Shall we go?'

I agreed and we tried to get away as quickly as possible. But although we left the food store straight away, the 'noseys' still followed us, and some of the children even threw rubbish at me.

When we got outside, we saw about five or six people carrying a middle-aged man, blood drenching his body and dripping all over the street. They were running towards the hospital. Red Guards were pursuing them and shouting, 'Stop! Bloody fuckin' bastard, stop! Bloody fuckin' Counter-Revolutionary, you deserve to be dead!' Then all the 'noseys' followed them instead.

My legs felt like they were made of cotton-wool and I felt dizzy. When I told Lao-Er, he said, 'Close your eyes, I am here, you are safe now.' Then he hailed a pedicab, and I asked the driver to close the curtains as we slipped away from that street of 'noseys'.

Almost immediately we heard another huge noise. The pedicab stopped for a while, then the curtain pulled open, and the driver said to us, 'Gee, another three dead bodies! A couple holding a child jumped out from a tall building together! The street is blocked by a sea of people. Would you like to stop here, or pay some more and I could take you home by another way?' We agreed to pay some more.

It must have been about two o'clock in the afternoon when we

71

finally arrived home. To my horror, the fire was still burning, but even larger and higher! The whole street was filled with the smoke, all coming from our garden. Our gate was now pulled down, and there was an audience sitting on the ground, from the garden right out into the street. The 'Struggle Assembly' was taking place. Nana, Mum and Dad were kneeling on top of the table-tennis table, in front of the garage, facing the crowd. Some of the Red Guards were standing behind them, with army belts in their hands, pushing their boots into my parents' backs. My sisters were standing beside the table with their heads down. In front was our large old mahogany dining table, its broken legs propped up with bricks. The local policeman and six other cold-looking men sat at it, with a megaphone before them. A Red Guard beside them held a portable megaphone, while another held Mao's Red Book and led the assembly in shouting slogans.

When they saw Lao-Er and I walk in, one of the Red Guards shouted at me, 'Come here!' and directed me to stand beside my sister. Lao-Er said very quickly, 'Look, these are her medicines, she is very ill now, the doctor said she has to be in bed immediately, not allowed to stand. She must have these medicines every four hours and change the wound dressing twice daily.'

'Fuckin' bloody bitch! You feign death!' one of the Red Guards growled at me, and Lao-Er hastily took one of my arms and indicated that I move as quickly as possible.

To my horror, I saw that the whole house had become a ruin – totally smashed and destroyed in just half a day! Broken glass, furniture, clothes, shoes, books, papers, photos, records, hair and bloodstains covered the path. Inside the house, all the glasses had been smashed, none of the door or window glass was left, not even the mirrors. Pictures, vases, flowers, wine glasses, plates, rice bowls, cups and saucers were all smashed to pieces upon the floor. Were these the Four Olds that, without destruction, the Four News could not establish?

When A-Yee Nana saw us walking in she called out, 'Careful!' and then ran towards me with tears in her eyes. She held me tightly and asked in a very low voice, 'Are you okay?' I nodded, my tears pouring down. A-Yee Nana used her handkerchief to dry my face and helped me walk into my room. She carefully cleared all the glass off my bed and changed the sheets. Then she took me into the bathroom, helped to wash me and put clean clothes on me, and made me feel much better. But when she helped me lie down on my bed my whole body started aching, and when my head touched the pillow it was extremely sore. I tried to turn to the other side but my body could hardly move. A-Yee Nana gave me some painkillers with a cup of tomato, chicken and ham soup, which was left over from yesterday. She then whispered, 'Poor thing! Close your eyes, try to get some sleep. A-Yee Nana will sit beside you. You are safe now.' Lao-Er quickly used the broom to clear away all the glass inside my bedroom, and then the mop to swab my bloodstains off the floor.

Through the broken windows of my bedroom I could clearly hear the assembly still going on outside. A-Yee Nana sat beside me with her face towards the windows. And the painkiller sent me, dazed, to sleep.

But suddenly I heard A-Yee Nana call out, 'Oh, no! Your Nana has fainted! Don't move. Stay in bed. I will be back shortly.' She ran out and I heard a very loud shouting, 'Feign death! Bloody fuckin' bitch, you feign death!' Followed by more shouting of the slogans through the megaphone:

Down with Lee Li!
Lee Li feign death, must surrender, or be doomed to perish!
Down with Capitalist Class Lee Li!
Down with the cow's demon and snake spirit Lee Li!

Down with Counter-Revolutionary Lee Li!
Lee Li must confess!
Lee Li must make a clean breast of her guilt!
Leniency to those who confess their atrocities!
Severity to those who refuse!
Disobedience is a road to death!

I tried to sit up. I looked at the clock on my bedroom wall. Despite the glass face being smashed, the hands were still moving and I was shocked to see that it was almost 7 pm. I then moved to the window and saw that the crowds were already heading towards the street, and Lao-Er, A-Yee Nana and my sisters were carrying Nana into the house. I heard my eldest sister call out loudly, 'Quick! Give Nana some ice water! Quick!' Then Lao-Er ran towards my parents and tried to pull them up from the table-tennis table. He lifted the heavy boards from around their necks and helped them down. They stood there for quite a while, as if dazed, before they slowly made for the house.

The deathly silence was broken by the local policeman, who yelled out: 'Listen! Cow's demon and snake spirit Guo Jinren, Ling Yuxin! You two stay here tonight, but don't you talk or move. We will be back tomorrow!'

He carried on: 'My Young Fellows! My Fellow Red Guards! Should we allow only nine to occupy such a three-storied mansion, to have this kind of decadent dissolute Capital Class lifestyle, with three servants?'

'Of course not! A thousand times not! A million times not! A billion times not!' the Red Guards chorused.

'Well said my Young Fellows! My Fellow Red Guards! What should we do now?' he incited them further.

'Confiscate! Confiscate all!' they started shouting.

Rebellion is justified!
Revolution is justified!
Get rid of the Four Olds!
Establish the Four News!
Without destroying, cannot establish!

Before they finally left, the policeman threatened, 'Listen! Cow's demon and snake spirit Guo Jinren, Ling Yuxin! Now all your rooms have been sealed. You are not allowed to touch anything. Everything has to stay exactly where it is. You are not allowed to move. We will check tomorrow. If anything is touched, the consequences will be serious! You will be punished severely.'

Finally it grew quiet, and we were alone . . .

After the mob had left, I heard quiet footsteps on the stairs and saw A-Yee Nana and Lao-Er helping Nana up towards A-Yee Nana's room. Following behind were Dad, Mum and my sisters. Mum and Dad walked into my room. Mum bent down, put her face on my forehead and asked softly, 'Are you alright?' I nodded. Then they helped me out of bed and I followed them. A-Yee Nana helped Nana lie down on her bed, with us all around her. I could not even recognise her as my Nana. She looked so frail, and extremely pale and ill. With her hair half shaved, half unevenly cut she looked like a Holocaust victim. Nana opened her eyes to find Dad. When she saw Dad and Mum standing beside her, she asked Dad in a faint voice, 'Where is your father?' Dad just stared at her with no reply. Then she closed her eyes, her tears streaming down, and we all cried together in silence.

The beginning of September was the end of summer in Guanchou. Inside, the temperature averaged around 25 degrees Celsius, while outside it was more than 40. Throughout that endless Struggle Assembly in the afternoon heat, all the spectators, the policeman and the Red Guards wore their hats and placed themselves under the trees. Mum and Dad wore their tall dunce caps, and my sisters stood in the shadow of the garage. Only our poor Nana had had absolutely no protection from the merciless sun. How could our Nana, aged 68, be expected to cope with it? Since they had taken our Mum and Dad away she had hardly eaten anything or slept. This brutal persecution and humiliating abuse was aggravated by the pitiless sun, and now Nana grew very ill.

When A-Yee Nana brought Nana a cup of clear soup she shook her head. Then A-Yee Nana, with tears in her eyes, passed it to Dad, who said, 'Mum, please drink it for us all.'

'Mum, please drink it for Dad,' my mother added. Nana simply did not reply.

How changed Mum and Dad were in just two weeks. Both of them had lost a great deal of weight, and had been given the same haircut as Nana. Mum's vibrant personality and confidence had vanished and, with her bloodless cheeks, she looked absolutely gloomy. Dad's healthy looks had also totally disappeared and, with his wrinkled brow, he now looked just like a dull, old man. I looked at my sisters and realised that we, too, had had our youth swept away in the space of that one day.

'Leave Nana with me, and go have your meal. It's ready in the kitchen,' A-Yee Nana whispered. And so we went down.

On our way downstairs, we discovered that the whole house now had only six doors without sealing strips: Hua Yei-Yei's room, A-Yee Nana's room, Lao-Er's room and my room, plus a bathroom which was next to the kitchen. Inside the kitchen, none of the chairs had four legs. The kitchen table, with just two, had collapsed onto the floor, and even the lights were smashed.

Nonetheless, A-Yee Nana managed to cook us a very nice meal with tomato, chicken and smoked ham soup, steamed fish and steamed pork, with some green vegetables and rice. All the plates and bowls had been smashed, so the food stayed inside the pots. A-Yee Nana put our school lunch-boxes on the table for us to eat our meal from, but none of us were hungry.

'You must try to eat,' A-Yee Nana insisted. 'Think of it as a medicine, that you need it. You never know what tomorrow will bring. They may not allow you to eat all day, and then you will have had nothing at all.'

After the meal, we realised that we now had nothing – no clothes to change into, no beds to sleep in. Everything was sealed. From the few rooms open, A-Yee Nana shared her clothes with Nana, Mum and my sisters, Lao-Er shared his clothes with Dad, and I shared my clothes with my brother. Mum and my sisters shared my room with me, but they all had to sleep on the floor. That night was extremely hot, so at least they didn't catch cold. Dad shared a room with Lao-Er, Nana stayed in A-Yee Nana's room and Di-Di remained with Hua Yei-Yei.

Dad came down with Mum and listened while I told my sisters what had happened to me. My sisters cried in silence as I spoke. Dad and Mum were staring at us, so sombre. Then, in a whisper, Dad said, 'Listen, girls. Next time they ask you any of those kinds of questions, you should say that you know how bad your parents and grandparents are, and from now on you will draw a very clear line apart from us. You must learn to shout the slogans, such as "Down with Mum, Dad, Yei-Yei, or Nana". Do whatever is necessary to defend yourselves.'

'To protect yourselves is the most important thing. Mum, Dad, Yei-Yei and Nana all understand. We cannot bear to see any of you beaten like that,' Mum added. Then she turned to me with tear-filled eyes, kissed me softly and said, 'Sorry, this is purely Mum and Dad's fault. We have brought you all into the wrong world.'

I tried to get some sleep that night, but I couldn't even close my eyes. That dead woman's face kept appearing in my mind. I could still see her blood and brains, as well as the more-dead-than-alive man's blood. And I could even see the dead bodies of the couple and their child crumpled in a pool of blood. All the howling, the smashing, the burning, the cutting, the beating, the punching, the kicking, the bleeding and the chasing – I couldn't block it out. I asked Mum to put the bedroom light on, and she tried to switch it on but the bulb was smashed. Instead, she said soothingly, 'We've got moonlight,' pointing to the sky through the broken window. She added, 'Be brave. Mum will stay beside you. You are safe.'

For some strange reason the moonlight that night was not as bright as usual – it was dim and gloomy. I gazed at the moon's face and it was as though there were tears in its eyes.

So many questions kept running through my head. Where was our Yei-Yei? Why did they take him away? Why did they take Mum and Dad away for those couple of weeks? What had our family done that had anything to do with the Great Proletariat Cultural Revolution? What were the differences between the Intellectuals and the Revolutionaries, the Capitalist Class and the Proletariat? Why were the Intellectual and Capitalist Class so shameful, and the Revolutionary and Proletariat so honourable? Let's say, if the world were now filled with the Revolutionary and Proletariat and with absolutely no Intellectual and Capitalist Class, what would the world be like? Was this the real aim of Mao's Great Proletariat Cultural Revolution? Who were our persecutors? Were they really sent here by Mao? If so, what did Mao try to do for us, for this nation and the world? Why did Mum say it was purely their fault, that they had brought us all into the wrong world? Why . . .?

Yei-Yei always told us when we were young, how fortunate we were. World war and the civil war would never come back again. And today's peace was thanks to the thousands, millions and billions who had fought for our wellbeing, who had used their blood to bring change for us. He told us that we must study as hard as we could, to treasure today's happiness and peaceful life. As Chinese citizens, everybody had to be proud of themselves and of their nation. And in this life, everybody had to learn to treasure, to respect, to trust, to love, to care, to be proud and to make a determined effort to do well for themselves, their country and the world.

Ever since I could remember, I had always thought myself very fortunate. I had such a lovely grandmother, she was so beautiful. Everybody called her Pio-Long Nana (Pretty Nana). I was so proud of her beauty. She loved us dearly. And I had such a respectable, resourceful grandfather. He was looked up to by everybody – even my schoolteachers respected him. He knew everything – just like a live encyclopaedia. I had such a talented mother, I was so proud of her and of her pieces in the local newspapers and magazines. I had such a blooming father, full of love and liveliness. He made our lives so joyful!

I had always tried to remember what Grandfather said to us, and I studied very hard and always tried to be the top student in the class. The other pupils could not answer all the questions, but I was always able to. Sometimes I would be selected by my teacher to participate in the national primary school competitions, for writing or mathematics. Sometimes I would volunteer to stand up in front of the class to tell a story I had read at home, or to recite a Chinese classic poem taught to me by my grandfather. Sometimes I even brought friends home to ask Yei-Yei to give us extra lessons on the subject we were studying. But now I wondered whether my grandfather really said the right things to us. Did I really get it right? Were we really fortunate?

If, as Yei-Yei said, we really were fortunate, then world war would never come back again. But what about the political campaign? What was the difference between the 'Bloody War' and the 'Violent Political Campaign'? Yei-Yei once said, 'War signifies destruction and death!' And now, what about all the destruction and the deaths! What made one war a 'Violent Campaign' and another a 'Just War'? Also, if Yei-Yei was right, and we had all learned the lessons of love and pride, to treasure and respect, how could the same descendants of this teaching do such terrible things to their own people and their nation? Why did they hate us so deeply . . .?

Very early the next morning, A-Yee Nana carried in a tray of ginseng tea. She gently woke Mum up and said, 'Drink this first, it will give you energy for the day. The breakfast is ready as well. You'd better have it now, in case they come back early.' Mum thanked her and simply sat looking at the tea, the tears streaming down her face . . .

About an hour later, the downstairs door began to bang and I looked out and saw the local policeman and the other six cold-looking men who had sat before the Struggle Assembly the previous day. With them were about 20 Red Guards. Lao-Er ran up and told me not to move, to stay in bed. He closed the door and left me there.

Shortly afterwards, the door crashed open, as three Red Guards burst in and started shouting. One of them ran towards me, just like a mad dog, and seized my collar. He slapped my face and pulled me up from the bed. 'Fuckin' bitch!' he shouted. 'Are you deaf? Why are you still in bed? Get out!' I stood up quickly and, with bare feet, limped downstairs, followed by Nana, who had undergone the same ordeal.

After we gathered downstairs, the evil local policeman started his threatening talk again. 'Listen! Cow's demon and snake spirit Lee Li, Guo Jinren, Ling Yuxin and all the Worthy Progenies, today you must all attend a very important public judicial Struggle Assembly! You must be earnest and frank! You will not be allowed to move. If any of you violates the laws, the consequences will be very serious. You now have five minutes to get ready.'

He then turned to A-Yee Nana, 'Today, you will all participate in this political movement and attend the assembly as well!'

'Alright! If you want us proletariat to attend this assembly you have got no right to give us such short notice and to order us to get ready in five minutes. We need more than an hour to get ready. Otherwise we won't go!' A-Yee Nana answered defiantly.

The policeman looked at his watch, then back at her. 'No, it's nearly eight o'clock, and the assembly is held at nine. We must leave here by half past.'

While the policeman was delivering his threatening speech, I had noticed A-Yee Nana whispering to Lao-Er. Nodding his head, Lao-Er ran out. Shortly after, he returned with about a dozen peasant straw hats (wide-brimmed), and he put a small towel inside each hat to give it extra protection against the sun. He gave us one each. A-Yee Nana then quickly passed each of us a bottle of cold water and a small packet of biscuits.

'Come with me,' beckoned Lao-Er. I followed him upstairs and he helped me put my school running shoes on. 'Take your medicine with you,' he said, 'and don't forget, if the assembly is not finished by lunchtime you must have it!' I nodded. Then we all stood downstairs to await the local policeman's next order.

Suddenly he shouted at Dad, 'Where is your bloody son?' Immediately five or six Red Guards ran upstairs and we heard Di-Di screaming. Hua Yei-Yei begged them not to lay hands on him. Holding one of Di-Di's hands, he led him down, with the Red Guards following. Then the policeman yelled again, 'Quick! Quick!' and we were forced to leave at once.

It took us about 25 minutes to reach the square. Poor Nana, she had to be helped by A-Yee Nana and Lao-Er to keep on walking. My head wound was pounding again and I felt dizzy too. Mum stopped to find me some painkillers but one of the Red Guards kicked her buttocks and shouted, 'Fuckin' bitch! Who said you could stop? Are you trying to escape?' Mum lost her balance, but luckily she was holding my school bag and her head hit that instead of the hard ground. Dad and I quickly helped her to stand, but when she insisted that I needed a painkiller the other mad Red Guard seized her collar, and slapped her face: 'Fuckin' bitch shut up!' I felt terrible and apologised, 'Mum, sorry! It's all my fault!' I saw tears welling in Mum's eyes. Dad whispered to me, 'Close your eyes, Mum and I will help you walk.'

Suddenly we heard slogans being shouted behind us, and the noise was growing closer. Several military trucks were moving slowly towards the assembly square, and on the front of one there was a man with a tall dunce hat upon his head. Hanging from his neck was a big wooden board covered with some words and a big red cross. His body was tied with rope, and two policemen gripped his neck. Other policemen holding guns stood behind them. A second truck was packed with Red Guards holding Mao's Red Book as they led the people who were shouting slogans:

Political power grows out of the barrel of a gun!
Stay resolute — suppress, execute the Counter-Revolutionary!

Stay resolute — suppress, execute the long-term secret Japanese war criminal!
Stay resolute — suppress, execute the most heinous Japanese traitor!
Stay resolute — suppress, execute the long-term secret Japanese spy!
Long live the Mighty Dictatorship of the Proletariat!

Behind this terrible procession followed lots of children throwing rubbish, such as watermelon skins, rotten vegetables, and stones.

As the trucks drew closer to us, I heard Dad gasp. 'Look, it's Dad's name!' I couldn't believe this was our Yei-Yei. In one short month, Yei-Yei looked so totally changed. He looked exactly like an old, ill, emaciated, poor country peasant. If his name had not been written on the white board we would not have believed this was our Yei-Yei. He used to be strongly built, tall and full of vigour and vitality.

The truck passed us and entered the assembly square. Nana had not even realised it was our Yei-Yei on the truck! The policeman started shouting again, 'Quick! Listen, quick!' and shoved us in. We had been reserved a place, very near the platform. And now, all around us stood policemen, not Red Guards. The atmosphere in the square was extremely tense and expectant.

Political power grows out of the barrel of a gun!
Stay resolute — suppress, execute the long-term secret Japanese war criminal!

Suddenly slogans were again being shouted through the speakers. Then there was a commotion at the rear as two policemen seized Yei-Yei's neck and pushed him kneeling to the middle of the platform. Another three policemen held guns, and followed behind. Then, about six or seven uniformed policemen marched in. One of the policemen opened the proceedings with a fierce address:

'Comrades! Fellow Red Guards! Today we have invited you here to tell you of an appalling crime that has been hidden for nearly three decades, ever since the Japanese war! This one in front of you, who slipped out of the net, is a long-term hidden Japanese war criminal, a first-class Japanese traitor, a long-term Japanese spy, who caused the deliberate deaths of millions of Chinese and owes heavy blood debts! This family before you are wolves in sheep's clothing who have swindled, hoodwinked and struck right at the heart of the innocent masses of China. They discriminated between love and hate and who was really a friend and enemy, and have voiced their grievance! They went scot-free into hiding, to wait, and create a suitable opportunity to stage a comeback!

'Our great leader Chairman Mao points out explicitly: "Our enemies are all those in league with imperialism – the warlords, the bureaucrats, the comprador [bureaucrat] class, the big landlord class and the reactionary section of the intelligentsia attached to them."

'Our great leader Chairman Mao repeatedly admonishes us: "Who are our enemies? Who are our friends?" This is a question of the first importance for the Revolution. The basic reason why all previous revolutionary struggles in China achieved so little was their failure to unite with real friends in order to attack real enemies.

'We must remember Chairman Mao's admonishment: "The enemy will not perish of himself. Neither the Chinese reactionaries nor the aggressive forces of US imperialism in

China will step down from the stage of history of their own accord." And the imperialist and domestic reactionaries will certainly not take their defeat lying down and they will struggle to the last ditch.

'And every Communist grasps the truth: "Political power grows out of the barrel of a gun."'

Following this policeman's lengthy diatribe, many Red Guards marched up to the platform vehemently condemning Japanese crimes of aggression during the Japanese war, on behalf of their parents and grandparents. They were extremely upset that their families had been killed by the Japanese. Their intense anger over the blood debts owed by the Japanese and Japanese traitors now made them strongly demand that the Party and the government exact recompense for it in blood.

Political power grows out of the barrel of a gun!
Stay resolute — suppress, execute the Japanese war criminal!

The slogans echoed again and again as the assembly went on and on. By the time I checked the clock at the top of the posters it was nearly two. Our poor Yei-Yei could no longer kneel. His head was leaning on the frame of the white board around his neck and his body was curled close to the ground. We stared at Yei-Yei with fear, as the atmosphere in the square grew ever more oppressive and frightening.

Suddenly, one of the Red Guards, aged about 15, after delivering his long indignant denunciation, ripped Yei-Yei's dunce hat off and threw it to the ground. Then he took his thick army belt off his waist and ferociously lashed Yei-Yei's head with the huge brass buckle, yelling, 'Bloody slipped out of the net, long-term hidden Japanese war criminal, first-class Japanese traitor, long-term Japanese spy! You've caused the deliberate deaths of millions and owe heavy blood debts! Now it's your turn! This blood debt will be paid by blood!'

The heavy brass buckle continued to lash Yei-Yei's head. It gave out a dreadful sound, and I just couldn't bear to watch! But our poor Yei-Yei neither screamed nor moaned as the blood and white brains from his head sprayed all over the platform and he collapsed into the pool of blood . . .

About 10 or 15 minutes later a doctor, guarded by a few policemen, rushed onto the platform. The doctor bent down, felt Yei-Yei's pulse and said, 'He's dead.'

The policemen standing beside this doctor looked at each other, shaking their heads, and the whole square fell into a dead silence . . .

Yei-Yei, dead? No! No! Noooooooooooooooooooooooooooo! It couldn't be! My whole body was trembling, my ears were roaring, and my heart almost jumped out of my throat. Nana collapsed in a deep faint. Dad sat there with his staring eyes, utterly numbed. Mum squeezed one of my hands, nearly breaking my fingers, and her whole body shook. Di-Di screamed out and tried to run over, but he was held back by Hua Yei-Yei. All my sisters were banging their heads on their knees, sinking into a flood of tears . . .

The Struggle Assembly had been disrupted by this unexpected event, and the policemen who sat in the front row closed their folders without delivering their preplanned final judgement. They simply stood up and marched out. The policemen who stood on the platform took hold of my grandfather's arms, dragging him down from the platform. And the silent audience spontaneously dispersed.

Then lots of the old people, who I had never met before, clustered round us. Some of them put wet towels on our heads, some of them gave us cold water, some of them held our hands, and some of them even put money in our pockets. One of the old men whispered through his tears, 'That band of fatuous rulers! Where are their hearts? To allow such a little bastard like that to beat his ancestors' saviour to death! Where is his heart? Be strong! Live! One day they will be punished by Buddha. This blood debt will be repaid by their blood.'

Will be repaid? I wished that it was possible. Our hearts were broken . . .

Shortly afterwards there was a shout: 'Quick! Quick! Quickly get on the truck!' They herded us into the truck. Hua Yei-Yei suddenly stood up and ran with Di-Di back towards the other side of the square. They caught the eye of a policeman. 'Stop! Stop!' Several mad Red Guards ran after them and one of them grabbed Di-Di and threw him back into the truck.

Hua Yei-Yei cried and banged his head on the ground: 'Buddha! Buddha! Where are you? Buddha, please open your eyes and look. Buddha, how could you abandon these innocent people? Buddha, where are your hands? Buddha, please reach out your hands and help! Buddha, I beg you, please! Buddha . . .'

And this, then, was the story of my grandfather . . .

As I walked through the streets after my meeting with Yee Bing my mind and heart were full of those dreadful events of 17 years ago. When I got back to work it was lunchtime. As I came through the gate one of my colleagues called out to me through the café window, 'Hey! Sheng! Come here. We're all waiting for you.'

But when I walked into the café, to my disgust, the ugly Human Resource Manager was sitting right at the front, near the door, eating his lunch while reading the newspaper and looking perfectly relaxed. I just couldn't help it. I strode towards him, grabbed his paper and threw it onto the floor.

'Who told you?' I yelled at him. 'Who told you that my grandfather was a criminal with heavy blood debts? He was an innocent! He was one of the innocent victims massacred by your bloody, ugly, dirty, heartless Party!'

His head snapped up, and he stared at me for a while. Suddenly he rose, thumped his hand on the table loudly and shouted back, 'You! You fuckin' bloody bitch! You fuckin' bloody Counter-Revolutionary! You fuckin' insulting our Great, Glorious, Right Communist Party of China! You fuckin' fuckin' —'

Everyone in the café was dumbfounded — what was going on? Then one of my colleagues yelled out in my defence, 'Don't swear! Please don't swear!'

'No! Please don't swear!' All the people in the café followed her example and yelled it too.

The Human Resource Manager went red and tried to leave. But before he went he scowled at me and shouted, 'You'll pay for what you just said! Our Party has an account to settle with you! Our Party won't forget you!'

Afterwards everyone clustered around me, to find out what had happened. 'Have you said anything to him? Why is he suddenly swearing at you? Why? Tell us!' One of my closer colleagues, Lao Zhu, walked over to me and cautioned, 'Sheng, listen! Go home. You are overtired.'

Lao Zhu was a talented artist and a very good friend of mine. He was the department head of Art Design at our company. He also came from a similar family background to me and understood better than anyone what I was going through. He had lived through the same nightmare.

When the Cultural Revolution was launched Lao Zhu was a first year art student in the Guanchou Art School. The local propaganda arm of the Cultural Revolution movement went to the school to find some young students to paint the posters of

Mao's portrait to go up in the city and mobilise the public to actively participate in the campaign. Lao Zhu was one of them. They had to stand on very long ladders, and use oil paint to paint Mao's portrait on the tops of high buildings and on tall walls. The paintings had to be very accurate as well. Day after day, building after building, from sunrise till sunset, he was exhausted. One day, when he was halfway through painting Mao's hair, he suddenly felt dizzy and fell off the ladder. His face hit the wall, and his nose bled. A kind passer-by found him and took him home on his bicycle.

But at the moment he slipped, he accidentally painted a long line right through the middle of Mao's face, and the oil paint made a huge mess of the poster. It was the early evening, just as it was getting dark, and so he and the passer-by hadn't noticed it. Early the next morning he was arrested by the Guanchou police and labelled a Counter-Revolutionary. They claimed he used the painting opportunity to vent his grievance against the Great Leader Chairman Mao, on behalf of his so-called Anti-Communist Capitalist Class Family. He was locked up in jail for eight long years! This nightmare began just a few days after his twentieth birthday.

I took Lao Zhu's considerate advice, and with a saddened heart and in a sombre frame of mind I left work and went back home.

I had had enough! All I wanted now was to close my eyes, shut out the dreadful world, fall into a deep sleep and never be woken again . . .

Four

人權在何方？

Where Are Our Human Rights?

Nobody was at home, and I soon fell fast asleep. Next thing I knew, my mother was shaking me awake. 'Lao Zhu is here, he wants to see you now. What's happening?' she said, and rushed into her room and rang my father and Da-Bo.

Da-Bo (which means 'bigger father') was my godfather. He was also my grandfather's godson. Da-Bo's father had been one of my grandfather's staff. His mother died when he was born and when he was 12, his widowed father died from TB. The extended family asked my grandfather to be merciful and take this poor child in, to be a factory worker, as they were far too poor and old to care for him, and he had to make his own living. My grandfather accepted him and found tasks for him to do, suitable to his age. And so, he bought the newspaper, dusted the office, made cups of tea and fetched morning tea and lunch for all the office workers. He did very well, paid his boarding-house fees, and saved. He then asked the factory's accountant to help with his writing and sent all his money to his grandparents. My grandfather was most touched. Three months after he had started working at the factory, Grandfather decided to pay for his education and he sent Da-Bo to boarding school. From that time, he became a member of our family, a best friend and an older brother to my father.

Da-Bo was now a heart surgeon. A physician with high moral standards, he was also a warm, good-natured person, with an easy manner, kind-hearted and very unselfish. He was also the only surviving member of his family. Da-Ma ('bigger mother'), his wife, died from an unknown illness in a labour camp during the Cultural Revolution. Their son – an outstanding medical student at Guanchou University – committed suicide during the Anti-Right Campaign in 1957.

When I walked into the living room, Lao Zhu was sitting on a sofa by the window, his eyes fixed on the sky, looking obviously worried. My mother came in, softly closed the living-room door, and turned the stereo on (a habit of safeguarding private conversations developed by Chinese families during the Cultural Revolution). There was a gentle knock on the door and Li-Yee entered with a tea-tray and some coffee and sliced lemon cake.

Soon, Da-Bo arrived and not very long after, my father came home too. Everyone looked deeply disquieted. The music stopped, and there were some gentle greetings, then a strained silence fell upon the room. I started to realise that I had got myself into deep trouble.

Mum opened the conversation calmly. 'Tell us, what's been happening?'

After my explanation, Lao Zhu looked panic-stricken. 'You – you – actually did blame the Party in front of him at lunch-time?' he stammered.

I nodded. All their eyes fixed upon me, in a shocked silence. The tension was unbearable. I excused myself and rushed out of the room.

I lay on my bed, staring at the ceiling and desperately questioning myself. 'What have I done? What's the matter with me? Am I awake? Have I been having a nightmare?'

Then the door opened. When Dad walked in, I didn't wait for him to speak. I jumped up from the bed and cried, 'You are an unworthy father! Accepting the Party's "sugar-coated bullets". You are as short-sighted as a mouse, seeing no further than what is under your nose! Where are Yei-Yei and Nana's bodies? Did they really deserve to die that way? It is seven years since the Cultural Revolution ended, but Yei-Yei is still being slandered and libelled and you have done absolutely nothing – you seem to have forgotten it all! You –'

'Stop! Please stop! I cannot bear to hear those words from your mouth. It hurts!' Dad was shouting and trying to shake me out of my crying. His face had turned white as a sheet and his tears streamed down and dropped onto my forehead. It was the first time in my life that my father had shouted at me. It was also the first time that I had hurt him so deeply, and without saying a word of apology. I will always regret this, as my father had far, far, far too much to bear in his life.

After my grandfather's public trial, the truck drove us endlessly along country roads, then mountain tracks. The bumping, swinging and jolting made us badly sick. My head and arm were extremely sore, so Mum cradled my head on her chest to ease the jolting. Dad sat on the truck floor to pillow Nana's half-unconscious body. Di-Di sat beside my eldest sister and continually asked where we were going. After two nights the truck stopped before a crumbling little temple and we were ordered out.

'Listen! All get out now! Quick!'

None of us moved. In fact, none of us dared move, as we were too frightened and unsure of what lay in store for us. But, again, the ugly bullying yells dislodged us from the truck.

This temple lay in our native home, Fei-Yn, a very poor village of Ku-Shan province, about 2000 kilometres from Guanchou. (Later I discovered that this temple had been donated by my great-grandfather.) It was about 100 square metres, but only two and a half walls still stood there. The roof had collapsed. Inside, the floor was littered with broken candles, glass, smashed images and bloodstains. Dad picked up a length of wood, perhaps a part of the wall. He brushed it clean and helped Nana lie on top, then directed Di-Di and I to sit beside her.

When a Red Guard saw Nana lying on the board he kicked her and shouted, 'Stand up, cow's demon and snake sprit Lee Li! Don't feign death! Get up!' Nana kept her eyes closed and did not respond. Then he turned on my brother and I and shouted more of the same. But we dropped our heads down, curled together on a corner of the wood and merely trembled.

Revolution is justified!
Rebellion is justified!
The enemy that does not surrender is doomed to perish!
Down with the Counter-Revolutionaries!

Suddenly, hundreds of slogan-chanting locals, wearing red armbands printed with 'Red Guards' in Mao's own hand-writing, and holding Mao's Red Book and paper flags with slogans written on them, marched towards us. They halted in front of the temple. A policeman stepped forward and began his rebuke:

'Listen! Counter-Revolutionary Ling Yuxin, Anti-Revolutionary Capitalist Class Guo Jinren, cow's demon and snake sprit Lee Li and all the Worthy Progenies, here is the place for you to carry out your forced labour!

'From now on you must be earnest and frank, and if you work hard enough you will redeem your souls. This is your last opportunity, under the strict local Party and Red Guards' supervision, to transform yourselves and begin life anew!

'You must obey our local Party and Red Guards' surveillance! If any of you go wrong or override our local Party and Red Guards' discipline and our laws, the consequences will be worse than you could ever imagine! .

'You must kneel down before our Great Leader's image, admit your errors and ask for punishment every single morning, and then again at night!

'You must confess your atrocities and accuse and expose each other, separately, to our Fellow Red Guards on a daily basis!

'You must, you must, you must, you must, you must and you must!'

He then continued:

'Fellow Red Guards, now we must unmask and expose these Class Enemies' ugly features and souls to the light of day, and parade them through the village in public disgrace, and mobilise the people to keep their eyes open, heighten vigilance, and watch the movements of these Class Enemies.'

And then my parents and sisters were marched in humiliation through the village, while we were left behind to take our situation in.

Eventually Nana stood up and said, 'You two remain here and take care of each either, Nana is going to the toilet.' My brother burst into tears. 'No, Nana, you must not go anywhere, I'm afraid!' Nana stared at him numbly, pleading, 'Let Nana go.' Then she moved stiffly outside. Suddenly she made a U-turn, bent down to kiss us, and then left.

We waited and waited, but Nana did not return. I was terribly worried, and thought that Nana could not find her way back. My brother and I tried looking for her around the temple. We couldn't see anybody, but the sense of emptiness around the ruin was echoed by the wind whistling across the desolate landscape.

'Where is my Nana?' Di-Di started crying.

About two hours later, a police jeep pulled up outside the temple. The driver rushed in and yelled at us, 'Fuckin' Worthy Progenies where is everybody? Fuckin' tell me!' We dropped our heads with no reply and he eventually left us alone.

Much later, the dreadful slogan-shouting heralded our family's return. Then the policeman rushed into the temple and once again began his reproving. Finally, he yelled:

'Comrades, Fellow Red Guards, I have uncovered a new tendency of Class Struggle! A Counter-Revolutionary committed suicide to escape punishment and resist our people, our Party, our country and our Great Proletariat Cultural Revolution! We must keep our eyes open, heighten vigilance, and watch the movements of these Class Enemies!'

Then he turned to my father and shouted, 'Counter-Revolutionary Guo Jinren! I order you to come here and identify this body.'

Dad numbly lifted his head, stared at him for a while, then moved stiffly towards the police jeep. The policeman opened the door, and there was Nana lying on the floor. Her singlet was wound tightly around her neck, and was attached to a broken

95

tree branch at the other end. My father took one look at her and collapsed, while all around us the slogan-shouting again broke out . . .

After seven years of torture, in 1972 my sister, brother and I returned to Guanchou. Unfortunately my other sisters were forced to make their lives elsewhere and did not get the opportunity to return to Guanchou until much, much later. Mum and Dad had to wait another three long years, for the final investigation, before obtaining their Guanchou residents' permits. Eventually, they too returned.

But our old house had been confiscated and was occupied by a local Communist Party family, so we stayed temporarily with A-Yee Nana, our previous housekeeper. She did her very best and squeezed us all into her only room, about 12 to 13 square metres, in a Guanchou slum district. At night we were like tinned sardines, arranged neatly on her floor.

This room was part of the largest, and best, house in the slum neighbourhood. It was an old-style Guanchou building but terribly run-down and filthy. It looked near to collapse – one foot in the grave already! There were two living rooms and six bedrooms, with no bathroom and toilet facilities, and only a tiny kitchen. A water tap was attached outside the kitchen window, connected from the inside. The kitchen contained 12 briquet cookers, about 25 cm by 25 cm square and 40 cm high. A very old-fashioned Chinese cooker, it used egg-shaped fuel made from coal powder and mud – it took 30 to 40 minutes to boil a kettle of water. So, 12 briquets, 12 families.

A total of 94 people lived in the house with A-Yee Nana. Her room was just above the kitchen, and during the summer the heat from below was over 40 degrees Celsius – the floor felt like it was boiling. The room was not just for sleeping, but also had to be used for sitting, eating, washing dishes, washing clothes, drying clothes, bathing and toileting. Every day we waited outside in a long queue to get water and carry it up, then we had to carry it down again after it had been used. Very often the water was in short supply, and we would have to wait two or three hours just to get one bucket.

The dreadful thing was, the neighbours all seemed to be fighting from very early morning, till they exhausted themselves late at night. For a bucket of water or a tiny wee space, they might fight each other until skulls cracked. Each time they fought, the floor would squeak and the walls would shake. Theft was an everyday occurrence; money, clothes – even your dinner would disappear from the middle of your table. Obscenity was their mother tongue.

Life for us at that time was just like an old Chinese saying: 'Huan Tong Bu Huan Yao' – 'the same medicine, only differently prepared', or 'the same old stuff presented as a new concoction'. We lived our lives in a constant state of terror.

When our parents returned, Mum got a job offer straight away, as a cotton cloth manufacturing worker. More accurately, it was ordered rather than offered. It was her first official government job in her life. Her monthly salary was only a bit higher than a new employee – 32 yuan. At that time it was worth about US$18, now about US$4. In the second year, she reached the average income of 36 yuan per month.

Mum was now over 50, and the job was far too harsh for her. Especially after 10 years of inhuman torture, her health was very run-down. She had to run between 36 cotton-weaving machines for exactly eight hours a day, six days a week, on a three-shift system. Her legs were starting to swell, and soon swelling crept over her whole body. This extremely demanding work, aggravated by poor living conditions, meant that Mum began to suffer from another health problem – sleeplessness. One night shift, she collapsed in front of the cotton-weaving machines. This finally led to the end of her ordeal. Supported by the doctor, she obtained a 'Qualified Leave Post Retirement'. She retired instantly.

Meanwhile, Dad kept waiting for his employment orders. Every day he went to the local Implement Policies of Party office to beg for a job for himself and a commendation for the family. Mum, after her retirement, would roll up the bedding every morning to make space to move. Then she would sit on top of the bed rolls, with her blank eyes fixed on the ceiling, and pass her days silently. She looked so sombre.

One Sunday morning, Mum was sitting there as she always did. Suddenly, she gave a shout of excitement – 'A spider!' We saw it slowly descending from the ceiling to the ground in front of Mum. She then made everybody lift up their feet while her darling spider marched jubilantly away, like a Big Hero! Mum, with a large smile, said softly, 'Thank you spider. Thank you spider.' The Chinese believe that:

In the morning, spider brings you some good news;
At lunchtime, spider brings you a visitor;
In the evening, spider brings you a god of wealth.

Mum's beautiful smile was a gift to us all – a gift we had missed for years, and had almost forgotten.

And, yes! A week later, Dad got a job as a thermos manufacturing worker. The factory was previously owned by Grandfather. The monthly salary was about the same as before the Cultural Revolution – 850 yuan; worth at this time about US$500, now about US$100. Compared to the average monthly income of 36 yuan, this was a Western country big-boy millionaire's salary indeed! At this stage, the Party did not worry too much about it though. In fact, in Guanchou, after the Cultural Revolution, very few people with the same background as my father were still alive. Perhaps only a couple of dozen, and they were now very old, with my father possibly the youngest among them.

Dad requested to cash his first month's income payment in advance, and we escaped from this dreadful place and moved into a cheap hotel in a safe area that same day. I had my first shower and slept in a real bed for the first time since the Cultural Revolution.

About a month later, the Guanchou Conglomerate of Industrial Enterprises (the head office of the thermos factory) offered Dad a job as a financial advisor. But it was on a loan basis only. That meant that although Dad now worked only for this organisation, he was still on the staff of the thermos manufacturer itself. They still had to pay his salary, health care, retirement pension, even funeral expenses. After the Cultural Revolution, Thursday became known as 'Cadre Work Day'. This meant that every Thursday the higher-up workers had to do manual labour at grass-roots level. So, Dad had to go to do manual labour in the thermos factory once a week. It didn't worry my father too much, so long as he had a secure job to occupy his time and reasonable pay to support his family.

After my father started his job, we obtained a flat. Compared to Western living standards, and our old home, it was a very small place. But, by the average living standards after the Cultural Revolution – especially compared to A-Yee Nana's place – it was like heaven!

About this time, Mum broke down in front of the family, and vowed that she would never write a single word again. She felt that she had been the cause of all the pain and suffering we (along with our innocent grandfather) had endured for the past 10 years. So she decided that she would stay at home to help with our delayed education and to look after the family.

And so, now, Dad recovered with a peaceful place to stay,

an interesting job to occupy his day, and a reasonable pay to support the family. The Guanchou Conglomerate of Industrial Enterprises treated him with courtesy and consideration, and with the care of his beloved, devoted wife he worked extremely hard for enormously long hours. That enabled him to numbly put everything behind him.

Later, after I heard Lao Zhu leave for home, Da-Bo came into my room. He bent down, kissed my forehead and said solicitiously, 'I am terribly sorry about what has happened.' He paused and struggled to control his emotions. He then continued, 'Lao Zhu said this afternoon, after you left, that your company's Human Resource Manager called an urgent Party meeting, for all Party members, the senior executives and department heads to attend. At the meeting he pointed out sharply that you had acted against the Party. He also issued an urgent circular note to all staff members on behalf of the Communist Party Committee of the company. Here is a copy.' He handed it to me. It read:

Urgent Circular Note

No: GZ.HEF.1001 83-6-21

To: All Party members of the Company.
        All Senior Executives of the Company.
        All Department Heads of the Company.
        All Staff Members of the Company.

CC (File): Head Office of the Local Party Committee.
        Head Office of the Local Industrial Committee.
        Taido Sub-Police of Guanchou.

Re: Suspend Guo Sheng from her position as Director of Finance pending further investigation and a decision.

Guo Sheng, political background of family of origin – *Counter-Revolutionary*.

Our great leader Chairman Mao admonishes us – In a class society everyone lives as a member of a particular class, every kind of thinking, without exception, is stamped with the brand of a class.

On 21 June 1983, 12.30 pm, in the canteen of the company, Guo Sheng uttered an appalling malicious culmination of words and deeds against the Great, Glorious, Right Communist Party of China and vented her class grievances on behalf of her very intricate and complex Counter-Revolutionary family. Clearly, it was about her grandfather, who was a long-term secret Japanese war criminal, Japanese collaborator, and secret Japanese spy with heavy blood debts, who was exposed in 1966.

Therefore, this announcement, given by urgent circular note to all internal and external Party members of the company, states that the Party of the company has decided to take urgent action to immediately suspend Guo Sheng from her position of Director of Finance, pending further investigation and a decision.

This urgent circular note takes effect from today, 21 June 1983, 3:30 pm.

Hereby ends urgent circular note.

I was utterly dumbfounded. I simply stared at the note and began crying.

'Don't cry – listen, it's not the end of the world,' comforted Da-Bo. 'We could still do something together to remedy it. Can

you hear Da-Bo, Sheng? Answer me – please answer Da-Bo!'
Da-Bo was standing in front of me and shaking my shoulders
with both hands.

My bedroom door was open, and through it I could see
Mum and Dad standing there, staring intently at me.

'Your Mum, Dad and I have already spoken to Dong Bo-Bo
and he will fix it for you. Don't worry!' said Da-Bo.

Dong Bo-Bo (Dong was his family name, and Bo-Bo means
father) was a well-known Guanchou psychiatrist. He was also
the head of the Psychiatric Institute. Dong Bo-Bo was an old
friend of Da-Bo's, and his wife and my mother were the best
of friends. They were also our godparents.

'Tomorrow I will take you to his hospital to see him, and he
will arrange to get a medical certificate for you, for being struck
down by the stress of your heavy study load and extremely
demanding job,' Da-Bo continued. 'He will say that it led to a
mental breakdown, or derangement, or something like that.
Then they will have to retract this circular note. If they don't,
the institution, the hospital, even the doctor could defend you.'

'No way! I'm not going!' I screamed with anger. 'Can't you
understand it's purely a threat? I won't sell my soul. I know this
ugly, bloody-minded man very well. He is grasping at power,
bringing pressure to bear. I don't care! It's not the Cultural
Revolution any more. I can't let him carry on insulting Yei-Yei's
name. Yei-Yei must be cleared at once. The Guos must be able
to stand tall again. Seven years have passed and you did nothing,
so I have done it. I will see that the truth comes to light. And
nobody will stop me. I must do it! And now!'

'No! You can't. It's impossible.' cried Mum and Dad
simultaneously, bursting into tears and rushing towards me.
Once again, Dad used every ounce of energy to hold and shake
me, crying out, 'No! It's suicide. You will end up locked in jail
until you die.'

'I don't care. Do you hear me? I don't care!'

Da-Bo collapsed to his knees in front of me, reached out and cried, 'Yes! Yes! You must care! It's power. Do you understand? Power! In this society the real truth is *power*! Have we got any? Can't you remember the death of your Da-Ge? ('big brother', Da-Bo's only child.) Da-Bo can't bear to see you become a shadow of your Da-Ge!'

He was referring to the tragedy in 1957, at the height of the Anti-Right Campaign, when Da-Ge was in his final year at the Guanchou University Medical Faculty. He was planning, after he obtained his medical degree, to go to the Soviet Union to complete his Master's degree, so that he could be a first-class specialist like his father. An ambitious and outstanding scholar, he sailed through all his examinations, but he could not pass the political investigation of his family background. This puzzled him. He thought his father was an orphan, his mother was a housewife, and his maternal grandfather was a humble country teacher. Neither Capitalist nor landlord, they seemed as clean as everybody else! There must be some mistake, like maybe the same name but a different person. Everybody agreed, especially his parents. Eventually they suggested that he question the Institute of Higher Education Students Studying Abroad Office. The answer was:

'You have been very dishonest to the Party of this institution. At the time you applied for admission, you did not tell the real truth about your family's background. Such as the person who is related to your father. You should have been rejected in the first place. You have wasted our time!' the official said rudely.

'I don't understand what you are saying. Are you sure you mean the person called Zhen Wei (his own name) and the son of the heart surgeon Zhen Dawei? My father is an orphan!' Da-Ge replied angrily.

'Come on, young fellow. Don't play me for a fool. We are far too busy. If you really don't understand what I have said, you should go home and ask your father who his surrogate father is.'

'I beg your pardon?' laughed Da-Ge uncontrollably, and said, 'You mean Guo Ci-Xiang (my grandfather)? You must be mad! He is not even our blood relative. He is just a kind-hearted man who sympathised with my orphan father's plight and helped my late grandparents bring him up. You must be mad. You must be mad!' He thumped his hand on the desk and walked away.

When Da-Ge returned home, an unexpected phone call came for his father, from the Chief of the Communist Party Committee of the University. He pointed out that his son had openly disregarded the Party official, the Party, and the Party's policy, and demanded a written self-criticism before the next day's classes started.

Da-Bo understood that it was not the right time for his son to cause trouble for himself. He also knew his son very well — that it would be impossible for him to accept this kind of madness. So he drafted the self-criticism for Da-Ge himself, and begged him to copy it.

'No way, Dad! You must be mad too!' Da-Ge refused, terribly upset. He took the paper and tore it into pieces.

The next morning Da-Ge went back to university, but he never returned. He committed suicide.

With the pain of this memory, Da-Bo's face turned white as a sheet, he broke out in a sweat, shook, and his hands turned as cold as ice. (I learned later that this reminder of Da-Ge's death caused Da-Bo such a shock that he was unable to operate at the hospital for almost six months.)

Together, Mum and Dad gently helped him over to my bed, while I rushed into the kitchen to get a glass of water. Da-Bo's mouth was trembling and his tears were streaming down as Mum helped him drink the water.

'I'm so sorry Da-Bo! I'll go with your tomorrow, Da-Bo. I'm so sorry –' I cried in regret.

Da-Bo stayed the night. Early the next morning he rang his rooms and cancelled all his appointments. He took me to Dong Bo-Bo's hospital. He looked extremely pale. Before we left home, he said to me, 'Listen, don't worry, all you have to do is keep silent – say absolutely nothing, not even hello. Will you remember?'

I nodded and we left in silence.

Upon our arrival at the Psychiatric Institute, a woman doctor in her late fifties met us at the front door. She greeted us warmly, but I didn't respond, only followed her expression-lessly into her room. She started asking me questions, but I didn't answer these either, and made no eye contact. I was too scared to look at her, in case she discovered that I was tricking her. Suddenly, she stood up and left the room. Da-Bo followed her, and about 10 or 15 minutes later they returned.

'She'd better stay here. She can get better care and treatment, and she will recover more quickly,' the doctor said to Da-Bo.

'Oh, no, no,' Da-Bo shook his head and countered, 'Her mother will be terribly upset if she stays here. But, doctor, if she could obtain the best treatment, it would be very much appreciated.'

'Certainly!' she answered quickly and wrote out a prescrip-tion and a medical certificate for three months off work. Then she said to Da-Bo, 'This is the best medicine for her current condition. I will give her three months' supply. If there are any changes either bring her back here or give me a call. And you must make sure that she has complete rest and avoids any stress for three months at least. A holiday would probably do her good.'

Then she turned to me and placed her hand on top of mine. 'Sheng, can you hear me? Answer me!' she said. Still I did not answer. She continued, 'Now, you go home with your father. Those pills will make you feel happy and sleep well and your father will take you somewhere nice for a holiday. Afterwards, you will feel as good as new – fit, happy and able to go back to work and study again. Smile? Yes? Come on, Sheng! Say yes!'

Once again I reminded myself – *keep silent*!

Da-Bo thanked her and we left for home. On our way back, I felt dreadful. Was I really having a mental breakdown? Was I really mad? Why did I have to act like that? Why didn't I allow myself to show my real feelings and tell the truth? Why? Was I a person? A human? If so, where were my rights? Where were our human rights? I wanted to scream! But when I lifted my head to look at Da-Bo his face was so pale, and his expression so extremely grave, that I swallowed down the pain.

And it still remains inside of me – a heartfelt sorrow, far beyond expressing . . .

We arrived home in silence. Mum opened the door, whispering in my ear, 'Listen! Keep silent. They're here,' as we walked in. The Deputy Chairman of the company's Communist Party Committee, the ugly Human Resource Manager, and the head of the company's medical clinic were seated in our living room. I decided to ignore them and passed them by silently, heading for my bedroom.

They left about an hour later. Before they went, I heard the Human Resource Manager demand loudly, 'Who is the doctor? Who issued this medical certificate? How come she has no past history of mental illness? Here is our Party's doctor, she will re-examine her some time tomorrow.'

During the Cultural Revolution vast numbers of doctors were held for investigation and decision. Some were sent to labour camps, some were forced to labour at their former work places – doing work such as cleaning the floors and toilets, sterilising the instruments, washing dishes in the kitchen and so on. Then the farmers, factory workers and other labourers were trained up as doctors – these people were known as 'Barefoot Doctors'. The head of the company's medical clinic was just such a Barefoot Doctor. I knew she was a party activist and loyal member, but I wasn't so sure whether she could write her own name or not.

'Yes! What a great idea! It would be very much appreciated doctor, if you could give us your valuable time to re-examine her. She is rather run-down now. She badly needs a medical specialist to give her a thorough examination, then she will get the right treatment and recover quickly. We are all terribly worried,' answered Da-Bo in his extremely diplomatic way, but rather sour and sharp.

Next morning Da-Bo came by very early, as he knew that things would not be quite as simple as that. And, only 10 minutes after his arrival, the doorbell began to ring. Da-Bo quickly turned to me and said in a whisper, 'Go! Quick! Into bed!' And I hurried to my bedroom.

Then I heard the Human Resource Manager ask very loudly, 'Where is she? The ambulance is waiting downstairs. We have discussed her case with the Psychiatric Institute's Party Committee, describing her appalling words and deeds against the Great, Glorious, Right Communist Party of China. They can tell her illness is very serious and that she badly needs to have electric shock treatment – the sooner, the better.'

Da-Bo rushed in, fumbled open the pill bottle, quickly tipped two sleeping pills out on his trembling hand and said, 'Quick, swallow these. They won't harm you. Quick! Close your eyes and go to sleep.' With that, he ran out.

'No, I'm terribly sorry. You can't. She's my daughter, I have to take full responsibility for her whilst she's ill. I can't let anybody take her from this place, unless the doctor advises us in person.' I heard Mum say firmly.

Then I heard Da-Bo say, 'Yes, you are correct, it's your responsibility, as the mother of your daughter. Nobody is allowed to take your sick daughter away without your permission. To my knowledge, no professional body is allowed to make any kind of judgement without seeing a patient first, nor give any kind of treatment without consultation with the patient or the patient's relatives.

'However, you are perfectly right,' continued Da-Bo to the Human Resource Manager. 'Sheng's illness is indeed serious, and she needs good treatment. As suggested by the specialist yesterday, she must have a three-month treatment of oral medication, and we must make sure that she is resting well and avoids any stress during that time. It was also suggested that perhaps a holiday would do her good. Maybe the specialist is right, maybe she is wrong. I myself am a specialist – in heart surgery – but I am not specialised in psychiatry. So, if your company could assist us through the professional body to find an alternative treatment for her which will do her good, it would be most welcome and gratefully accepted. But we must discuss it with the medical specialist in person first!'

But it was as if Mozart was being played to a mad dog, so little notice did this man take of Da-Bo's words of reason.

'Listen! Don't waste our time. The ambulance has already waited downstairs far too long. She must go with us now,' the Human Resource Manager yelled out rudely.

'No! Not before we see the medical specialist in person,' said Dad desperately.

Meanwhile, the sleeping tablets were taking effect, and I fell into a deep sleep. Next thing I knew I felt somebody pulling me up by the arms and shouting at me, 'Quick! Get out of bed! Don't feign death! Quick! The ambulance is waiting for you!'

There was much arguing, and suddenly I heard Mum screaming, 'No! No!' and Dad and Da-Bo were shouting, 'Stop! Stop!'

I struggled to open my eyes, and to my horror, there were four uniformed male stretcher-bearers standing beside my bed. Thank God! The powerful tablets meant I could not even open my eyes properly, let alone know what exactly was happening.

I awoke in the middle of the night, extremely thirsty. As I went to the kitchen for water I noticed a suitcase sitting in the hallway. On my way back to bed, I found Dad waiting by my bedroom door. He held me tightly, dropped his head on top of my forehead, his tears streaming down, and cried, 'I'm so sorry. I'm so terribly sorry that that happened to you . . .'

I woke up very early the following morning and again felt extremely thirsty and hungry. I went to the kitchen and drank three full glasses of cold water at once, then made myself some breakfast. I found that Da-Bo had stayed the night, and soon Mum, Dad and Da-Bo all got up and sat with me while I ate my breakfast. But instead of the usual morning greetings, they all kissed and cuddled me sorrowfully.

Then Da-Bo opened the conversation. 'Did you see the suitcase in the hallway?'

I nodded.

'It's for you,' he continued. 'We all believe that the safest thing for you now is to go to your Da-Jei's (my eldest sister, who lived in West Gin province – Da-Jei means big sister) for a while, to let things cool down a bit. So, after your breakfast, check and see if there is anything we haven't packed. You will have to leave by 10 o'clock this morning – the flight is at 11 o'clock. It takes about three hours to get to Kiuing (the capital city of Gin province), but there is no further air travel after Kiuing. You will have to wait two or three days there, as the buses are not regular. But your Mum and Dad will stay with you until you meet your Da-Jei. She will take you home with her on the bus. It is a long journey. You will both have to take care of each other.'

I could only nod helplessly in reply – like a speechless, powerless baby.

Da-Bo saw us off at Guanchou airport. He held my hands and said, 'Be strong! Remember, we all love you. Whatever you are, you are always our pride. Whenever you need us, we are always there for you. We will never, ever abandon you or let you down.'

I looked at him and, once again, my tears poured down. I knew those words came from his heart's core. I knew with utmost certainty they loved me dearly. But I wondered then if I deserved them. What had I ever done for my family? What could I ever do?

I simply drooped my head down, and, following Mum and Dad, disappeared into the entrance of the terminal.

Five

沉默

Silence

When I reached Da-Jei's home, Mu-Long, a small town of Gin province, my little nephew, GuoYi (Da-Jei's only child), pulled his little hand from his nanny's and flew towards us crying, 'Mama! Mama! My dearest Hao (great) Mama is home!'

He was a very good-looking, extremely chatty wee fellow. With a pair of moon-shaped shining eyes, a small thin-lipped mouth, an erect nose – all sitting so well on his little chubby face – and with his fascinated, puzzled expression, he was just like a little emperor getting to know his kingdom. He was about to turn four, and his young mind was always busy, and his mouth was always questioning. He liked to follow me around and ask his thousands, millions, billions and zillions of questions. Why this? Why that? Why? Why? And why? However, for the first couple of days his inquisitiveness gave me a headache. I was in absolutely no mood to answer him and told him to 'Be quiet!' He was extremely upset, cried and asked his mother, 'Why doesn't Xiao A-Yee (Little Aunt, he called me) love me?' That made me feel rather guilty, so the next day I tried to be very patient, and to answer his constant 'Whys?' Once started, though, he never wanted to end!

Each morning, he liked me to help him out of bed, bath him, dress him, feed him breakfast, then take him to kindergarten. He liked me to pick him up again in the afternoon and cook him some dinner. Afterwards we would all go for a walk, then I would put him to bed and read him a 'Guanchou Children's Story' (any kind of story that I told him, he always called a Guanchou Children's Story). Together we would disappear into story world. He would always make me promise not to go back to Guanchou and to stay with him for ever. I would have to say, 'Yes, I promise!' Then he would give me his big smile, kiss me and say, 'Good night Xiao A-Yee, I love you,' and drift off into his sweet dreaming.

One morning GuoYi asked his mother for permission to stay home with me. I was so glad to have his company. Da-Jei then thought that she should have a day off too and take me out. I had been there almost a week, and she was always busy with her work. I stayed at home alone and she had found some books to help occupy my time.

'You seem in a better mood today. Would you like us to take you to town and have a special time?' Da-Jei asked.

I agreed.

'Bravo, Mama! Bravo, Mama!' GuoYi clapped his little hands in great excitement. 'Mama, Mama,' he said, 'Xiao A-Yee can buy me lots and lots of Guanchou Children's Stories, and toys, and lollies!'

But we'd decided too late, for the morning bus had already gone. We would have to wait for the midday bus, then catch the late afternoon one back. GuoYi then decided to take his three-wheeled bike with him, but he couldn't remember where it was. His mother wanted him to find it by himself, but pointed in the right direction – the garden. He was a bit upset, but out he went.

Meanwhile, I began to unpack my suitcase – something I hadn't bothered to do yet. Since I had been at Da-Jei's I'd spent most of my time catching up on sleep, then sitting around feeling sorry for myself. When I opened the suitcase and found all my university textbooks lying on top, I looked at them, and then looked at my watch. It was the fourth of July, a month after Yee Bing's birthday, a week away from the end-of-year examinations, and two months away from my birthday. How totally everything had changed! The realisation over-whelmed me – my job lost, my dream quenched, my life turned upside-down . . .

I automatically moved the textbooks to the table, and found a few cassette recordings lying underneath. One of them, as Da-Bo knew very well, was my favourite – Mozart's K. 466 in D minor. It's a very passionate piece, with great emotional intensity. I put it into Da-Jei's wee tape recorder, turned it up – as loud as I could – and invoked the blessing of God on this helpless woman, the daughter of a 'Politically Handicapped Tribe', a so-called Intricate and Complex Counter-Revolution Family. And my memory went back to . . .

The day before my sister, brother and I returned to Guanchou, Mum and Dad tearfully said to us, 'They might part Mum and Dad from you forever, and so, you must promise to take care of yourselves and look after each other. Be strong. Make Guo proud. Be Guo's survivors. Survive for your Mum and Dad; survive for your Yei-Yei and Nana; survive for this "Humbled Tribe" of Guos. In this country, nobody knows what will happen tomorrow. You must always remember that you were born into a "Politically Handicapped Tribe". Wherever you go, it will always be the same; whatever you do, your ancestors are always

113

with you. You have to face this grim reality, keep within the bounds of the rules, and toe the line. Whenever they bring humiliation upon you, make sure you do not complain; do not disagree and do not shed a single tear. Seal your lips; say absolutely nothing. Swallow it, and conceal it all within your heart's core. You must try to be cheerful, learn to survive, to live, and to wait for the day when truth returns.'

And so, with Mum and Dad's tearful words, we returned to Guanchou.

At the time of our return, the storm of the Cultural Revolution had just started to subside, although the people were still seized with the terror of uncertainty. Therefore, the three of us seemed like some dreadful pollution – like three filthy courses of bilge water. The people were terrified that we would turn their families into a fetid puddle by association. The only person able to, and prepared to, have us was our former housekeeper, A-Yee Nana. However, she had to lie to all her neighbours and tell them that we were her blood relatives, her grandnieces and grandnephew.

But, in a way, she wasn't lying. She made a far better grand-aunt than our real blood grand-aunt, and the richness of her heart was far beyond expression. She loved us dearly, and we loved her more than we could trust ourselves to say and far more than words have power to express.

A-Yee Nana was a typical old-fashioned Chinese Buddhist. She was born into a very poor country family in Leo-Long, in the north of China; she was the third of twelve children. When my grandmother married my grandfather, old Chinese custom held that a girl meant nothing; after marriage, her duty was to be at home, raising the family and looking after her husband, her father-in-law and mother-in-law. But my grandmother's parents thought that this was not for their beloved and educated darling daughter and wanted to provide her with help in the house. At the same time, A-Yee Nana's parents wanted their eldest son to be married, but the family were far too poor, and had no money to do so. They decided to sell their daughter to a rich family as a servant, so that she could have a better life, and there would be money for their eldest son to marry. This way, the family line would be safely carried on. Therefore, the deal was done; although A-Yee Nana was just 15 she became a servant in my grandparents' home. Later, my grandparents found her a husband, but she refused, as she had committed herself to Buddha already.

At the end of 1968, A-Yee Nana had heard that the Local Cultural Revolution Movements Organisation was rehabilitating previous Guanchou residents to their former positions and redressing the mishandled cases. Some of the families had been returned to Guanchou already. She wanted to let us know the news, but she could not write a single word. Then she remembered that our grandmother's blood sister was still living in Guanchou. She went to ask for help with the letter but she was screamed at and reviled.

'What? What do you want me to do for you?' my grand-aunt screamed at A-Yee Nana. 'Do you want to destroy our family? They are guilty! They deserved this punishment. They should admit that their guilt will be there till they die. Do you understand, they are a stinking pile of night soil, a filthy course of bilge water! Leave me alone! Let my life stay pure. I don't want anything to do with them. Now, be off with you. Flunky! Flunky! Have you forgotten your station? For shame! For shame! Our vast Working Class shame on you! Our Great Proletariat shame on you!'

This furious burst of tongue-lashing shocked A-Yee Nana into rage. She stepped up, slapped our great-aunt's face and said, 'You heartless bitch! Have you forgotten all they have done for you? And yes, remember what you said today, for one day

115

your sister will punish you for your words.'

On her way back home, A-Yee Nana just couldn't stop her tears, and couldn't believe those words had come out of my great-aunt's mouth – the one who used to be her sister's little darling!

A-Yee Nana then decided that she was going to pass the news on to us under her own steam. The train to Fei-Yn went only as far as Long-Miao (the capital city of Ku-Shan province) and no further public transportation was available. So A-Yee Nana walked more than eight hours to Fei-Yn. She also tried to carry as much food with her as she could. It was a very cold winter and after the long walk and with about 20 kilograms of food on her back, by the time she arrived she was completely soaked in a cold sweat. When she saw us she couldn't utter a single word. Her face had turned white as paper and she fainted on the spot.

In A-Yee Nana's words: 'At that time, I believed strongly. I could write no word, but I could speak, I could walk, I had Buddha in my heart and I could pray for Buddha's help and bless you all.' When she returned to Guanchou, she vowed to herself: 'I must do my best to help this innocent family get out of hell!'

And so she went to the Local Cultural Revolution Movements Organisation office, the Local Implement Policies of the Party office, and the City Citizen Neighbourhood Committee to beg for a review of our case, and she asked every single day for the return of our Guanchou residents permits!

Four long years later – thanks to her enormous effort and Buddha's helping hand – half of her dreaming came true. My sister, brother and I were returned to Guanchou.

By then, my brother was no longer a little boy, but almost 17. My sister was 22, and I was 20. My brother was 1.60 metres tall, but only 39 kilos; my sister was 1.66 metres tall, and 32 kilos; I was 1.59 metres tall, and 30 kilos. Our ragged clothes were so patched up that you could hardly find any original fabric. Our toes were poking out from our tattered shoes. Our bodies were covered with itchy spots, bitten by the mosquitoes and the fleas, and by the local lice that had infested our hair from the day we'd arrived in Fei-Yn. A-Yee Nana met us at the railway station. When she saw us get off the train, she ran towards us with both arms open wide. She kissed us, and cuddled the three of us together while her tears streamed down her face. I felt as though they were our precious Yei-Yei and Nana's open arms, kisses, cuddles and tears.

It was a summer morning, and A-Yee Nana took us to her home straight away. Luckily, there were not many people around, so A-Yee Nana used a piece of old sheet to cover a small corner behind the kitchen. Then she used a hose extended from the kitchen tap, and we had a wonderful wash with clean water. She gave us some of her own clothes to change into and threw all our old ones away. When our clothes were on the ground, the large fat fleas were jumping, floundering and desperately hunting around for our blood to drink for their last supper!

After our wash, A-Yee Nana gave us each a big glass of milk to drink and then she cooked us pork steaks, fish, chicken and ham soup, green vegetables and steamed rice. We had nearly forgotten the taste of milk and how delicious meat, fish, soup, fresh vegetables and steamed white rice were! We wolfed it all down at once and were still hungry. Then she fried some eggs for us. At Fei-Yn, we had drunk the muddy water from the river, our main food was sweet potato, corn and a very small portion of flour and brown rice. Our vegetables were cabbage, potato and pumpkin. We hardly saw any kind of meat, fish or green vegetables – not to mention milk or chicken and ham soup!

After we ate, A-Yee Nana found our hair still contained lots of lice, and so she gave us some fruit and said, 'You three rest now, I'm going to the nearest chemist to get some Ba-Bu (a kind of Chinese herbal medicine, to kill lice) and to buy you some clothes and shoes. I'll be back shortly.' And off she went.

Not very long after she left, I felt sick, and quickly grew dizzy and began to vomit. Then so did my sister, then my brother. A-Yee Nana hadn't shown us round the house, and so while we searched about for a toilet, we vomited all over the place – inside A-Yee Nana's room, outside her room, in the hallway, on the stairs, the kitchen floor, in the kitchen sink, outside the kitchen, and everywhere. The whole house stunk! The neighbours grew angry and yelled at us: 'What's going on here? Fuckin' stink! Bloody pumpkins! What are you doing here? Are you drunk?! Fuckin' pumpkins, get out of here!' Such dreadful yelling, that we felt as though we were still in Fei-Yn. We dropped our heads down, silenced, and then quickly found a broom and mop to try to clear up.

When A-Yee Nana returned, she was shocked and pulled us into her room to ask, 'Tell me who is sick?' My brother pointed to my sister and I, and said with a sad expression, 'She started first, then she, and last was me.' My brother still acted like a 10-year-old in front of A-Yee Nana. He was worried she might growl at us for making such a huge mess, so he tried to blame both of us before himself!

'How are you feeling now?' she asked him anxiously. A-Yee Nana had not changed either, in her eyes our brother was always going to be her darling little baby boy. She rushed downstairs and told her neighbours not to worry, she would clean it all up. And she returned with a bucket of water and let us wash ourselves and gave us some water to drink. Then she quickly opened the herb bottle, sprayed the Ba-Bu on our hair, covered it with a face cloth and told us to sit and wait for an hour then repeat the whole thing twice more.

By the time we had rinsed through the third lot, A-Yee Nana had finished cleaning up as well. She looked very tired. She was now 70, not as sprightly as when we were young. She let us try on the new clothes and shoes that she had bought for us and asked us whether we wanted any dinner. None of us did. In fact, we had sore stomachs again already. A-Yee Nana suggested that we have an early night. She moved her table and bed against the wall and made some space for us to sleep on the floor. About midnight, my stomach was terribly sore and I got diarrhoea, followed by my brother and sister. A-Yee Nana was terrified, she thought it must be food poisoning and she wanted to take us to the hospital. But the area she lived in had neither public transport nor telephone services at night. Suddenly she remembered that her neighbours had bicycles, and she asked if they would take us to the hospital.

Luckily, that night we met a real doctor, not a Barefoot Doctor. This doctor was about my father's age. He asked A-Yee Nana what we had eaten that day, then quickly sent us to the laboratory for some blood and bowel tests. When the report returned to him, he said, 'Good, good, very good! There is no bug found.' He then began questioning A-Yee Nana:

'Are you their mother?'

'No, I'm their great-aunt.'

'Where are their parents?'

'At home, Doctor.'

'Home? Where?'

'Countryside, Doctor,' A-Yee Nana replied, then added, 'They are very busy at work, as they are very good Proletariat Class over there.'

'And these children have just arrived in Guanchou?'

'Yes, just today, Doctor.'

The doctor nodded, then asked A-Yee Nana, 'How did you manage to get here with these three? It's a long way!'

'Helped by our neighbours, Doctor.'

'Are they still here?'

119

'No, they have gone, Doctor.'

Once again he nodded, then called the nurse and said, 'Put them into beds now – including her.' He pointed to A-Yee Nana. Then he continued, 'They have all got the same food poisoning. I want to keep them here for observation till tomorrow morning, then run a second bowel test. If it's clear then they can go home, otherwise they need to be treated straight away.' He turned to A-Yee Nana and said, 'Do you understand? You four all ate the same food, so *you* need to stay here for observation as well.'

Early the next morning the nurse woke us up and asked for a bowel sample. I heard the doctor say to A-Yee Nana in a whisper, 'Be patient! Don't expect to fatten them up in just one day. They have just returned from the countryside. The kind of life, and the food they had over there, I know very well. I myself just returned 18 months ago. Remember, the first week or two they must have very plain soft food, then gradually add some rich foods, such as meat, or fish, and so on. But certainly not milk – it's far too rich! When their diet returns to normal, then they will be able to have the foods that you gave them yesterday.'

A-Yee Nana thanked him and we left. I saw him as we said goodbye – frowning as he tried to stop the tears flowing down his face.

After that night, A-Yee Nana prayed even harder – every morning and every evening, with no intermission! She did not just pray for our parents' safe return, she also prayed for the three of us to obtain jobs. Sometimes I woke up in the early morning and would see A-Yee Nana already sitting on her bed, her Buddhist beads in her hands, deep in morning prayer. Every evening she was always the last one to bed, and she always prayed before she went to sleep. During the daytime, she kept visiting the Local Cultural Revolution Movements Organisation office, the Local Implement Policies of the Party office and the City Citizen Neighbourhood Committee, to beg for our parents' return and for work for the three of us.

According to the City Labour Planning Policy, for every two members of a family, one must be sent to do farming in the country, and the other can be a manufacturing worker in the city. Luckily, at this stage our family had seven members – four still in the country. Thanks to A-Yee Nana's huge effort, Buddha's help, and that loophole in the policy, we soon obtained jobs one after another. We all had the same kind of job offer – manufacturing workers. My sister was assigned to a clothing manufacturer, my brother to an electrical equipment manufacturer, and I was sent to work as a hand-embroidery worker.

Being able to work in the place where we were born was a godsend for us. We only had to work eight hours a day, six days a week, and even had some extra public holidays off. This was easy compared with life in Fei-Yn, where we worked from dawn till dusk each day, Monday to Sunday, all year round and had absolutely no breaks. Also, there was no hard physical work involved, no heavy loads to carry. We all received a regular income of 17.80 yuan per month to begin with, which for us was very good money compared with Fei-Yn, where we only received 6 yuan per person each month. However, by far the most important thing for us was that there was a great hope – to be treated equally as fellow humans!

When we received our first pay, together we bought A-Yee Nana a winter jacket, a woollen scarf and a pair of woollen gloves. She had been incredibly generous to us, buying us all new clothes, but her own had not been replaced since we left Guanchou seven years ago. Also, it was a way of expressing special thanks to her from our hearts' core. A-Yee Nana was so pleased. Her tears flowed down her face, she cuddled the three of us together and said, 'How wonderful! How special! A-Yee

Nana loves them! Especially because they come from you three. How exciting it would be if your Yei-Yei and Nana were still alive and they could see them and admire them too.' Here she stopped and began to sob violently.

Then we decided that we were going to give her all our income to help pay for our living expenses, despite knowing that it was not enough to cover all the money that she spent on us. Since we had been at A-Yee Nana's, she had tried to build us up, feeding us every day with the best food, while she herself hardly ate anything. She had outfitted us from top to toe, from underwear to jackets, from summer clothes to winter clothes. When we told her our plan, she was extremely upset and refused: 'No! A-Yee Nana has got enough. You must keep it for yourselves, you are growing, and you need some money to buy things for yourselves that you really like. A-Yee Nana could not bear to see you three so thin, so sad.' Then we told her that if she was not going to accept this money, we could no longer stay there with her. This really worried her and she relented, making the three of us very happy. 'Okay, my three ancestors – you win! I will keep the money for you, but I won't touch it. If you ever need it you must always ask. Promise?' And we promised her.

After we had been at A-Yee Nana's for half a year, our hair turned extremely shiny, our faces turned pink, all the itchy spots disappeared, our skin turned smooth, and we all put on heaps of weight. But all the time we were gaining weight, A-Yee Nana was losing hers. And the more weight she saw us put on, the more she worried about our parents.

The time drew close to the Chinese New Year, and we heard that we were to have five days off. We wondered if we should use this holiday to go back to Fei-Yn to see our parents, and we asked if she agreed. However, right from the beginning she said to us, 'No, I don't think it's a good idea.' My brother burst into tears and so she said to us, 'Okay, Di-Di, you can go, but not you two girls.' Then we began crying too and she tried to explain that it wasn't because our brother was her favourite, but purely for the safety of us girls, especially for my sister. She was now 1.66 metres tall, and with her slender figure, long straight legs, shining thick black hair, her face as smooth as a boiled egg out of the shell, and lovely features, she was acknowledged as the prettiest girl in the area. Every day after she finished work there were always very dangerous-looking men following her home. Consequently, A-Yee Nana walked her to and from work each day. But she still couldn't prevail on us, so in the end she said, 'Well, then, I will have to go there with you!' Once again, she compromised.

The New Year's holiday started on New Year's Eve. So we left Guanchou the day after we finished work. We caught the seven-thirty evening train to Long-Miao. After a 36-hour journey, on a slow train, we finally reached Long-Miao on New Year's morning. From Long-Miao to Fei-Yn took us another eight hours on foot. It was another cold winter, so the day before we left Guanchou, A-Yee Nana borrowed long, thick army winter coats and hats from her neighbours to keep us warm. Also, the coats and hats covered us up and made us extra safe while walking through the desolate and uninhabited countryside. We also carried lots of clothes, food and medicines for our parents. On this kind of poor country road, there were often robbers hiding there to steal food and money, and to rape the women.

When we finally arrived at Fei-Yn about three o'clock in the afternoon, Mum and Dad did not recognise us, only A-Yee Nana! When Di-Di saw them, he ran towards them, followed by my sister and I. Mum and Dad stood there numbly for a while, then the six of us collapsed together in a flood of tears. Mum and Dad still could not believe the three of us were standing there in front of them. Dad wondered, 'Di-Di – is that you? You are almost taller than your Dad!' He then looked at my sister and marvelled, 'Ji-Ji is that you? You look exactly like your mother when I met her at Chong-Sa University.' Lastly, Dad turned to me, kissed me and said, 'When Dad looks at you, it feels like he is looking in the mirror at himself!' Then Mum and Dad hugged A-Yee Nana and said simultaneously, 'Only half a year! How changed they are. They are healthy and safe now, but you are so thin. All your blood goes into their veins.' Mum and Dad thanked her again and again.

We stayed the night there, then returned early the next morning. While we were there, we were terribly hungry, but none of us touched the food that A-Yee Nana brought for them. Before we left, Mum and Dad said repeatedly, 'Mum and Dad won't worry about you any more! You are safe now! Remember, if anything ever happens to Mum and Dad, A-Yee Nana will always be there for you, and you shall never be alone.' Then they added, 'You three are now young women and a man, no longer little girls and a boy. You have to help A-Yee Nana, don't let her do everything for you. Make sure A-Yee Nana eats the same food as you do, don't let her save everything from her teeth for you – you have to look after her as well. Understand, A-Yee Nana's good health and long life is up to you three. She is your security and safety. Treasure it!'

It was a very exhausting and emotional visit. Two days to get there, two days to return. This only left us one short afternoon and a night with our parents. However, after that visit we were all alarmed by their poor state of health and loss of willpower. They were both extremely thin – even thinner than six months ago. Worse, they seemed to have lost all hope and desire for peace. A-Yee Nana cried all the way back to Guanchou. She kept saying that it would be the last time we would see our parents, as she felt it was unlikely Mum and Dad could carry on surviving. She reminded us that their words were true – that

124

she would always be there for us, and that we must help look after her in return.

A-Yee Nana's despondent words reminded me vividly of the night after Nana's death when I saw Mum and Dad sitting in a corner of the dark room and heard them whispering.

'Your mother was right. She really did the right thing for herself. She is now at peace,' said Mum.

'Yes, you might be right,' Dad replied.

'But what reason have we got to carry on our own lives for?' asked Mum.

'For our children!' Dad insisted.

'But our children are human too. Why should they have to suffer like this for us? They need peace too.' Mum began to sob.

Dad was silent for a moment, then he started whispering most insistently, 'No! We can't think that way. We can't do that to our children. Di-Di is only nine and a half, not even 10 yet. Far too young! They have not even begun their lives, so how could they be ended?'

Dad drew Mum into his arms and begged, 'You must promise me to wait until our children are out of this hell. Please promise me!'

We returned from that visit to our parents with such a terrible feeling of hopelessness that we began joining A-Yee Nana's morning and evening prayers every day. I also suggested that we should write to Mum and Dad every week, to let them know how much we loved them, missed them, and needed them. A Yee-Nana continued going to the Local Implement Policies of the Party Office and the City Citizen Neighbourhood Committee to beg for their rehabilitation and return to Guanchou every day.

But three more years were to pass before our persistent prayers, ongoing letters, and A-Yee Nana's unflagging efforts finally touched and moved Buddha and the order was given for our parents' repatriation to Guanchou.

Life seemed smoother after our parents returned. I felt as though the dreaded winter had passed and that spring was very much in the air.

Once I'd obtained my job at the hand-embroidery factory, I was trained up as an embroidery worker. It was purely handicraft, but very interesting. In fact, compared with the hard labour we'd experienced in Fei-Yn, it was a queen's task! Every day, I remembered Mum and Dad's words, and walked to and from work (saving 2.60 yuan per month for A-Yee Nana) then sealed my lips, put a smile on my face and played my part. I tried to work very hard, to do as much as I could. I listened very carefully, and learned very quickly. Soon, all my colleagues began to like me, especially the woman who taught me to embroider, who became very fond of me. I was commended for my keenness and enthusiasm. Later, I was even awarded a Commendation to the Advanced Individual.

Not long after our parents' return, a fellow worker collapsed and hit her head on a pile of embroidery scissors. Blood flowed all over the place and she died on her way to hospital. This was the first fatal accident in the industry's history. The Managing Director called an urgent staff meeting and requested a handwritten report from an eyewitness. Thanks to my dearest Yei-Yei's careful tutelage I was the only one in the whole workshop of about 100 workers that was able to do so. And so, I put my hand up and said nervously, 'I'll try.' My luck turned from that moment!

My report greatly impressed the company management – especially the Managing Director, who I later learned also came from an educated family that had suffered during the Cultural Revolution. Then they became aware of my other capabilities.

Shortly after, I was singled out for promotion to the accounts department. I was a bit nervous at first, as I knew my level of education was really only primary school grade. But I was encouraged by my father, who said to me: 'In this world, nothing is difficult for one who sets his mind to it. Where there is a will, there is a way! Constant dripping wears away the stone, little strokes fell great oaks and turn a dream to truth.' He then bought me a book-keeping book, which he read first, and taught me step by step. Within only a month, I began to work all on my own.

One morning, the Head of Accounts called me into his office and asked me how much spare time I had during the day, and whether I could help him. As he was a very radical Party member, the majority of his time was taken up by Party meetings and so he had great difficulties meeting the deadlines for his monthly reports. After that, I tried to finish off my own job in the morning, and used my afternoons to help him with his backlog.

Later, I discovered that in fact he was a very nice man – easygoing, a man who spoke his mind and had very high ambitions, but also a big heart. I was sure he'd make a great politician, but certainly not an accountant! It was purely a waste of his talent. We two got on very well. In some ways, we were perfectly matched workers. He talked extremely hard like a radio host, and I listened carefully and worked extremely hard like a machine. After about two months, the piles of papers and reports suddenly disappeared from his desk and the dreaded telephone calls petered out. I was promoted to be his assistant shortly after.

About six months later, he was unexpectedly given a Commendation to the Advanced Individual from Head Office for his high standards, outstanding financial reports and prompt reporting. He also received a promotion to Director of Finance and announced that I would be his assistant in this new appointment, and also his replacement as Head of Accounts. Two years later, he became Chairman of the Communist Party Committee of our company. Once again, I became his replacement as the Director of Finance.

To me, on the one hand it was just like winning the lottery, while on the other hand it proved the importance of my father's words to me: 'The easiest way to learn is by doing; the most important way to obtain an opportunity is by being willing to help others and not demand the credit.' It was just like the English saying: 'The proof of the pudding is in the eating.' Dad's words really guided my life in the right direction. Sadly now, all is gone . . .

Suddenly, Guo Yi was calling out loudly, 'Mama! Mama! Jei-Fung-Jung Susu is coming! Xiao A-Yee! Xiao A-Yee! Jei-Fung-Jung Susu is looking for you.' Jei-Fung-Jung means 'Liberation Army', Susu means 'uncle'. Chinese children were all taught at kindergarten that anyone from the Liberation Army is a most respectable person, and that they had to be addressed as 'Uncle'. Da-Jei jumped out from her bedroom, rushed towards the front door and he walked in. Da-Jei stared at him, her face went pale and she backed away. She had absolutely no idea who this stranger was. From the army? No – where were the shoulder-straps and insignia? A policeman? They don't dress that way. Plain-clothes man? No, it couldn't be! My company Human Resource Manager come down to spy on me? No. Surely not. Then who was he? Who was this stranger? And, so, she turned to me.

I couldn't believe my eyes – it was Yee Bing! When he saw me, he rushed forward and stopped right in front of me, placing his hands upon my shoulders.

'Are you okay?' His voice was hoarse and breathless.

I was utterly stunned, I couldn't make a sound.

It was Guo Yi who broke the silence. 'Jei-Fung-Jung Susu, I am Xiao Guo Yi, this is my dearest Xiao A-Yee, and this is my dearest Hao Mama, and this is my bike! Mama and I are taking Xiao A-Yee to town, so she can buy me lots of books, toys and lollies. Would you like to come with us?' Guo Yi was introducing, telling, inviting, and rapt with excitement all at the same time.

'Oh, yes! I certainly would.' said Yee Bing with a big smile, bending down and patting Guo Yi's little head.

I just looked at them both, and didn't know whether to cry or laugh. I quickly turned the stereo off and got up to introduce Yee Bing to Da-Jei. They greeted each other and shook hands and Da-Jei asked him to sit down. However, poor Guo Yi was put to bed straight away. Da-Jei knew her son well, and that he understood far too much for his age.

'How did you find us here? It's a long way from Guanchou – you must be exhausted,' Da-Jei asked after an awkward silence, trying to be friendly.

'Well, it was, but I am revived now, thank you,' replied Yee Bing politely.

'But how did you find us here? I mean, my dwelling?' Da-Jai stuck firmly to her original question.

'Well, I was helped by my father's friend.' Once again, Yee Bing gave nothing more away.

'Who is this friend? Does he know us? Do we know each other?' Da-Jei fixed him with her stubborn eyes.

'No, he doesn't. Just a friend of my father's. Or rather, one of my father's subordinates,' he replied nervously.

'Ah!' Da-Jei replied loudly, nodding in comprehension.

Yee Bing's head snapped up, his eyes met hers, and he flushed crimson as he suddenly realised Da-Jei was no soft cuddly teddy bear. Later, long after, he said to me, 'I never met such a tough woman as your Da-Jei in all my life! She is as stubborn as a stone, as tough as an India rubber ball. She really should be a politician. What a waste in such a small town.'

'Now, tell me, what is the aim of this trip?' Da-Jei's questioning became more aggressive.

Yee Bing was stunned. He bit his lip, dropped his head, and fixed his eyes on the ground.

'Mamaaaa!' Suddenly Guo Yi was crying. Da-Jei jumped up from her chair, ran into her bedroom, and returned with her son in her arms. Yee Bing had time only to sigh deeply and fix his eyes on me longingly before the conversation was switched to another channel.

'Mama, I'm hungry! Mama, I'm hungry!' demanded Guo Yi. Da-Jei quickly put him down and went into the kitchen.

Then Guo Yi said to Yee Bing, 'Jei-Fung-Jung Susu, are you hungry? Would you like to have some lunch with my dearest Hao Mama, my dearest Xiao A-Yee and I?'

Yee Bing looked at him, simply shook his head and managed a rueful little smile.

'No! Jei-Fung-Jung Susu, you must have some lunch with us. Otherwise you will starve yourself to death,' Guo Yi said with his most serious expression, and ran to the kitchen. 'Mama, Jei-Fu-Jung Susu is hungry too.'

Now Da-Jei had no choice but to let him stay. Neither the bus nor the train left for Kiuing on the same day – they only came twice a week. Therefore, there was no possibility of him returning to Guanchou today.

And so, Guo Yi had a new best friend. I no longer seemed important to him. Taking Xiao A-Yee to town, her buying him lots of books, toys and lollies – he had forgotten it all. Jei-Fung-Jung Susu was his idol. He asked Yee Bing to put his army hat onto his head first. Then he went to his room, got his toy gun, asked his mother for some scarves and asked Yee Bing to tie them onto his body, to make him a 'Most Powerful Army'. Then followed his thousands, millions, billions and zillions of questions – all about guns, armies, fighting, and even the war.

That night Yee Bing slept in Guo Yi's room, while Guo Yi, Da-Jei and I shared the other room. After we went to bed, I heard the front door open, and saw Yee Bing walk around in the garden until two o'clock, when he returned to bed. In the morning, Yee Bing asked me whether I would like to go to town with him, but I felt in no mood to go with him anywhere, and he went alone.

I stayed at home with Guo Yi while Da-Jei went to work. Yee Bing returned at lunchtime. He brought Guo Yi a children's storybook, a mini classic poetry book and a box of chocolates. He brought me a book on Gin province, with a rose flower bookmark, and whispered softly, 'I'm sorry. I couldn't find any flowers, so hopefully this will cheer you up instead.' He also brought some little lemon cakes for our afternoon tea, as he knew that anything with lemon was always my favourite. He had bought himself some T-shirts, trousers, underwear, socks, toothbrush, toothpaste, face cloth and so on, and I suddenly realised that when he came yesterday he had only his university textbook bag with him.

Da-Jei came back home very late that night, and already Yee Bing was replacing me, lying beside Guo Yi on his bed with the children's story he'd bought him that morning. When Da-Jei walked into the bedroom and saw Yee Bing holding her sleeping son in one arm, while he held a children's book in the other, also asleep, she was most touched. Gently closing the bedroom door, she sat beside me and muttered, 'This can't be like him?'

'What do you mean?' I asked.

'I mean, is he really like that?' Da-Jei looked very puzzled.

'Like what?' I asked.

'Full of love.'

I simply looked at Da-Jei, at a loss for words, as Yee Bing walked in. He was wearing his new T-shirt and trousers and, after his wee nap, was looking rather fresh and handsome.

We went outside for a walk. But as soon as we were alone, he suddenly stopped and held me tightly in his arms. He hung his head and began to cry. 'I'm so terribly sorry. Please forgive me! It's all my fault that this has happened.' He blamed himself again and again. Finally, he kissed me softly, held my hands and sat me down on the ground beside him. Then he straightened his legs, fished out a set of keys from his pocket and put them onto my palm, saying, 'These are the keys to our home!'

'Our home? Where is our home?' I was totally bewildered.

'After that row with my parents, I decided that I must move away from them at once. The sooner the better! I know that according to the old custom, "Neither a decent woman nor a decent man should leave their family before the marriage", but I had to do it! All my parents care about is power. They need humbling.' Suddenly he stopped and struggled with his emotions.

Then he continued, 'Now, I still want us to be married on your birthday. What's our study for? To be totally honest, when I decided to do my Masters degree, it was purely for you. I wanted to reach the same level of education as your parents. But all that study only gives us a piece of paper. You have already become a Director of Finance without it. We aren't a young girl and boy any more, we are already over thirty. We must remember that the human train goes just one single way! And then it's gone forever and never returns. Sheng, our children also need young, youthful, blooming parents. I must suspend my studies at once and find a job, so that we can start a family. Life is so short. We must make the most of it. Otherwise we shall regret it one day. Our parents have the right to bring us into this world, but they have no right to decide our destiny and future.'

He stopped and began to kiss me, before he continued, 'Now I hope you understand why I didn't see you the next day. I was concentrating on finding a flat for us through my father's contacts. Also, I wanted to give you a surprise. At lunchtime on the third day I finally got the key to a three-bedroomed flat very near to your parents. I was so happy! I ran straight to your work and found out what happened from Lao-Zhu. I was shocked. If I hadn't got this stupid idea to give you a big surprise, I wouldn't have left you alone for such a long period. I'm terribly sorry! I'm so stupid!'

I still didn't know what to say, but he carried on, 'I found out from your Da-Bo that you had gone with your parents to your Da-Jei's, but Da-Bo said he couldn't remember her home address or where she worked. Once again I was helped by my father's contacts. Then I found that the tickets were all fully booked, and even my father's contacts couldn't get one. I was just like the ant crawling on the hot pan, I didn't know what to do. Then on Monday morning, on my way to my lecture, I suddenly thought I'd go to the airport and see if there were any cancellations or emergency seats. And I was just in time! There was one seat, but the plane was departing in 10 minutes and I had no time to ring home. In the end I phoned Wu-Ma from Kiuing airport. Then, when I got off the plane, there was a bus to Mu-Long. People said I was really lucky – if I'd been five minutes later I would have had to wait in Kiuing for two days until the next one. Now, you see, everything is coming our way! Sheng, give me your hands and come to me! Come to me entirely! Let us start our life together and for ever! Sheng, I cannot live without you. Please accept me once more. Quickly! Say yes! Please repeat it. Please say it once more. Sheng, please talk to me.' He was gripping my arms, shaking me, and demanding a satisfactory answer.

I was lost for words, my voice not quite under command. 'I'm sorry,' I finally managed to get out. 'Let's discuss it some other time – I want to go home now.' I felt weak and sick, and I wanted some water. We returned to Da-Jei's immediately.

After Yee Bing had been staying with us for a week, Da-Jei had softened and grown more friendly towards him. She'd even offered to let him stay as long as he wished. One night, after she returned home from work, Guo Yi ran towards her and said, 'Mama! Mama! Listen! I can recite a poem! Mama! I can recite a poem!' Then he cleared his little throat and, standing extremely deferentially, recited two classic Chinese poems, one after the other, until he was nearly out of breath.

Not waiting till her son had finished, Da-Jei ran towards him, kissing and cuddling him through her tears. 'Tell Mama who taught you?' she asked him.

'Jei-Fung-Jung Susu taught me,' said Guo Yi, pointing at Yee Bing with a proud smile.

'No, he is not Jei-Fung-Jung Susu, he is Yee Bing A-Juo (maternal uncle),' his mother corrected him.

Yee Bing jumped up from his chair and said, 'Thank you Da-Jei!' with tears in his eyes, but a huge smile. He then cuddled me tightly and whispered in my ear, 'Your Da-Jei approves of our relationship. Say a special thank-you to your Da-Jei. Quick! Say it!' I could tell this happy moment was from his heart's core.

The next day Da-Jei arranged for Yee Bing to take Guo Yi to a children's movie and she had a very long talk with me. She thought Yee Bing was a very sensible, responsible, ambitious young man, full of love and energy. She believed that both of us were truly in love, and that I should accept him. She also suggested that I should return to Guanchou straight away, to get married, and to start our new lives.

However, Da-Jei also knew our mother very well and that it would not be so easy to change her mind. But she thought Guo Yi might be able to soften and break this deadlock a bit. So she wrote a long letter to our parents saying how much her son missed them, and was hoping to see them in Guanchou and so on. She included a tape recording of Guo Yi's recitation of the classic poems Yee Bing had taught him. A few days later our parents received this letter and rang Da-Jei at work at once to ask me to return to Guanchou with Xiao Guo Yi as soon as possible, as they couldn't wait to see him any longer.

At the same time, Yee Bing's parents demanded that he return as well. So Yee Bing arranged tickets. We took a sleeping berth train, which meant that we could rest any time we wished. It took five days and four nights to get to Guanchou. It would be a very long journey but he thought that, as it was Guo Yi's first long train trip since he was able to walk and talk, it would enable him to see more, and we two could spend more time together.

When Guo Yi heard that he was going to Guanchou with us he clapped his little hands. 'Bravo Mama! We are going to visit Pohpoh and Gohgoh (maternal grandfather and grandmother) – they can buy the whole of Guanchou for us!' But when he heard that his mother was not going he was very upset. 'Mama, why aren't you going with us? If you're not going, I won't go either,' he declared.

It was a very understandable reaction, as Guo Yi had never been apart from his mother for a single day since he was born. It seemed rather hard for both of them and I started wondering whether it was such a good idea.

Then Da-Jei said to him, 'You go with Yee Bing A-Juo and Xiao A-Yee on the first train, and Mama will finish work, then catch the next train to meet you for Chinese New Year.' It was rather adult talk, but when Guo Yi heard the words 'next train'

135

he got the message and was satisfied.

Next morning, after Da Jei had left for work, Guo Yi asked Yee Bing, 'Yee Bing A-Juo, why can't we wait till my Hao Mama finishes work, then we can go together?'

'Because Yee Bing A-Juo cannot wait to show your Xiao A-Yee her new home!' answered Yee Bing, shooting a tiny challenging glance at me.

'Will my Pohpoh, Gohgoh, Mama and I all stay at Xiao A-Yee's new home?' continued Guo Yi.

'Nooo! You will stay at your Pohpoh and Gohgoh's. I'm sorry. Your Xiao A-Yee's new home is for Xiao A-Yee and Yee Bing A-Juo only.' Yee Bing said, looking at him with a serious expression.

Guo Yi was terribly upset and said, 'If it's our Xiao A-Yee's new home, why can't we stay but you can?'

'Aha! You know why? Because your Xiao A-Yee is no longer yours – as soon as we arrive in Guanchou, Xiao A-Yee shall be mine straight away,' teased Yee Bing, trying to upset him even more.

'No! It can't be. My Xiao A-Yee's name is Guo Sheng, and my name is Guo Yi – we're all Guos! Guos always belong to Guos and you are Yees. We never will be the same family.' Guo Yi could talk rather amazingly for his age.

'Aha! Now I know you are a little dummy. Why can we never be the same family? We certainly can! Your Xiao A-Yee and I are getting married as soon as we arrive in Guanchou. As soon as we are married, your Xiao A-Yee shall be called Yee Sheng and no longer Guo Sheng, and she definitely will belong to Yees, not Guos.'

Having lost his battle, Guo Yi burst into tears, but Yee Bing then said very quickly, laughing and shaking his head, 'Oh no, you aren't going to cry? You shall be a big brother very soon. And your new brother will be called Xiao Guo Yi too, so then he shall be Guos and definitely will be yours! Smile! Quick! Smile!'

As soon as Guo Yi heard that he would be a big brother and have a little brother called Xiao Guo Yi as well he stopped crying and asked Yee Bing to promise him that his little brother must be called the same name as him, and must be his, and Yee Bing did, and the war ended.

Really, Yee Bing and Guo Yi were the best of friends, and Da-Jei also became fond of him. Yee Bing seemed so much happier, cheerful and full of courage. After we had arranged our return, he said to me, 'I'm sorry I've pushed you so hard lately. I really should have given you more time to think and to work out everything for yourself. I know it will be hard for you to discuss this with your parents, so don't worry, leave it to me — I'll talk to them and I believe they'll be just like your Da-Jei, and accept this relationship as well.'

He paused and frowned at me briefly before he resumed, 'I never appreciated your family as deeply as now — especially your grandfather and your father. I feel so sorry for your father. Those cheerful daily expressions that we see, are they really from his heart's core?'

Once again he stopped, and muttered determinedly, 'I must do something for your family! I must do something for your guiltless family!'

Then he took my hands and said earnestly, 'Sheng, please understand our marriage is not just for ourselves, it's for the Guos as well! Listen, don't worry too much about my parents. I know them well. The best thing to do is give them space for a while, but we must get married as soon as possible and start a family at once. Once we have our child and their grandchild, they will accept us and love us again. Then the Guos will become part of the Yees, and it will be their duty to help us clear your grandfather's name, make restitution and purify the Guos' political life. Together let us do something for the innocent Guos!'

I was deeply touched by what he was saying, and by what he had done for me lately. Such strength of emotion stirred the grief and love within me and, not waiting until he had finished, I buried my head into his chest and sobbed as violently as a heart-broken child.

Nonetheless, the sudden decision to return to Guanchou gave rise to very mixed feelings for me. My mind had absolutely no room for fantasy, it was fully occupied by a dreadful storm of questions. What would happen to my job now? What about the medical certificate? Would I still have a job, or would I be driven out of the company? What would people's reaction be? Would they treat me as a mad person and look down on me? What would Mum, Dad and Da-Bo's response be after I returned home with Yee Bing? And when they heard that Yee Bing and I still planned to be married on that same day, would they sit down and listen to what we planned to do for ourselves, for the Guos, and all the subsequent generations of Guos?

The day we left, Da-Jei came to see us off from Mu-Long station. She said to me, 'Be strong! Do whatever your heart instructs you to do; decide whatever your heart commands you to decide. Remember – the world always belongs to the Capable General!'

When the train started its engine, Da-Jei waved us off and called out to us: 'I wish you well – good luck and good news for you both!'

'Yes! Thank you, Da-Jei!' beamed Yee Bing, holding my hand, smiling confidently and waving back.

Six

無辜的生命

Another Innocent Life

As Da-Jei waved cheerfully to us from the platform of Mu-Long station my thoughts turned involuntarily to the tragic events of her own life . . .

Although Da-Jei means eldest sister, in fact Da-Jei wasn't our older sister – she was our cousin. Da-Jei was my father's only sister's only child. My parents were unable to tell her this family secret until after the Cultural Revolution – when Ni-Ni (Da-Jei's name) was almost 29.

When Da-Jei's mother was just 22, in her second year of university, she accidentally became pregnant. In those days if a young girl of her family background – 'A Proud Upper-Class' – had a child before marriage it involved a great loss of face. Not just for herself, but for the whole family. Therefore, she was far too scared to tell her parents. She went with her boyfriend (her classmate, who was one year her junior) to the countryside, Quan-Sa, near Guanchou, to have an abortion – helped by one of their close friends. Sadly, they were cheated by their friend's childless aunt who acted as a traditional doctor and offered them a supposedly very secure abortion remedy. But, instead, she gave her a remedy for the safety of her embryo. Later, they were told that it was very unfortunate, but the abortion had not worked for her. It was far too late to do anything by then, and she had to prepare to give birth to this child. However, the woman told her she would let her hide at her home until the baby was born. Afterwards, she said that they could leave the baby with her and return to Guanchou, and nobody would know. In their naivety they trusted her completely and thought it was the best and only option for them. They took up her offer, and lied to their parents that they were going overseas to study for half a year, then they went into hiding in her house until the baby was born.

Unfortunately, the one in whom they placed their trust was evil, and the place in which they stayed was an open grave! There was no medical care whatsoever. When the time came to give birth, Da-Jei's mother had a severe womb haemorrhage, and before they found a doctor, she died. Da-Jei's father was so distressed that he left her there and ran away, without even giving her a birth name!

Nevertheless, her mother's friend's aunt was desperate to keep the baby, and wanted to get rid of her mother's body as soon as possible. So she hid Da-Jei in another place and reported to the police that she had found a dead body in the river beside her house.

By the time my grandparents arrived there, Da-Jei's mother's body was in the river! This was a shocking moment for my grandparents, and many years later my grandmother still could not face a river. After we were born, we were never allowed to go near a river or even a swimming pool, and consequently none of us ever learned to swim!

However, my grandparents never believed it was the real story of their daughter's death. When they discovered the true story, my own parents had just married. So my grandparents took the child home, and the family shifted to a new place. Then, publicly, this child became our parents' first child – our eldest sister – and the story has been covered up ever since.

When the Cultural Revolution broke out in 1966, Da-Jei had just turned 19. She had some of our grandfather's features – an olive complexion, dark and clear – and she was quite tall, almost 1.64 metres. With her well-proportioned melon seed-shaped face, full bust, sloping shoulders, long graceful neck, fine head of dark, shining and straight hair, she was greatly admired among all her friends. She had a great passion for drama and as a little girl she dreamed that, once she grew up, she would be a famous actress.

The day the Red Guards broke into our house, Da-Jei was dressed in pure white and in the middle of a play – *Romeo and Juliet* – in front of the mirror in her room. The next day, when we were sent to Fei-Yn, these were the only clothes that she had on. When the locals saw her, she seemed like a Hollywood film star because of her beauty. Some of the local children followed her everywhere, and they spat and threw rubbish at her and accused her of being a Yang Gui (Western ghost). Then, some of the local evil men planned something wicked . . .

On our arrival in Fei-Yn, my head was covered by thick bandages, and my right arm was set in plaster and supported in a sling made from another big piece of bandage, so it all looked rather serious. Consequently, nobody forced me to do anything. Di-Di stuck very close to me, and we dropped our heads low, to avoid being noticed.

Not long after, the weather grew cold. We could no longer sleep on the mud floor. Dad found some big pieces of wood and joined them together to make a big bed for us all. But some of them were thick, and some of them were thin, so Dad found straw for us to lie upon, then covered it with a worn-out sheet that we were given by the locals. The sheet was so thin, we were always itchy from the straw.

One morning, after our parents and sisters had gone to work at the farm, my brother said to me, 'Jei-Jei (sister), I'm itching.' I pulled his jacket up, and poor thing, his back was covered with red itchy spots.

'I know,' I said to him, 'me too.'

'Is there anything we can do?' He looked like he was about to cry.

Then I remembered that just a couple of hundred yards from the ruined temple that we were staying in was the People's Commune Cultural Revolution Office where I had noticed some newspapers in their rubbish bin a few days earlier. 'Let's go and get some newspapers,' I suggested, and as there was nobody around, we took all the newspapers we could find and put them on top of the straw. Mum, Dad and our sisters didn't even notice. They worked so hard each day that, as soon as they had eaten at night, they fell straight to sleep.

One morning before they went to the farm, Dad said to me, 'If the sun comes up, don't forget to pull the bedclothes off and let the straw get some sun. It may dry out a bit, and then we won't get so itchy.'

So as soon as the sun came up, Di-Di and I stripped off the bedding and found that all the newspapers had fallen to pieces. We removed the papers and left the straw to dry under the sun. After I'd used my good hand to tidy up the scraps of newspaper I suggested to my brother that we go in search of fresh supplies. But when we reached the office, we saw people inside. We tried to slip away with some papers unnoticed, but it was too late. We were caught by an angry man who shouted, 'Stop! What are you doing here?'

We stopped and he ran towards us. 'Show me, fuckin' bastard, what's in your hands?' he demanded of my brother. When he found there were some of Mao's photos in the newspaper and that they'd been ripped up, he kicked Di-Di's buttocks, and slapped his face, thundering and screaming, 'Reactionary! Counter-Revolutionary! You dare to tear our treasure, our Great Leader Chairman Mao's photo, into pieces!' The kicks and punches fell like a storm. My brother held his head, bent down and screaming with pain. I quickly jumped over and pulled him behind me, begging, 'Don't beat him! Beat me! It was my idea. Beat me –' And I was immediately arrested.

There were about eight or 10 men in the room, and I was pushed kneeling onto the middle of the floor. The same man began to threaten: 'Xiao Counter-Revolutionary! We order you to accuse and expose who abetted you to do this? We know it wasn't your own idea, but that your parents abetted you. They deeply hate our Great Leader Chairman Mao, and they use you children to give vent to their great class hatred. Now! We order you to tell the truth, then you can go back to your family, otherwise you will be locked in the jail till you die! Do you know how serious this reactionary event is? It's an astounding Anti-Revolution event! It's an appalling Anti-Revolution crime! You children would not dare to do this! Only your Counter-Revolutionary parents would!'

Then another man banged his belt onto the table and screamed 'Quick! Xiao Counter-Revolutionary, quickly tell the truth! If you don't tell the truth, we will beat you to death now!

I told them that our parents always taught us to respect and love our Great, Glorious, Right Communist Party and our Great Leader Chairman Mao. And I said it was purely my idea, as we had all got itchy spots from the straw, and I thought the newspaper could help a bit.

But none of them believed me. Not waiting until I finished, the first man jumped up from his chair, thumping his hand on the table loudly and shouting, 'What rubbish! Xiao Counter-Revolutionary! How dare you fabricate a story to protect your Counter-Revolutionary parents!' Then the other man threw his thick army belt onto the ground in front of me and yelled 'Fuckin' bastards! Xiao Counter-Revolutionary you dare to tell a lie in front of us!' A third man was slapping my face viciously and vigorously kicking my buttocks and legs as he shouted, 'Okay! You don't want to live, you want to die, I know. Can you remember how you had your head and arm broken? Haven't you had enough? Do you want some more? Okay! We will give you some more!'

I was screaming with pain and begging, 'Don't beat me! I didn't tell a lie! It's truth –'

Suddenly the beating stopped. Someone pulled my head up and I found my nose was bleeding badly, the blood pouring everywhere. Then they shoved and kicked me into a ghastly damp and dark room and I lost my balance, falling onto the ground. Before they shut the door, they scowled and threatened: 'Xiao Counter-Revolutionary! You wait! We will make you tell the truth very quickly!' The door closed, leaving me in pitch-darkness. I sat on the mud floor, my whole body aching, and sobbed inconsolably.

Suddenly, something heavy dropped on my head. It quickly moved onto my body and started to bite me. I screamed and jumped up and found that my left leg could hardly move. From the light through the crack under the door, I saw a band of huge rats, almost as big as kittens, swarming over the floor. My hackles rose, I was trembling with shock and fear.

Then I heard some footsteps outside. I hobbled slowly towards the door. Through the crack, I saw my parents and sisters, their heads down, silently walking towards the People's

Commune Cultural Revolution Office, followed by several Red Guards.

'Dad!' I cried out hoarsely. They all stopped and tried to locate me. But a guard yelling, 'Fuckin' . . . ! Who told you that you were allowed to stop here? Do you want to corroborate statements with your daughter? Get moving quickly!' shoved them on.

'Dad! I'm here! Dad! They've locked me inside! Dad –' I was screaming in despair. I saw Dad turn his head and run towards the door, but one of the Red Guards quickly pulled him back and slapped his face and forced them to move on. I exerted every ounce of my energy to bang on the door and screamed, 'Let me out! Let me out!' Eventually I grew exhausted, and fell asleep.

Next thing I knew, Dad was calling me from outside the door: 'Sheng, are you there? Dad is here, outside. Are you okay? Sheng, answer Dad!'

I opened my eyes but the light had gone, and it was now so black I couldn't even find the door crack, let alone see Dad outside. I cried, 'Dad, where are you? Dad, I can't see anything –'

'Sheng, are you by the door?'

'Yes, Dad.'

'Don't be frightened now, Dad is outside the door and near you.'

'Dad, my head and arm are sore, and I think my leg is broken too –' I began to sob violently.

'Sheng, listen to Dad, don't cry. It's the middle of the night. If people hear us, we will get beaten again,' Dad whispered urgently from outside.

He then continued, 'Sheng, can you hear Dad? Be brave! Dad is here with you. Sheng, stop crying, take a deep breath and use your hand to examine your leg. See whether there are any lumps and if there is a particularly sore area.'

I did as he said and cried, 'Yes, Dad, on my left leg, just above the knee there is a big lump and it is extremely sore.'

A pause. 'Listen, don't cry. Tell Dad what happened this morning.'

After I told Dad everything, he said, 'Listen, tomorrow, if they come, you just tell them that your father knew it, but your mother and sisters truly didn't know.'

'No! Dad, it's a lie!' I was terrified that if I lied to them that Dad had known, they would lock him in jail and beat him to death.

'Sheng. Your leg is probably broken – if you don't get it treated straight away, you will get an infection. And if that happens, you might either lose your leg or die. Don't worry about Dad. Dad is much stronger! Say it. Please say it for Dad tomorrow.'

'No! Dad! I won't!' I was scared, and cold, and hungry, and I sobbed this through the door to him.

Dad then whispered again, 'Where are you now?'

'By the door.'

'Here, use your hand to find Dad's finger, in the crack in the door, then sit down and lean onto that spot and Dad will do the same – it can warm you a bit.'

And I did, and I was so relieved. When I touched Dad's finger, it calmed me down and I felt safe that Dad was right there on the other side of the door, and very soon I fell asleep.

But then the rats started crawling all over my body again, and started to bite me. I woke up screaming, 'Dad! Rats, Dad! Rats!'

Once again, Dad whispered urgently, 'Don't scream, Sheng. If you wake people up we will get beaten again.'

This cautioned me into silence.

'Sheng, can you hear Dad? You must try to get some rest.

Dad will help you make some noise, so that the rats won't come near you.' Dad started using his shoe to bang on the gap between the door and the ground. He made a 'pi-pa, pi-pa, pi-pa' noise, and after a while I fell asleep once more.

Next thing I knew, there was shouting: 'Counter-Revolutionary! What are you doing here? Tell me! Are you wrecking our cellar? Yesterday your family committed an appalling Anti-Revolution event and now here you are wrecking our cellar! Stay here! Don't move! I'm going to report!'

Through the crack in the door, I saw Dad staring numbly after the man until he disappeared. Then he whispered to me insistently, 'Remember, you must say what Dad told you before.'

'No, Dad. I can't!' I cried.

Then they came back. The man in the front was the same man who had beaten my brother, threatened me, and kicked me into this cellar yesterday. My father stood up from the ground and said very calmly, 'I have been waiting for you to come to correct what I said to you yesterday. Now I remember that in fact I did know. But my wife and the other children truly don't know. I think I should take the full responsibility for this. Could you let my daughter go back to her mother, she needs to go to the hospital very urgently as she has a broken leg.'

This man slapped my father's face and shouted, 'What? Who told you? How do you know that your daughter has a broken leg? Don't play your Anti-Revolution tricks! Counter-Revolutionary! Tell us! Why did you lie to us yesterday? Why did you waste our time? Why? We know it was you. Counter-Revolutionary, we order you to make a clean confession first.' He then waved his hand and shouted, 'Take him away!' and a myriad brutal hands seized my father's shoulders and led him off.

'No!' I shouted, 'My father lied! My father never knew that

before! No! It was all me!' I was screaming through the crack in despair.

About lunchtime, the door suddenly opened, and a man stood in front of me and yelled out, 'Xiao Counter-Revolutionary! Tell us why you told a lie. Your father has confessed already, but you still carry on the lie. Do you want to die here? Now, I'll give you five minutes to think! If you tell us the truth, that it was your father who abetted you to do so, then you can go back to your family. Otherwise we will beat you to death here!'

I curled up on the floor in silence, and trembled.

'What? Refuse to talk?' About four or five men jumped in and started shouting at me.

'Then I said, 'It is the truth. My father never knew that before. It's purely me and for the particular reason that I said to you before.'

Immediately the shouting came again from all sides: 'Fuckin' bastards! Xiao Counter-Revolutionary you are even bolder than your father! Okay! You want to die!' And again the belts, the kicks and punches rained down on me until I fell unconscious.

The next thing I remember, Da-Jei was calling me: 'Sheng, can you hear Da-Jei? Sheng, do you want some water? Sheng? Can you hear? It's Da-Jei! Do you want some water?'

I slowly opened my eyes and saw my sisters and brother all standing around me, but no Mum or Dad. My brother's face was extremely swollen and all covered with bruises. I asked where Mum and Dad were, and Di-Di cried, 'They took them away . . . Jei-Jei, are you sore? Jei-Jei, you've got a black eye, you've got a swollen leg, you've got so many bruises on your body. Jei-Jei, this is all my fault . . .' And the five of us sank into a flood of tears.

A whole week passed, and still we hadn't heard anything about our parents. My left leg was extremely sore, swollen and unable to touch the ground. One morning after my sisters went to the farmland, I asked my brother to help me find a piece of thick wood. Supporting myself with this stick, half walking, half jumping, I hobbled to the People's Commune Cultural Revolution Office. Again, the same cunning man was there, but by himself. When I saw him, my hackles rose and I began to tremble, but I kept moving forward until he saw me. However, strangely enough that day, when he saw me, he neither shouted at me nor beat me, but smiled an insidious smile.

'I knew you would come,' he grinned. 'Now, tell me, what have you come to lie about this time?'

'No, I didn't lie, I told the truth,' I replied quietly. Then I begged, 'Please believe me, it's the truth. It's purely me, not my parents, they didn't even know about it. Please let my parents come back. Let my parents come back, and lock me up again.' And I began to cry.

Then the man said slowly, 'How can I prove that you have told the whole truth? Tomorrow morning come back here with all your sisters and brother, and tell it all again in front of them and let them say whether everything you claim is true or not.' And here he stopped. Then suddenly his smile disappeared, and he yelled, 'Get out of here now! Come back tomorrow morning! Make sure you bring *all* your sisters!'

Next morning we all went there. He made me repeat it again in front of my sisters and brother. He then said he wanted to question my sisters separately in the next room. After he had questioned two of my sisters and told them to go back to the farmland straight away, he told me and my brother to leave immediately. But he kept Da-Jei there.

An hour or two later, Da-Jei returned. When she saw me, she sobbed violently. My brother ran to her and cried, 'Da-Jei,

149

did he beat you? Da-Jei, are you sore? Da-Jei, your bottom is bleeding! Da-Jei, don't cry! Da-Jei, if he hears, you will get another beating! Da-Jei, don't cry . . . '

And our parents were returned the same day . . .

But when we saw them, we were shocked. My brother screamed, 'No! Mama, Dad! . . . No! Mama, Dad!' They had swollen faces and black eyes, and were covered in bruises.

Early next morning, the same cunning man came. When Da-Jei saw him, her face turned white as a sheet. She quickly slipped into a corner and curled there trembling. This evil man with his foxy smile said to our parents, 'From now on, you must be very careful! You see, without my help, you would never have come back here again.' Then he turned to me and asked, 'How is your leg? Show me.' After I showed him, he said in his most sympathetic voice, 'Oh no! Swelling like that! She must go to the hospital now.' He then said to my parents and sisters, 'You all go to the farmland as soon as your are ready. Just leave your eldest daughter here with her, and I will arrange a vehicle to take her to hospital.' And off he went.

We numbly watched him disappear. My sister went over to Mum, buried her head into Mum's chest and sobbed violently, 'No, Mama, I cannot stay here! No, Mama, I'm going with you! Mama, I'm afraid . . .'

'Tell me, what's the matter?' Mum asked anxiously.

'He beat Da-Jei yesterday. Da-Jei got a bleeding bottom,' my brother cried out.

Mum stared frozenly at Di-Di, then asked Da-Jei, 'Have you got your period?'

'No, Mama . . . No, Mama, it's not –' Da-Jei sobbed even more brokenly.

Suddenly, our parents' faces turned white. Mum, with her voice shaking, said to Dad, 'You stay here with Sheng – we had better leave here before he returns.' And they all rushed out.

Barely a few minutes later, this cunning man returned with Da-Jei beside him. Da-Jei stood there quivering. He scowled at Dad and commanded in a great rage, 'Do as you are told! Get out of here! Go to the farmland immediately!'

After Dad had left, a truck pulled up outside. Da-Jei helped me climb in and then she quickly jumped in and sat beside me. But this man yelled out, 'No! You come down. You are not to go with her, you stay here with me.'

Da-Jei began to sob, and begged with a trembling voice, 'Please let me go with my sister.'

'Remember what I told you yesterday? Don't be foolish – refuse a toast only to drink a forfeit! Do what you're told and get down now. And immediately!' the man shouted.

Then the truck took me to a small clinic. There was no laboratory or X-ray facility and no doctor either, only a few nurses. One of the nurses said to me, 'Your leg looks very much like it has got a fracture, but I can't tell exactly where it is. Anyway, it's too swollen, and too late to do anything. I'll put it in splints to stop the broken part from moving.'

While she put the splints on my leg, I heard the other nurse go out to talk to the driver: 'What's going on over there? Why did the head of the Cultural Revolution office send her here? This family was not sent here for recuperation! Where is his Class Stand? They deserve to be dead.'

Then the truck driver replied, 'Maybe he regretted what he had done to this child. She's only a kid. Look –she has a broken head, arm and now leg, but her parents don't – well, who knows? I'd better go.'

I dropped my head down and returned in silence to the temple. I saw Da-Jei huddled in a corner together with my brother. When they saw me again, Da-Jei held me and began to sob. Then my brother cried, 'Da-Jei, did he beat you again? Da-Jei, don't cry. He said he will be back. If he sees you cry, you will get another beating. Da-Jei, don't cry . . .'

At that moment the cunning man walked in. 'What? Still crying? Remember what I told you this morning. Refuse a toast only to drink a forfeit! From now on, you don't go to the farmland. You stay here to look after your sister and watch your parents' words and deeds. You must report to my office when I order you to come,' he shouted at Da-Jei and marched away.

'Da-Jei, what did he tell you this morning?' I demanded.

'No! I can't tell you. He said if I told anybody in the family, we would all be dead straight away.' Da-Jei sobbed even more violently.

After that, he came and ordered Da-Jei to go to his office once or twice a day, each time for around an hour or two. When Da-Jei returned, she always had tears hanging in her eyes, then would fall into silence for the rest of the day.

Later, Da-Jei became very ill. She could hardly eat anything and was sick all the time. One morning he came again, and he saw Da-Jei vomiting in the sink. He stood behind her for a while, then he went away, and he didn't come back for almost two weeks.

Late one night, there was a flurry of knocking at the door. Dad jumped up, held his breath and listened cautiously for a while, then asked, 'Who is it?' Mum quickly got dressed and followed Dad to the door.

'Quick! Open the door!' It was this same cunning man.

Dad opened the door, and the man rushed in, closing the door behind him very quickly. He whispered to Dad, 'I want to have some words with you and your wife.' He then led them into a corner of the room and continued, 'You do know your real situation, don't you? I am helping you now. Here is a ticket for your eldest daughter to get out of here, to marry a very nice man in Gin. Here is his photo and address. You have to let me know by tomorrow morning. The train leaves very early the next day. I will arrange a vehicle to take her to the railway station and let her future husband know when to meet her.'

Not waiting until he finished, Mum said firmly, 'No thank you!'

'Okay! If you don't want my help, it's fine. It's up to you,' this cunning man said angrily. He scowled at Mum and left.

Once he'd gone, Da-Jei jumped up. She clutched Mum and cried in despair, 'No, Mama, I'm not going! No, Mama, I would rather die here with you! No, Mama –'

Dad and Mum hugged Da-Jei, and said, 'No. We won't let you go alone. We will live together and die together.'

Early the next morning, Dad suggested that Da-Jei should go to the farmland with them. They tried to leave as early as possible. To our horror, this cunning man waited for her there, and he brought Da-Jei back straight away. I heard him threaten her: 'Don't you understand you are pregnant? You have to leave here before it gets bigger, or people will see! Do you want to stay here and make trouble for me? Do you want your family all to die with you? Do as you are told and get ready, the truck will wait for you outside your door early tomorrow morning.' And he went.

After he left, Di-Di held her hand and made her sit beside me and comforted her, 'Da-Jei, don't cry, Mama and Dad said that we won't let you go alone, we won't let him take you away from us.'

'No, Di-Di, you're too little, you don't understand. Da-Jei must go, otherwise, you –' Da-Jei stopped, and sank into a flood of tears.

Before Mum, Dad and my sisters came back from the farmland, Da-Jei splashed cold water on her face, then told my brother and I not to tell our parents that she had cried all day. After we had our meal, Da-Jei said, 'Mama and Papa, I have decided to go tomorrow.'

Mum and Dad were stunned. They stared at her blankly for a long while, then cried simultaneously, 'No, Ni-Ni! You can't! We must live together and die together. We can't bear to see any of you bullied, taken away, or left alone! No, Ni-Ni, you mustn't go.'

My sisters were holding her too and cried out, 'No, Da-Jei, you can't! We live together, we die together!'

But Da-Jei responded calmly, 'Mei-Mei (younger sister), don't cry, Da-Jei will be okay.' Then she turned to Mum and Dad and said repeatedly, 'Mama, Papa, don't be upset, I'll be okay.'

That night none of us had any sleep, even Di-Di lay there with his eyes open wide all night.

The next morning, before Da-Jei left, she said to us, 'Look after yourselves, don't be too upset, I'll send you a telegram as soon as I arrive.'

Before the truck started its engine, Dad asked if he could see her off to the railway station, but the cunning man yelled at him, 'Don't forget why you are here!'

Da-Jei waved to us, her tears streaming down. Mum and Dad collapsed to the ground. We all sank into a flood of tears . . .

We waited, waited and waited to hear of Da-Jei's safe arrival. One week, two weeks, three weeks . . . nothing at all! Mum wrote several letters to the address, but got no rely. She became very ill, and couldn't even get out of bed to work. Dad started to lose weight. We kept going to ask this cunning man for news, but he gave us no answer. Then one day he said to us, 'Yes, it's very strange, I haven't heard anything about her either. Well, let me check with the driver first.'

Next day we spied the driver furtively looking around our place – I simply walked out and asked him whether he saw

Da-Jei off at the railway station or not. He replied vaguely and nodded, 'Ohhh, yeee, yeee,' and slipped away. Next day we heard that his body was found in the river. How? And why? Nobody knew. The dreadful thing was that nobody even intended to find out or investigate.

A few days after his death, we suddenly received a telegram from Da-Jei, saying that she had just arrived and that we would receive a letter from her soon. We waited about two weeks. A very short letter arrived, saying that she was okay, and that her husband truly was a kind-hearted man. But she didn't tell us who her husband was, or explain why there had been such a delay. Two months later, we received another note from her, saying that her husband would come to see us with her letter. We knew that she was unable to tell us the reason in her letter, as all letters to us were scrutinised first. In the end, we found out that Da-Jei was extremely worried about the safety of our Er-Jei (second sister), as Er-Jei was now 17, and she couldn't bear to see Er-Jei become her shadow and replacement. So she sent her husband with a letter to our parents, and she forged a letter from Er-Jei's so-called future husband and included a train ticket. Er-Jei was helped by Da-Jei's husband to leave Fei-Yn safely the following day.

However, we still didn't know why Da-Jei's arrival had been delayed, or the nature of the relationship between her husband and this cunning man. Her husband looked indeed a kind, simple and decent man. He was 16 years Da-Jei's senior, and was rather tall and strongly built, although a bit slow. But at least we knew that our Da-Jei and Er-Jei were safe now.

As it happened, we did not find out the dreadful answer to this mystery until after the Cultural Revolution.

The morning Da-Jei left the temple for the railway station, the driver had begun his questioning:

'Where are you going?'

'To Kiuing.' Da-Jei made the answer simple.

'What for?'

'I'm going to marry my long-time boyfriend,' Da-Jei answered as she had been told to.

'How long have you two known each other?'

'Since we were kids.' Again, Da-Jei answered as she had been instructed.

'But you are not from Kiuing? From Guanchou? Right?'

'No, I was born in Kiuing, we lived in Guanchou only for the last couple of years.' This too, Da-Jei had been told to say.

'Have you been to Kiuing lately?'

'Yes. I just got back from there before my family came here. So now they send me back,' she continued to lie.

'How old are you?'

'Twenty-five,' she lied once more.

'No! You certainly don't look twenty-five. You look so young, so beautiful – we have never seen such a beautiful girl as you before,' the man said as he stared at her with his mouth open wide and a foxy smile.

Da-Jei lifted her head and examined him closely, her hackles rising. This man was in his late forties, with a bottle nose, heavy beard, and a very dark and rough appearance. He looked extremely treacherous.

Suddenly, the truck pulled into the drive of a desolate and uninhabited countryside house. He said to Da-Jei, 'Come on, get down, and give me a hand. The truck needs some water.' And Da-Jei followed him, walking into the house.

After Da-Jei walked in, he slammed the front door very quickly, then forced her into a dark room. He lit a kerosene lamp and Da-Jei saw that the room's only window was covered by wood, with no natural light. There were bloodstains all over the walls. The earth floor was strewn with empty liquor bottles and cigarette butts. In the middle of the room was a wooden bed, and on top of the bed was a sharp knife and a whip. Da-Jei collapsed onto the ground immediately.

'You don't have to be frightened of me. Just like your boyfriend, I want to keep a woman to fuck with,' he leered, and began to take his clothes off.

Then he lit a cigarette, opened a liquor bottle and drank a big mouthful, with his naked body right in front of Da-Jei. He said, 'This room has been ready for you for ages! I've waited for the day you'd sit in my truck, and today you have and now you will be kept here forever. Get up! Quick! Take your clothes off quickly!'

Da-Jei knelt in front of him and begged, 'Please let me go! I beg you let me go! I am pregnant already –'

'Humph!' he snorted like a wild animal. 'Pregnant? Easy! You stay here and soon you will not be pregnant! Come on! Get up! Let me get rid of the baby first!'

Again, Da-Jei begged, 'Please let me go! I beg you –'

'What? Fuckin' bitch,' he roared. 'You want to go? Do you still want to go?' He threw the knife onto the muddy ground beside her, then he waved the whip and continued, 'Can you smell? There is a body underneath this floor! She lived here for almost 10 years. But she, like you, was stubborn. She tried to run away continuously. And now she is under here. Mind you, underneath here is not just one body!' he pointed with his foot to the ground. Then he pushed Da-Jei's head against the dirt and shouted, 'You smell it! Fuckin' bitch! Smell –' He seized her by the hair and pulled her up, pointing the knife at her chin. 'Fuckin' bitch! Take your clothes off quickly!' he shouted.

After that, Da-Jei didn't even know the time, or whether it was day or night. He always came and went at very odd hours. But each time he left he always gagged her mouth and tied her arms to the wall, then Da-Jei would hear him lock the door very carefully. And once the door was locked, Da-Jei could hardly hear anything.

One day, while he was with her, suddenly there was somebody banging on the door very loudly and yelling, 'Come on! Quick! We have to go now. Otherwise we'll never be able to get back before it gets dark. Come on! Quick!' And his face suddenly turned gray as ash. He then quickly put the kerosene lamp out, locked the door, and rushed off. But he forgot to tie Da-Jei up. Da-Jei then waited for a while. She found the kerosene lamp in the dark and lit it. She looked carefully around the room and discovered that the wood across the window was only held by nails, and his knife was on the ground.

Working swiftly, Da-Jei used the knife to dig a hole around the nails, exerting every ounce of her energy to lift the wood up. But sadly, under the wood there was a big piece of iron sheet, and she could not even see how he had put it on.

Time is life! Da-Jei picked up the biggest piece of wood she could find. Gripping it tightly, she backed up to the other side of the cabin, then exerted all her strength and charged forwards. The iron sheet ripped open like a huge mouth and the window glass shattered at the same time. Light poured in. Da-Jei's emotions were beyond expression. Cutting a long piece of cloth from the sheet, she hastily tied all her tickets and her future husband's letter, photo and address to her waist, underneath her jacket. Then she scrambled out the window. But she didn't even know which way to go.

Then she heard a burst of train whistles. Da-Jei ran towards the sound and found the railway track. When she saw a little boy playing on the ground she ran to him and asked him how far away the railway station was from there. The boy just said, 'I don't know.' She then asked this boy where his mother was. Again he answered, 'I don't know.' Da-Jei almost wept.

All of a sudden, the little boy's mother was standing right

in front of them and told her: 'The railway station is miles away from here, about two to three hours by foot.' Da-Jei's heart sank.

Then, when Da-Jei asked her how to get there, she answered, 'There are two ways. One is a safe way, but takes much longer. It is by the transportation road. The other way is a short cut, through the hills and farmland, but it's too dangerous for a stranger to take. You would easily get lost and there are hardly any people to help.' She then added, 'You had better go by the transportation road, there are many trucks and vehicles. Who knows, somebody might give you a ride there.' Then she began to question Da-Jei, asking where she was from and where she was going . . .

Now time was precious. It was life or death! The transportation road was far too dangerous for her, as she could easily be caught by this man. She decided to take the short cut, but she didn't know which way to go, or how to get there. It was far too risky to reveal anything to anybody before she got out of there. So, without answering the woman's questions, Da-Jei begged her: 'Da-Jei ('big sister' is the polite way for Chinese to address a stranger like this), please help me get to the railway station by the short cut, my husband is dying and I have lost my way! Da-Jei, I beg you . . .'

The woman stared at her for a while, then said to her son, 'Okay! Let's help her get there.' On their way to the railway station, she put her arm round Da-Jei's shoulder to comfort her and said, 'Don't cry, your husband will be okay.'

Once Da-Jei arrived at the railway station, she knew she must take the next available train as a matter of emergency. She found that there was one to Shinzhong province, the next province from Ku-Shan. It was up in the north of the country; Kiuing was down in the south. The train was leaving in seven minutes. She had no money and her ticket was only to Kiuing.

The train attendants were all standing at the front of the train checking every ticket strictly. She just stood there, her heart almost jumping out. Then she noticed a few passengers with big bags trying to get onto the train as quickly as possible, as it was about to leave. She quickly rushed in front of them, saying, 'Excuse me, I must go first, I've left my bags on board,' and she ignored everybody and jumped aboard.

Once on, she acted as if she was looking for her bags, moving from one carriage to the next. Soon everybody became aware that she had lost all her bags. She sat down crying, and people all thought she was upset because somebody had stolen her luggage. Then some kind passengers gave her some food and drink, and some of them even gave her money. About 35 hours later, Da-Jei arrived safely in Jingchu, the capital city of Shinzhong province.

After she got into Jingchu station, she quickly looked up the timetable for the next train to Kiuing and sent a telegram to her future husband. She waited at the station for another 10 hours. Once again, she used the same trick to get onto the next train. As soon as the train started its engine, she sobbed loudly and then she was violently sick. This time not only the passengers had sympathy for her plight, even the train guards took pity on her. They put her into a sleeping berth carriage, and the passengers gave her lots of food and drink, and looked after her all the way to Kiuing.

Da-Jei was on the train for exactly five days. Before the train arrived at Kiuing, Da-Jei got her future husband's photo out and studied it closely to make sure that she wouldn't get the wrong person.

When she met him at the station, she even forgot that the man in front of her was a stranger. She was so relieved, she buried her head into his chest and wept. It was a lovely morning, the sun was shining peacefully, and the birds were singing. He took her straight to the marriage registry office in Kiuing, and they got legally married. He then took her to catch the next bus to Wnning, a small town about eight hours away from Kiuing. After they arrived at his home, he said to her, 'We are legally married now, but I won't touch you until you are ready to be my wife.' Then he arranged for Da-Jei to occupy his room and he made himself a temporary bed in the kitchen.

Da-Jei's husband was the cunning man's eldest son, by his first marriage. His mother died when he was four. Later, he was brought up by his maternal grandparents in this small town. Since his mother died, he had seen his father and his siblings no more than two or three times. He had never been to Ku-Shan. He never knew exactly what his father did. He didn't even really know what his father was like, or just how many siblings he actually had.

However, at the age of 35, he was content to be a shop assistant in a small rice store in the same town where he grew up. He obtained a regular income from it – far better than if he worked in the farmland. There was no hard physical labour involved. He lived alone in a very small flat near the rice store, left to him by his grandparents. He had never been married before, and had never had any female friend in his life. He had never even dared to dream of marriage and little thought he would be married one day. He was a very simple, plain and gentle-tempered country man. He was also a man with no talent, no interests, no hobbies and no ambitions whatsoever. He hardly read a newspaper or listened to the radio. He had never touched a book or listened to music in his life. But he was a truly kind man with a big golden heart.

After Da-Jei arrived there, she had a very severe womb haemorrhage. The doctor found that she had miscarried and that both her womb and vagina were severely injured and badly

161

infected, and that she had a high fever. She was transferred from Wnning's small town clinic to Kiuing hospital by ambulance. Then she was kept there for almost a month. Her husband slept on the hospital floor the whole time and looked after her. He said to her: 'You have no relatives, no family here, and now I am your husband. It is my duty to take full care of you, look after you and make sure you are safe now.' Before he took Da-Jei out of the hospital, the doctor said to him, 'I am so sorry to let you know that your young wife's womb and vagina are permanently injured and she will never be able to have a child.'

Her husband wept and and said to Da-Jei, 'I am sorry. I am terribly sorry for what they have done to you in your life.'

Later, he found out that it was his birth father who had done this to her. He vowed to Da-Jei that once she had fully recovered, he was going to Fei-Yn to slap his face. And that led Da-Jei to contemplate how to help my Er-Jei escape a similar fate.

One month after Da-Jei got out of hospital, under her husband's tender care she had speedily recovered. She made a plan, and said to her husband, 'I don't want you to go to Fei-Yn to slap your father's face, but I do want you to go there to help my eldest younger sister escape from there, and to warn your father to make sure that my family no longer gets bullied, and are kept 100 per cent safe there.'

And he did. He went to his father's office, slapped his father's face and said, 'Now her family is in your hands – if any of them gets bullied or raped I will kill you straight away!'

Then, like a big hero, he returned with Er-Jei to Wnning.

In the following years, Da-Jei got very little good sleep each night. She always woke up in the middle of the night with some dreadful nightmare. Sometimes she was woken by her own sobbing. Sometimes she was woken by her own screaming. Each time she woke, her whole body, her hair, even the bed sheets, were soaking wet with sweat. Her husband always got out of bed, ran her a bath, changed the sheets and then carried on with his day.

One night, Da-Jei again had a dreadful nightmare. She was screaming and her husband woke her up. Once again she was drenched in a cold sweat. Her husband did as usual, and ran her a bath. But, as she sat in the bath, she still couldn't stop her tears. Her husband put his arm around her shoulders, kissed her softly and said, 'Don't cry, I am here, you are safe now. I love you, I swear I will take full care of you and nobody can mistreat you again. Try not to think too much about the past. Let's think of it this way – if it weren't for that dreadful nightmare, we would never have been able to meet each other, and I would never have been able to have such a beautiful, attractive young wife – I would have been alone forever!'

Then he added, 'I should really thank our Great, Glorious, Right Communist Party! Thanks to our Great Leader Chairman Mao for launching and mobilising this Great Proletariat Cultural Revolution! They bestowed upon me an angel; they brought you into my life; they brought me happiness; they gave me hope. Without them, I would never have been able to have you and love you.'

Da-Jei's heart was broken. She fully understood what her husband really meant. He was purely trying to comfort her, to soothe her and to show his heart – the true love in it towards her. But to Da-Jei, it was like a sharp knife through her heart, that she could no longer bear! And she began to realise that in this marriage there was no love, but a heartfelt gratefulness only . . .

Once Da-Jei had fully recovered she got to know the locals. She found herself a job in the head office of the rice company, in Mu-Long, the next town to Wnning, as a cashier. It was the largest company in this small town. She swiftly familiarised herself with the job, but it soon got boring. Later they found that she was far too bright for such a position.

When the Cultural Revolution started, Da-Jei had been in her last year of high school. She had a great passion for drama, and of course – thanks to Yei-Yei – her Chinese was far more advanced than anybody else in her age group. With her strong and charismatic leadership style, she soon fitted into the company and became very much admired. Six months after she started she was promoted to be an office manager in the General Manager's office. A few years later, the General Manager retired and she took his place. And so, her demanding job cheered her up, enriched her heart and became an integral part of her life.

Ten years after her marriage, at the beginning of 1976, Da-Jei unexpectedly became pregnant. It brought back all her painful memories of 1966. It was far too difficult for Da-Jei to carry on this marriage. She couldn't let this innocent unborn life be tainted by this unforgettable and unforgivable piece of history.

However, Da-Jei knew her husband very well. He needed a wife for company, someone to share with. Also, by this time she fully supported him, both emotionally and financially. So, first she found him a wife, and then she moved out with an emptied hand, leaving him with all their assets and savings to support his new marriage.

It impacted on her tremendously, and so, in need of her family's support, she returned to Guanchou. And it was at this time that the family's secret about Da-Jei was told – that, in fact, Mum and Dad were her aunt and uncle, and we were her cousins. Da-Jei was almost shocked into a coma.

These were the memories that churned through my mind as

I watched Da-Jei wave off me, Yee Bing and Guo Yi at Mu-Long station on our way back to Guanchou.

Even before the train had begun moving, Guo Yi had already made billions and zillions of friends. He named all his new friends Huo-Che Susu and Huo-Che A-Yee (Train Uncle and Train Aunt). He started busily introducing himself straight away: 'I am Xiao Guo Yi, this is my dearest Yee Bing A-Juo, this is my dearest Xiao A-Yee, and they are getting married. Yee Bing A-Juo is going to show Xiao A-Yee her new home and I shall stay with my Pohpoh and Gohgoh. The new home is for Xiao A-Yee and Yee Bing A-Juo only. Because I am Guos not Yees.' Here he suddenly stopped and became very upset.

'No, you shouldn't be unhappy that your dearest Xiao A-Yee will be a bride and your dearest Yee Bing A-Juo will be a bridegroom,' one of his Huo-Che Susu consoled him. 'You should congratulate them!'

When we arrived at Guanchou, Mum, Dad and Da-Bo all met us at the railway station. Before Guo Yi left Mu-Long, Da-Jei had shown him our parents' and Da-Bo's photos. So, when Guo Yi got off the train and saw them, he ran with his little arms opened wide, straight towards them. The three of them were holding him, kissing him and cuddling him, full of joy. Eventually they put him down on the ground, and he began his busy introductions at once.

'Pohpoh! Pohpoh! This is my dearest bridegroom Yee Bing A-Juo. This is my dearest bride Xiao A-Yee. Yee Bing A-Juo is going to show Xiao A-Yee her new home and Xiao A-Yee is now his, called Yee Sheng, and no longer mine. I shall be a big brother, Xiao A-Yee is going to bring me a little brother very soon. He shall be called Xiao Guo Yi as well and he certainly will be mine!'

Mum went red and stammered, 'No, Darling, you are over-excited. You are talking nonsense. Please keep quiet for a while, Pohpoh has a headache.' Mum looked totally shocked. The smiles had all vanished and conversation was abandoned. There were polite, but rather distant greetings, as we went to the taxi station.

The limited seats divided our party in two. Mum, Dad, Da-Bo and GuoYi automatically entered the first car, while Yee Bing and I took the second. Yee Bing held my hand and said, 'Did you notice how shocked your mother was? How flustered your father and Da-Bo were? Very understandable, after the night-mare that their own flesh and blood went through. If I was them I would be the same – maybe even worse. Don't worry, leave it with me. I believe I will be able to discuss it with them rationally and they will be the same as your Da-Jei, and will understand and accept our plan.'

The taxi had almost reached my home when Yee Bing suddenly pointed to a tall flat building and said, 'Excuse me driver! Could you please stop here?' It was an old 1930s French-style block, located in the same area where I lived, about 10 minutes' walk from my home.

'Here is our new home,' he announced and I followed him up. Yee Bing took me around within a minute or two. Inside, the flat was almost empty. An old military office desk with two chairs sat in the middle of the living room. Some of his university textbooks were lying upon it. Two old military single wooden beds were shoulder to shoulder against the wall of the master bedroom. The other two rooms were simply empty.

He sat down on the edge of one of the beds, made me sit beside him and said, 'Before you go home, you must promise me once more that our wedding day – the ninth of the ninth – shall be kept forever and never change.'

I merely stared at him and truly did not know what to say, but I nodded.

Ignoring my silence, he said, 'There is one thing that I do have to remind you, and that is, it will be unlikely – maybe impossible – that we can have any kind of public marriage ceremony. Maybe only you and me together, at the registry office. Is this okay for you? I am terribly sorry, but it will have to be so.'

'Why would you feel sorry about that?' I finally managed to speak. 'Why do we need a public ceremony? It's our dream, our life, it should be kept for ourselves. I prefer to have something rather special and unique between you and me only.'

'Yes, you might be right,' he replied slowly. 'Well, how about our new home? Do you like it? It's okay for me. I was brought up in a military camp, so I am already used to the furniture and wooden beds. They bring back fond memories of my childhood. But they may seem far too harsh for you. I'm sorry! But just remember, it won't be forever. I promise you – once I've got a job, the first thing I'll buy you is a comfortable bed, and believe me, one day, I will bring our standard of living back to what you had at your parents, maybe even better!' He suddenly stopped, bit his lips and looked at me with a remarkably confident smile.

'Why should you feel so sorry about it?' I protested. 'You've got no money, but nor do I. Our parents are our parents. There's no point in expecting anything from anybody else. Whatever we can afford, whatever we have, we should accept and be happy to have. By now you should understand, this marriage is purely for love, not for money. I love you, not the money,' and I stopped. I couldn't say another word, I felt so insulted and cheapened. It seemed that all I was expecting from this marriage was money!

After a pause, I added coolly, 'Please remember, I, Guo

Sheng, am marrying for true love, not money.'

I could never have predicted that my anger would so deeply touch Yee Bing. His tears rolled down, he put both his arms around me and kissed me softly. 'I love you! I love you more than ever, Sheng. I can no longer wait. I want you to be mine entirely. And now! Do you hear me? I want you now . . .'

When I did not respond, he continued, 'I envy you that your grandparents and your parents brought you up in such an accomplished way. They made you so special and unique. You are so sophisticated, you know just how to love and you dare to love.' He then stood up and moved slowly towards the window.

He stood there, gazing fixedly outside for a while, before adding, 'In fact, I do love my own parents very deeply. But sadly, they have misinterpreted the real meaning of human morality and love. They followed Mao through the Long March when they were teenagers. They vowed to contribute their whole lives to the Red Revolution and the Party and they really did! They were totally brainwashed by Marxist Leninism and Mao's thoughts. They truly believe that the real meaning of human morality is to devote oneself to the Class Struggle. They have participated in battle after battle, war after war, campaign after campaign, until the killing and death are insignificant in their eyes. The huge gap between your family and mine is aggravated by this lack of respect and understanding.' Suddenly he stopped and sighed deeply.

Then he turned to me, placed his hands on top of mine, and continued, 'In the meantime, I think the best way is to leave them. I know it will hurt them very much, as I am their only son. But we have to move on our way, build our life and our future together – to have our family first. However, in the future, I beg you to learn to understand and tolerate them – I am their flesh and blood.'

I was dumbfounded. Learn to *understand* them? I didn't think I possibly could! I would never be able to understand this ugly piece of history for as long as I lived. However, to learn to tolerate them, maybe. I had learnt tolerance the hard way. But instead of saying something, I stared back at him blankly. A chill ran through me . . .

Again he continued, 'But your parents are totally different from mine. I know you love and respect them very much and I now love you, so I have to learn to love and respect them as well. It is my duty. I must help you work it out with them, and make sure that they are happy and agree to our marriage. Surely they won't be as inflexible as my parents –'

Suddenly we realised it was almost dinner time, and the conversation had to be abandoned. He kissed me and then added confidently, 'Can you promise me that you will go home, have a hot bath, put everything behind you and have a good rest? I will come to see your parents tomorrow.'

I nodded mutely.

After we arrived home Guo Yi invited Yee Bing to stay for dinner, but he said, 'No thank you. Yee Bing A-Juo is too tired and needs a good rest. But I will come to see you tomorrow.' And he left.

I had a bath at once, and overheard Mum ask Guo Yi to repeat what Yee Bing had said. Afterwards I went straight to my room and heard Mum in her room yelling at Da-Jei over the phone. I picked my own phone up carefully and listened.

'What have you to say for yourself? I trusted you and sent your sister to you to look after, but it ended up that you sold her! Why didn't you tell me that he was there, and they'd got married already and that she's pregnant? How did he find her there? Did she ring him up? When did they get married? I can't believe you didn't tell us!'

'Sorry, Mum. Please calm down a bit,' Da-Jei finally managed to get a word in. 'I'm not quite sure what you're trying to say. You mean they're married already and she's pregnant right now? I never knew that! Who told you? Did she tell you this herself?'

Then Mum repeated what Guo Yi had said to her. Da-Jei laughed very loudly, then said, 'Mum, don't be so naive. You've taken Guo Yi at his word and he's not even four yet.'

'But children don't tell lies!' Mum retorted angrily.

'Mum, listen, I'm not going to argue with you,' interrupted Da-Jei. 'I suggest you just ignore what your little grandson says and listen carefully to what your mature daughter has to say. I had a very close look at Yee Bing during the time he was here. I found him to be a very sensible, responsible, ambitious young man, and full of love. I believe both of them are truly in love. They are mature adults, they should be able to make their own life choices. We should respect and appreciate that. I think Yee Bing is very wise, he even pointed out what Dad always says to us – "Yesterday has gone past, it's history. We should make the most of today and do the best for tomorrow."'

Mum was furious. 'What?' she screamed. 'You mean we should forget everything they've done to us? Don't make such a hasty judgement at such an early stage. Please don't steer your sister's life into misery and suffering forever. She has suffered enough!'

'Mum, let me finish,' Da-Jei broke in. 'As a mother myself, I believe I have the right to bring my son into this world, but I don't have the right to decide his destiny. He should be able to choose his own.'

To my surprise, Dad was on the other phone, and chorused, 'Yes, she's hit the nail right on the head. She is perfectly right. It's *her* destiny.'

Now Mum was yelling at both of them. 'Exactly! It's her

destiny! Love is blind! She is now at the crossroads, she needs support. You two have no feelings for her but I do!' Mum began crying, and the conversation came to an end.

I was utterly numbed. No tears, no screaming, just a desperate wish that I had never been brought into this wretched world and had never come to understand the meaning of true love.

I dropped the phone and fell, with nothing to break my fall but the hard wooden floor . . .

Seven

殘酷的命運

Cruel Destiny

The doorbell rang, and Mum answered it. There was Yee Bing, with a confident smile and a big bunch of flowers. Mum looked at him numbly, neither smiling nor greeting. When he passed the flowers to her, she was like a person waking from a sudden daydream, but she recovered very well. She held the flowers and smiled, saying, 'Oh, the smell is marvellous. How beautiful! Guo Mama (a polite Chinese term for a close friend's mother) loves flowers. Thank you! It's very kind of you. Please do come in. Please do sit down.' She gently closed the door, and added, 'Guo Mama is going to make you a nice cup of coffee.' With that, she went.

This was my mother – a typical Chinese mother. One could even say '*a typical old-fashioned Chinese mother*'. She never liked to reveal her true feelings in front of people, unless she felt it was absolutely necessary. When necessity demanded, she could be very well-mannered, but sharp. And, for the sake of a mother's dignity, she always stood her ground, permitting absolutely no room for discussion or compromise.

Soon my mother returned with a tea-tray and her first-rate coffee. Everybody dutifully began to admire it. Finally, Yee Bing opened his conversation:

'Guo Mama, Guo Bo-Bo, and Da-Bo, today I have come to express my sincere apology to you all for the big mistake that I accidentally made. I regret it still. I would like to discuss it with you, so that you will understand what the situation really is. And, I would also like to take this opportunity to solicit your opinion, as I sincerely wish to unite my life with Sheng's and build our future together. We are committed, and would like to be married on her birthday – the ninth of the ninth – this year. We would also prefer not to have any kind of public ceremony, so that we can create something unique and special of our own.'

Mum was speechless. That gave Dad an opportunity for his response:

'No, Yee Bing, there is no need for any apology. It wasn't your fault. It was just unfortunate. Guo Mama, Da-Bo and I fully understand. Also, Guo Bo-Bo believes that you two are mature and sensible young people, so there is no need to solicit our opinion on your own commitment and dream. As long as you two are engaged, you certainly should be congratulated. If there is anything further you would like to discuss, you are most welcome, and we would appreciate it.'

Recovering her power of speech, Mum interrupted, 'No! You are wrong! Please be sensible. Do not confuse these young, innocent lives. He is perfectly right – for such an important thing they should certainly solicit both their parents' opinion.'

There was an uncomfortable pause before Mum pressed on. 'Have you discussed this with your parents? What is their opinion? Do they agree? Are they happy for you? Are they prepared for it?'

Yee Bing regained his composure very well, nodding

repeatedly as Mum continued, 'Guo Bo-Bo, Da-Bo and I are very much delighted that you are a good friend of our Sheng. We are very fond of your diligent, earnest qualities. Yet please do understand, Yee Bing, no good will come of you getting involved with the Guos – especially with our political background. You are your family's only child, and so your marriage is extremely crucial to them. And so too for your own political life, as the son of a Revolutionary family. Therefore, I believe there is no need for any further discussion. However, I do agree with Guo Bo-Bo, there is no need for any apology either. It wasn't your fault, it just came to pass. Extremely unfortunate, but we should be able to swallow it.'

After another awkward pause, she added, 'Love is blind – please do accept Guo Mama's words, stand up high and see the future. The world belongs to you, Yee Bing! Heaven bestows on you a solid foundation, so treasure it!'

Yee Bing, Dad and Da-Bo were shocked into a stunned silence. Eventually Yee Bing asked in a low voice, 'Is there no room for further discussion?'

'Sorry! In being solicitous of your family's political life and your bright future, I must state it very clearly – No! There is no room for any further discussion! Please do value yourself, uphold your family's honour, and – full stop!' Mum finished, emphasising each word very distinctly.

Another dead silence ensued. Finally Yee Bing stood up, said goodbye to them in a very dignified manner and left.

Dad lit a cigarette, took a deep puff, and then yelled out, 'These young lives aren't toys – they're flesh and blood beings with dreams and feelings just like you and I! It's true love! Do you understand? It's their hopes, their dreams, their vows, their life commitments, their future, their destiny! This refusal will hurt these young lives for ever! How could you be so unfeeling? Have you got no feelings?' He stopped and sat there for a moment with his head in his hands before saying in a trembling voice, 'No . . . I don't think you have any . . . You are as cold as ice . . . You are as hard as an iron rock . . . I'm sorry . . . I'm terribly sorry to say so . . . but . . . but, you are . . .'

After a brief pause, he added, 'Don't you remember your own life? Don't you remember our marriage? Don't you remember what we've been through together? Don't you remember how we struggled? Have you forgotten? Have you forgotten it all?' He lit another cigarette, stood up, and walked out, banging the door behind him.

Shortly afterwards, Da-Bo left without a word. It was the first time in my life I'd ever heard Dad yell at Mum, and with such harsh words. It was also the first time in my life I'd ever heard Dad slam a door. Mum simply sat dead-still in the middle of the empty room and began to sob . . .

My mother's father was an orphan adopted by a childless working-class family. His foster parents both worked extremely hard their whole lives. Eventually, in their middle age, they owned an iron factory. When my grandfather was 14 he was forced to abandon his schooling to carry on the family business, which had turned out extremely well and grown very large. Sadly, the merciless devil snatched those unfortunate lives, and his foster parents both died one after the other, over a very short period, turning my grandfather into a very rich man at the age of just 29.

Hungry for a young, beautiful wife, he went back to the orphanage in Wei-Zo, a poor country town in northern China, that he came from. He picked out the prettiest girl, aged just 15, and brought her home to be his wife and started a family at once. However, not very long after the birth of their first child – my mother – when my grandmother was expecting their second, the doctors discovered that she had cervical cancer, and the child died before birth. Two years later my grandmother died also.

Not even waiting for his poor wife's body to cool, my grandfather remarried a young and wealthy girl straight away. However, according to old Chinese custom, for an upper-class, unmarried girl to marry a widower with a child involved a great loss of face. To remedy the situation, he travelled all the way back to Wei-Zo and paid for a temple to be built. Then he sent his three-and-a-half-year-old child to live there, and for good!

The day he took her up there, he put her suitcase down beside her and delivered his last words: 'You stay here, and wait to meet your mother one day.' With that, he left! This poor abandoned child just stood there numbly, watching this cold-blooded being disappear forever, then began screaming, 'Mama, where are you? Mama, where are you? Mamaaaa . . .' until finally, exhausted, she fell asleep.

When the sun rose, she rose and picked up her doll and started walking around and around inside the temple, continuing her daily lament: 'Mama, where are you? Mamaaaa, where are you? Mamaaaa, where are you . . . ?'

The monks put her into the servants' court, and she followed the servants around all day long, always waiting for her mother to meet her. Day after day, week after week, month after month, this poor forlorn child cried out with broken-hearted despair. Then, one day, as she was banging her doll, her hands and her head onto the image of Buddha and screaming, 'Where is my Mama? Tell me! Where is my Mama?' or, a huge crowd of yellow-uniformed monks knelt down behind her and began praying loudly, 'Do Evil! Buddha Blessing! Commit a Sin! Buddha Blessing!' Then one of the largely-built monks seized her collar and threw her onto the ground. Another monk with large fat hands pulled down her pants and held her firmly, while a third monk beat her bottom with a thick bamboo stick. She screamed, and screamed, and screamed, until finally a kind-hearted servant called Lu Ma knelt in front of the monks and begged for mercy: 'Do Evil! Beat me! Commit a Sin! Beat me!'

Later Lu Ma explained to the child: 'If anyone offends or violates Buddha's image this person commits a sin and does evil, and can be punished to death.' But that pack of wicked, beastly fakes, they were not real Buddhist monks at all. This poor child was their money-spinner! As in the saying, 'Kill a chicken to frighten the monkeys', they only punished her as a warning to others. The darkness inside that temple was inexpressible.

After this inhuman cruelty, the monks burned her doll, shaved her hair and gave her a string of Buddhist beads. But this unyielding spirit, this poor, forlorn orphan child thought: 'You have beaten me, shaved my hair, burned my only friend – my doll – now I burn your beads! So she threw the beads into the fire without being seen, and kept on waiting for her mother to come to meet her.

And still, when the sun rose, she rose. Except now she held nothing but two strings of her tears as she walked around and around the temple, every day crying, 'Mama, where are you? Mama, where are you? Mama, Mama, Mamaaaaaa . . .'

One summer night, as she crouched in a corner, with her head lifted towards the sky, weeping to the moon and the stars, 'Mama, where are you? Mama, Mama, Mama, Mamaaaa . . .' the kind-hearted Lu Ma squatted down beside her, dried her tears, and said, 'Xiao Ya-Tuo (Xiao means little, Ya-Tuo means servant), don't cry! Your mother cannot come to meet you any more.'

This was too difficult for a girl so young to understand, but at the word 'cannot' she jumped up from the ground, and using both of her little fists and exerting all her energy started banging on Lu Ma's shoulder, and screaming, 'Why not? Why not? Why? Why? Why?'

Lu Ma's heart was pierced. She held her tight and cried, 'Yes, she can! Yes, she can! Yes, yes, yes . . .'

Eventually she added, 'Xiao Ya-Tuo, maybe you are right, maybe she can. But she wants you to stop crying at once and look up towards the moon and stars to count 100 New Years first. Then she will be able to come to meet you.'

These tender words seemed to calm the poor child – for the time being, at least. And so she began counting the 100 New Years straight away, and Lu Ma became her bosom friend from that time forward.

Every day, the sun rose, Lu Ma rose, and she rose. Lu Ma washed the clothes, she washed; Lu Ma cleaned the house, she cleaned; Lu Ma ran to the kitchen, she ran; Lu Ma ate her meals, she ate; at the end of the day Lu Ma, exhausted, collapsed onto her bed, and she lay beside Lu Ma under the moonlight and continued her counting.

One New Year had passed by, and the next one was nearly coming, when Lu Ma told her that after this New Year she would be six!

'But why hasn't my Mama come to meet me yet?' she asked impatiently.

'Very soon. Very soon, I tell you,' replied Lu Ma. 'Once you have completely counted these 100 New Years, you shall be very surprised to see your Mama right in front of you!'

New Year's Eve arrived, and thousands and thousands of people arrived at the temple with their offerings of fruit, rice, cakes, sweets, wine, money, and everything else they could possibly offer in this world. Those false monks acted like real ones, all standing side by side with the biggest smiles that they could possibly show, and the sweetest tongues with which they could possibly utter: 'Buddha's blessing to you all!'

Those poor, good people were intoxicated with these hon-eyed words, not even realising that they were being duped. They lit the incense and the candles, kneeling on the ground, kow-towing and kowtowing and kowtowing, praying and praying and praying, and begging for their best wishes to the New Year. This carried on and on and on until the middle of New Year's day.

In the early afternoon, after the worshippers had all gone, the temple finally fell quiet, except for the busy tinkling of the monks counting their money, and the bustle of their servants collecting and sorting the food and preparing a feast to celebrate the abundance of another New Year.

By late afternoon the feast had finished, and all the monks were dead drunk and had slipped off to their rooms, while the exhausted servants had retired to their own quarters. The temple was empty except for this poor disconnected orphan child who, with her unyielding spirit, continued her counting.

Suddenly, an old yellow-uniformed monk appeared, holding out a packet of lollies with a wide smile as he walked towards her, saying, 'Come here, my pretty Ya-Tuo! Look, here is a lolly! Come here, my pretty Ya-Tuo! Look! Lolly!' and he waved the pack to show her.

'Lolly! Lolly! Loooolly!' she cried in delight and flew towards her treat!

The evil old monk bent down and kissed her, saying, 'Buddha's blessing, my pretty Ya-Tuo!' and with that, he picked her up and carried her into his room.

'Where is my lolly?' she demanded impatiently.

'Wait! Wait!' he said, beginning to take her clothes off.

'No! I don't want to sleep! I want my lolly! No!' she cried.

'No, no . . . you have to sleep first, then you can have your lolly,' he cajoled her.

So, for the sake of her dream lolly, this poor child happily accepted and let him take all her clothes off and put her to bed.

Then he said to her, 'Now, you have to close your eyes and sleep. And when you wake up, your lolly will be beside your pillow.'

And so, she closed her eyes and disappeared into her sweet lolly dream . . .

Suddenly, something hard rammed against her bottom. She was sore. She jumped out of the bed, naked, crying, 'I'm sore! No! I don't want to sleep, I want my lolly! Where is my lolly! No!' and she ran towards the door.

But the door was locked. She couldn't get out. That old devil jumped out of the bed, with his bare body, but three-legged, and he ran towards her. He lifted his small middle leg up and squeezed it into her mouth. The jelly was all over her face, her mouth, her nose, even her eyes.

She screamed and started banging on the door with both her little fists: 'Lu Ma! Lu Ma! Lu Ma, where are you? Lu Maaaa . . .'

Suddenly the window broke, and Lu Ma jumped in. She slapped his face and cried, 'You bastard! Is it not enough that you have done this to us our whole lives, and now you do this to her! Bastard! She is not even six yet!' Then she picked the poor child up, and holding her tight in her arms, carried her out sobbing.

Early the next morning, a huge crowd of the yellow-uniformed monks and women servants gathered. They were all kneeling on the ground and praying loudly: 'Do Evil! Buddha Blessing! Commit a Sin! Buddha Blessing!' Lu Ma was lying face down on the ground. Four largely built monks were holding her legs and arms very tight while another monk, holding a thick bamboo stick, beat her buttocks. There were no screams, no tears, just a dead silence . . .

Afterwards, Lu Ma warned the child: 'In this place there are no lollies, only poison. You eat it, you die! Then you will never be able to meet your mother again.' And she made the child promise her never to take a lolly from any of those monks and never to let any of them take her to their rooms again; and never to leave Lu Ma for a single minute!

From then on, after she had put the child to bed, and locked her in, Lu Ma would disappear each night. When she came back, tears always in her eyes, she never allowed the child to question, and silently rocked her to sleep. Later, Lu Ma used a cotton cloth to tie her tummy up to hide her pregnancy, then put her clothes on. Suddenly, Lu Ma disappeared for a day or two. When she came back, she stopped tying her tummy up in the morning. Then, later, she started again, and disappeared, and came back . . .

Another two years passed, and still the poor child counted. Lu Ma then told her: 'You are eight now. You are big Ya-Tuo. You are ready to fly!'

One spring morning, another crafty old yellow-uniformed monk, with a foxy smile and his two gold front teeth glinting brightly, called to her, 'My pretty Ya-Tuo . . . My pretty Ya-Tuo . . .' and started slowly moving towards her.

A chill ran down the girl's spine. She looked at him and began backing away, screaming out, 'Lu Ma! Lu Ma! Lu Ma, where are you . . .?'

But no reply! No Ma! Panicked, she saw the temple's back door opened wide. She turned and ran towards it. The old fox pursued her. Soon though, he had had enough, and stopped. But this poor disconnected orphan child kept running and running and running . . .

Hearing a chorus of sounds, like praying (poor child – that was the only sound she was familiar with), she followed them until she saw a strange place right in front of her. With lots of children! She was bewitched looking at them and thought, 'Who are they? Are they all little monks? Where are their yellow uniforms? Are they all little Lu Mas? Where are their aprons? Where am I now? Another temple . . .?'

Then a tall, kind-looking man, with a big smile, walked towards her. He greeted her kindly and asked, 'Child, what's your name?'

'Ya-Tuo,' she replied.

'Where do you come from?' he continued.

'Temple,' she answered.

'Temple? Temple? Mmmmm . . . Where . . .?' he asked, rather puzzled.

'Over there!' she pointed in the direction she had come from.

'You mean you've just been at the temple?' he asked.

'No, I am living *in* the temple. Just over there.' she corrected him a bit impatiently, and used her little finger to point repeatedly in the direction she had come from.

'Oh, no! No, child, it cannot be! It's a long, long way! Child, it's at least two hours to get here,' he said, shaking his head.

The poor child had never heard the word 'hours' before, but she got the message and repeated angrily, 'Yes! I *am* living in the temple!'

'Well, tell me child, where are your Mama and Papa?' he asked gently as he squatted down in front of her.

'I've got no Mama or Papa — they are all dead. But I've got Lu Ma,' she answered.

'Tell me, child, where is your Lu Ma? And how did you get here?'

'She is in the temple,' she gestured.

By now, all the children had crowded round her. Some of them even began inviting her to play with them.

'Can I stay and play with them?' she then asked.

'No, you have to answer my questions first,' he said.

Bursting into tears, she started banging on his shoulder with both her little fists and crying, 'Why not? Why not? Whyyy . . .?'

'Don't cry, child,' he soothed, taking her by the hand and leading her into the house.

Inside she met another kind-looking person, an old woman. 'Child why are you crying?' she asked her with a big smile. 'In this place everyone has to smile, then they can stay.'

My mother stopped her crying straight away, and asked with her tearful eyes, but a big smile, 'Can I stay now?'

'But, listen child, how about your Lu Ma? Where is she? She will be worried!' said the kind man.

'No! Lu Ma said I am a big Ya-Tuo now, eight, and ready to fly!' she responded firmly.

The two kind-looking people turned away and whispered to each other. Then they turned to her and said, 'Okay, child, you can stay and play. But, before you go out, you have to tell us once more and very clearly, where is your Lu Ma?'

'In the temple!' she answered very quickly and ran off to play with the other children.

About mid-afternoon, Lu Ma unexpectedly appeared at this place, and talked to those kind-looking people. Suddenly, Lu Ma knelt in front of them and cried, 'Please have mercy! Please keep this poor child for Buddha!'

Those two kind-looking people quickly helped her up, and said simultaneously, 'We will do our best . . .' and Lu Ma went.

The next thing this child could remember was Lu Ma shaking her in the middle of the night, and whispering, 'Xiao Ya-Tuo, wake up! Xiao Ya-Tuo, wake up! Xiao Ya-Tuo, it's Lu Ma! Do you hear? Lu Ma has come to say goodbye to you . . .'

After my mother awoke, Lu Ma said to her through her tears: 'Xiao Ya-Tuo, you stay here. From now on here is your home! You are safe now. But remember, never tell anybody where you came from. If they know, they will send you back. Remember, never come back to that temple! But come back to see Lu Ma when you're grown up.' She held her, sobbed and sobbed and, leaving a parcel of clothes beside the child, she left.

When Lu Ma stood up to go, she jumped up from the bed, desperately clutching at her leg and pleading, 'No, Lu Ma! You can't go! No, Lu Ma! You must stay too . . .'

This happy place was a local private primary school. The kind-looking man was the principal, and also the founder of the school. He was called Song Lao-Shi. Song was his family name, and Lao-Shi means teacher. He was a middle-aged bachelor. The kind-looking old woman was called Chen Ma. She was his housekeeper, and was in her late 60s.

They lived in a small cottage at the back of the schoolyard, with two other kind-hearted men. One was called Fan Yei-Yei. Fan means meals or tea, and of course, Yei-Yei means grandfather. He was the school cook, and all the children thought he was the best cook in the world! The other one was called Magic Yei-Yei. He was the school caretaker, and all the children thought he was the smartest Yei-Yei in the world; if anything went wrong, or didn't work, Magic Yei-Yei walked in, and it worked straight away! If any of the classroom furniture was broken, Magic Yei-Yei walked in, put some of his saliva on it, left it in the corner of the classroom, then told everybody not to touch it till tomorrow. Next day it stuck together like iron! All the children tried to use their own saliva to fix their belongings, such as a broken ruler, rubber or pencil, but not even paper would stick together. Magic Yei-Yei really was magic!

The cottage had three bedrooms, plus a study and a library. Song Lao-Shi occupied the master room. Fan Yei-Yei and Magic

Yei-Yei shared a room; and now this child was going to share with Chen Ma.

Chen Ma came from a very poor part of the countryside of northern China, called Lao-Zeng. She was a truly kind-hearted woman. Her husband died the second day of their marriage, when she was 14. According to old Chinese custom, a widow must stay in her late husband's home forever, and do whatever she is told by her parents-in-law. Three years after her husband's death, her parents-in-law decided that they were going to sell her, as they needed money for their second son to be married. The deal was done; a widower, 49 years her senior, bought her as a servant and wife. Ten years later her second husband died, and his son (her stepson) sold her to a local ruffian, a gambler, to pay for his gambling losses. This brute beat her every day after he drank or lost money in the gambling house. As per an old Chinese saying: 'Marry chicken, pay obedience to chicken; marry dog, pay obedience to dog.' And so, she stayed there with him and had 11 children. Sadly, only the second child, a son, and the eighth child, a girl, survived. Later, the son followed in his father's footsteps and became a heavy drinker and gambler. When her daughter turned 12 and her husband sold her into the brothel as payment for his gambling losses, Chen Ma could no longer bear it. Helped by Fan Yei-Yei, she ran away from him and found the secure job and safe home where she was now.

Next morning, Fan Yei-Yei cooked breakfast and Chen Ma called her in and pointed her to the dining table. But she walked into the kitchen, found a new corner, then sat down on the floor, crossed her legs and waited for her breakfast. But once again Chen Ma pointed to the dining table and said, 'Your breakfast will get cold.' My mother thought that Chen Ma must be talking to somebody else, so she remained in her corner and kept waiting. Suddenly, Chen Ma came over and stood in front of her, and said impatiently, 'Why are you still sitting here? Your breakfast is getting cold.' She pulled her up and took her to the dining table. But my mother picked up a steamed bun and returned to her corner. Chen Ma came over again and asked, 'What are you doing back here, not sitting at the table?'

'Lu Ma said we were not allowed to eat at the table, it's "Do Evil",' she replied.

With tears in her eyes Chen Ma pulled her up from the floor and held her hand, saying, 'Child, this is your home! Do you understand, it's your home? You are not in the temple any more!' And she led her back to the dining table.

After breakfast, Chen Ma took her into Song Lao-Shi's study.

'Good morning, child,' he greeted her warmly.

She looked at him without replying, not knowing what 'good morning' meant.

'Child, did you sleep well? Have you had your breakfast?' he asked kindly.

She nodded.

'Do you miss your Lu Ma already?'

Again she nodded.

'Do you want to stay or go back?' he asked, looking straight at her.

'Lu Ma said never to go back there,' she replied very quickly.

'Well, then, we will have to give you a proper name,' he said, then added, 'What would you like to be called?'

'I've got a name — Ya-Tuo!' she replied.

'No, child, it's not a name. Ya-Tuo means servant. You need a proper name.'

'What does servant mean?' she asked.

'Well, child it's far too hard for you to understand right now, but one day you will understand,' he told her. He stared at her for a while, then repeated, 'Tell me, child, what would you like to be called?'

186

'I want to be called Yu-Liong and Xin-Xin (Moon and Star). Lu Ma said that if I could stop crying and count 100 New Years towards the moon and stars then I would see my mother right in front of me!' she answered very quickly and shed some tears. But the tears were of happy longing for her mother.

'Yu-Liong and Xin-Xin! Yu-Xin? What a beautiful name! Yuxin! Yuxin! Beautiful!' Song Lao-Shi hugged her and tears streamed down his own face.

'Why are you crying, Song Lao-Shi? Don't you like this name?' she asked, rather puzzled.

'Oh no, child, I love it! I love it . . .' Song Lao-Shi sobbed.

After Song Lao-Shi had taken her round the house introducing her to everybody by her new name, they returned to his study and he placed her in an armchair facing him, put a book on her knee and said, 'Yuxin, it's a present for you, from me.'

Not even waiting till he had finished, she threw the book onto the floor and cried out loudly, in great disappointment, 'No! I don't want to be a monk, chanting Buddhist Scriptures! No! Lu Ma! Where are you? No! Lu Maaaaa . . .!'

Song Lao-Shi stood up quickly and said, 'Alright, alright, Yuxin, don't cry. Listen! It's not Buddhist Scriptures. Do you understand? Not all books are Buddhist Scriptures. Will you stop crying and let me explain to you? Will you stop?'

And she stopped.

'Listen, Yuxin, this place is not a temple. You are not in the temple any more! We won't make you be a monk if you don't want to. It's a school, a nursery, to enrich people *here*,' he said, pointing to his head, then continued, 'Soon you will understand, not all books are Buddhist Scriptures. Some of them are the quintessence of our humanness, and we could not possibly be without them! They make us wise and capable of performing miracles, to work wonders . . .'

Interrupting him, she asked, 'What's the meaning of humanness and quintessence?'

'You see, Yuxin, you've got so many questions already!' said Song Lao-Shi. 'Now, I tell you, all the answers are in there.' He pointed to the book that she had thrown on the ground. 'Now, tell me, can you read? Can you write?' he asked.

She stared at him, shaking her head.

That morning, Yuxin joined the class. She was the oldest one by three years, and her little hand had never touched pencils, papers or books in all her life. But from the moment she started, she was utterly absorbed and could hardly put them down. She became the hungriest girl in the class. She wanted to know everything, everything and everything, and all at once!

The spring went quickly, and soon the summer came, and the school holidays arrived. Song Lao-Shi seemed contented and spent a lot of time with her, teaching her reading and writing. She was completely fascinated.

One morning, Song Lao-Shi said to her: 'Yuxin, you are doing very well. Yes, surprisingly well. You are a genius! Indeed, you are a genius!' He stopped and looked at her, then continued, 'Today we are going to have a break. Soon we shall have a visitor and afterwards perhaps you can go home.'

'Home? I have no home! No! Do you want to send me back to the temple?' she cried. She burst into tears and wept, 'No! Lu Ma said, "Never go back to the temple." Here is my home. No! I am not going! No!'

Chen Ma rushed in and said, 'No, Yuxin, stop! Stop and listen. Song Lao-Shi will never send you back to the temple. He is finding you a real home. Your father's home! Do you understand?'

'No! You lie! Lu Ma said I have no mother or father – they are both dead!'

At this moment there was an unfamiliar noise, and a very handsome motor vehicle passed the window and pulled up in front of the house. The driver got out, opened the other door and a well-dressed gentleman got out. His brows were knitted as he walked towards the front door and pressed the doorbell.

'Shhhh . . .' Chen Ma said with her finger to her lips, then took one of Yuxin's hands and said, 'Come, sit with me.' Song Lao-Shi rushed to answer the door.

'Mr Ling? I am Mr Song. How do you do?'

'How do you do, Mr Song?'

'Your daughter is here, do you want to see her now or later?'

'Later.'

'Mr Ling, I am so glad that you finally made this trip. Ever since the day I chanced across your daughter at my school door, I have vowed to find her birth parents. The purpose of this invitation is to discuss your new arrangements for your child in person.'

'Sorry, Mr Song. As I explained to you before, with family matters as they are, it's very hard to make any new arrangements.' He then continued, 'Mr Song, I believe you are a bachelor, right? If you like you can have her. But you won't have to worry about the financial matters.'

Mr Song did not reply.

'Well,' the man continued, 'I must be leaving now. Here is a cheque, which I believe is enough for her until she marries.' And with that, he went.

A dead silence fell, and then Song Lao-Shi reappeared in front of Yuxin, his tearful eyes fixed upon her. Then he simply walked away.

The rest of the summer holiday went past quietly. Soon summer was gone, autumn had arrived, and the new school year began. Once again, Yuxin was hungry for knowledge.

Every day after school she remained at her desk, still absorbed in her textbooks.

One day Song Lao-Shi came up to her and said, 'Yuxin, bring your chair and your books and come with me.' He took her into his own library, which was next door to his study. 'From now on,' he said, 'this chair can stay here. After school I would like you to leave the schoolroom at the same time as your class-mates, come here and do whatever you like. You can draw, you can write, you can read, you can do anything you like here. Look, here are all my books. They will make you clever, and one day when you are grown up you may love them, and they will all be yours!'

She looked at him and said, 'They shall all be mine one day? Why can't it be today?'

'Oho! My dearest little Oliver Twist – you always want some more. Today? Now? Okay! Now! All yours! Right now!' Song Lao-Shi nodded his head with a big grin.

After that, Song Lao-Shi moved lots of children's books from the school library into his library and Chen Ma specially made a big thick cushion to replace the schoolroom chair. At the beginning, Song Lao-Shi would sit beside her, reading along with her. Later, she found this far too slow, and she preferred to read by herself.

Years at the school passed quickly. One summer morning as the school holiday began once more, Song Lao-Shi called her into his study and said, 'Yuxin, after this holiday you will be 14. You are no longer the little girl who burst through this school door six years ago. Now, this place has grown far too small for you and you are ready for the big world!' He paused, and looked at her with a confident smile.

Then he continued, 'Yuxin, I would like to send you to a boarding school in Guanchou for your further education. It's a big city, and you can learn lots there. Also, it's the place you came from 10 years ago and I feel sure that one day you will like to live there too.'

'A boarding school in Guanchou? But my home is here!' she protested. 'I would have to leave you, Chen Ma, Lu Ma, my friends and all the nice people here and I would know nobody there! No! I'm not going!' and she burst into tears.

'Yes, I know you will be scared to go, as you know nobody there. But, actually, you do have somebody there, and a new place, a home to go . . .' he broke off. 'Here is a letter for you,' said Song Lao-Shi solemnly.

Yuxin opened a very poorly handwritten letter in very broken Chinese. It read:

Wei Qing,

Your father has been too ashamed to write this letter to you. I had to leave you alone ten years ago for family reasons.

Mr Song has written to me several times and said that you are a real genius, and that his place is far too small for you, that you need a bigger place and a better education. Your father is very pleased for you, as he has never had a proper education. Therefore, I shall pay all your education and living expenses in Guanchou.

On weekends, if you have no place to go, you can come and stay with us. But, do call me uncle.

Your father,

Rong-Hua

When Yuxin had finished this letter she shouted, 'It's not my father! Lu Ma said I had no father or mother, that they were both dead. Who is he? Who is this man called Rong-Hua? Who is Wei Qing?'

'Yes, Yuxin, Rong-Hua is your birth father. Your mother died

191

when you were three, but your father didn't. Wei Qing is your given name,' Song Lao-Shi replied in a very low voice.

Yuxin was shocked to tears. 'What? My father is living? He abandoned me 10 years ago but is too afraid to be called father! No! I am not going! I don't want his money. I don't want him to pay for my education and living expenses. I don't want anything to do with him! He is not my father! My father is dead!' she cried vehemently and ran out of Song Lao-Shi's study.

The whole house sunk into a gloomy silence. Nobody mentioned the matter again until the very end of the summer holiday.

Then one morning Song Lao-Shi walked into the library, sat down beside her and put an arm around her shoulders. He kissed her forehead softly and said, 'Yuxin, I love you. I want you to be my daughter.' She lifted her head slowly and looked at him, not knowing what to say. But she could see a father's genuine tenderness expressed on his benign face. It was the first time in her life that she had received a father's kiss, straight from a father's heart. She buried her head into his chest, sobbing violently like a heartbroken child . . .

That night, Chen Ma cooked a beautiful dinner and surprisingly Lu Ma turned up to join them. Yuxin was overjoyed to see Lu Ma and pulled her chair to the corner of the table between Song Lao-Shi and Lu Ma, as she felt this was the first time in her life that she had a father! This was also the first time in Lu Ma's life that she could sit at the dining table for her dinner! Song Lao-Shi lit the candles and they had a big celebration. It was the happiest moment of this orphan child's life.

Chen Ma was extremely busy over the next few days. She roasted rice, sesame, peanuts and walnuts, and then mixed them with sugar and ground them into flour and put them into tins. She sliced steamed buns and dried them under the sun and prepared lots of pickled vegetables.

One morning, Song Lao-Shi called her into his study again and said, 'Yuxin, sit down. Today, I want to have a few father's words with you, which means you have to listen and obey! I don't want to hear any such word as "No" from you!' It all sounded very serious, but there was a big smile on his face.

'First of all, good news! Your boarding school arrangements are fully made and all you have to do is attend by next Monday. Secondly, you don't have to stay with anybody else during the weekends. It's been approved by the school that you can stay there, although there are no meals provided. Therefore, Chen Ma is now preparing enough food for you to keep you for half a year. Thirdly, my school holiday has been extended another week, so I shall go and stay in Guanchou with you for one week, until you settle into your new place. Fourthly, I would like you to write to me at least once a week and tell me about everything, everything and everything! Such as your study, your accommodation, your weekend food, your spare time, your reading, and your health. And I will write back to you every week as well. Lastly, any questions?' Song Lao-Shi stopped and looked at her with a fatherly concern.

'Who is going to pay for my education? My boarding school fees?' she asked.

'Ah! Good question. Very good question indeed. I would like to say, gradually it will be yourself!' He paused and nodded before adding, 'Yes, I am sure in the end, yourself.'

With a broad smile Yuxin looked at him, rather puzzled, and said, 'You mean . . . you mean that I shall be working as well, while I am studying?'

'Oh, no! A girl of your age – how could you do both? Let me explain it to you properly,' he answered hastily. 'If you do well in school or at university you can apply for a scholarship. Once you obtain a scholarship your studies will be paid by the school or university or by some other organisation.' He stopped here and nodded. Then he added, 'Child, always remember! The world will never be conquered by a human's tears, but only by a human's unyielding willpower.' And again he nodded and looked at her steadily, then murmured, 'Yes! I can see you already have it!'

Those years at Song Lao-Shi's had been the happiest in Yuxin's life. Between them, and thanks to Lu Ma, Song Lao-Shi and Chen Ma had made a home, a haven for her. She was set to enter the big world and began her new journey confidently.

Yuxin was sent to an affiliated middle school of Chong-Sa University, which was the best (and most expensive) private school and university in Guanchou during those years. The majority of the students came from very wealthy families. The school provided the students with excellent accommodation, meals and care during the school week. The school weekend started midday on Saturday. All the students were allowed to go home for their lunch. For the first Saturday, Yuxin was the same as the rest; Song Lao-Shi was waiting for her at the front entrance, and took her out for lunch. Then he escorted her back to her hostel and introduced her to some of the chairmen of the school, who all came from the countryside and stayed in the hostel during the weekend as well. They promised Song Lao-Shi that they would take care of Yuxin, and told her that if she needed any help to just ask them. Song Lao-Shi taught her how to manage her weekend meals, and then rushed back to Wei-Zo for his school's new year.

Yuxin stood at her window after seeing Song Lao-Shi off, and as the evening approached, the dusk closed in and it grew dark. But the whole floor's lights were switched off by the usual weekend timing procedure. She thought someone might be able to help her, but when she opened her door, it was pitch-dark in the hallway. She could not even see which way to go.

What was worse, she was dying to go to the toilet! She sat on her bed, beginning to sob, and soon she lost control – her clothes and bedding were soaking wet.

The following Monday, it was the hottest news and spread all over the place. Everybody knew that she had wet her bed. When her classmates also found that she was unable to speak the local dialect they began to mock her, copying her accent, and looking down on her. They also gave her a very cruel nickname – 'Wet Pants Pumpkin' . . .

It was a very painful lesson for her to learn in her first couple of weeks out in the big world. No Song Lao-Shi, no Lu Ma, no Chen Ma, nobody! Nobody knew her, nobody understood her, nobody protected her or helped her. She felt very much alone, shamed, humiliated, and could no longer bear to stay. During a study break, she slipped away from the classroom, back to her hostel room, and wrote to Song Lao-Shi:

. . . Song Lao-Shi, I am frightened, I am cold, and I am alone! Song Lao-Shi, I beg you to come and take me home! Song Lao-Shi, I can no longer bear this discrimination and humiliation! Song Lao-Shi, I beg you to take me home . . .

Barely a week later, Song Lao-Shi turned up at her door. When she saw him, she threw all her textbooks, pens and papers onto the floor, ran towards him and buried her head into his chest. 'Take me home!' she cried, 'I beg you, take me home now . . .'

'Child, tell me what's been happening! Child, stop crying and tell me what's been happening?' Song Lao-Shi gently stroked her hair. Then he took her out of the school for a walk.

After Song Lao-Shi had learned all about the first couple of weeks in her new place, he said, 'Child, do you remember what I told you? The world will never be conquered by a human's tears, but only by a human's unyielding willpower. Do you understand? It means that a human's tears will never be able to move the world, but only a human's determination. It's the beginning of your life! If you give up now, you give up your whole life. Listen to me Yuxin! Never give up!' Then he opened his bag, took out a very small roll of red paper, and passed it to her. It said:

Where there is a will, there is a way!

'Now, hang this above your bed,' he urged, 'and when anything upsets you, always look at it and remind yourself – "I am the one who is going to conquer this world!" It's power! Remember, child, one day you will move, conquer and shake this world.'

Song Lao-Shi stayed in Guanchou overnight, and early the next morning he caught the train back to his school. After he had left, the school headmaster made a most touching and sincere apology to her on behalf of the school in front of the class, then all her classmates gave an apology as well. And so, Yuxin's feelings of self-consciousness and inferiority ended and she longed to move, to conquer, and to shake the world!

In no time at all she became the top student of her class. Her Chinese was far more advanced than any of the others in the same year. Three years later, she won a scholarship to Chong-Sa High School. Then another three years later, at the age of 20, she won a scholarship to Chong-Sa University to study Eastern Literature. And a year later she accidentally met a young man three years her junior who was later to become my dearest father!

My father started his university studies when he was 17. He was the youngest in his class, about two years junior to most, as he had skipped a grade twice during the years he studied at Chong-Sa middle and high schools.

At this time, my father was dying to own an Austin car, but Yei-Yei and Nana were not very keen on it. In those days, if you owned a car, it also meant you had to employ a driver and supply him with accommodation, meals and so on. Most importantly, they were worried that the car would disturb his studies. But they did not want to disappoint him too much, so Yei-Yei said, 'Well, this is your first year in university. If you are still doing as well as you did at high school, such as being the top of your school, then by the end of the year you can have a car.'

So this young man's goal became to fight for an Austin car! But this young woman was still the same – fighting for her own education. For this young man the year passed far too slowly, but for this young woman it passed much too quickly! Eventually, they both reached their last day, and waited impatiently for their final results.

When the headmaster awarded medals to the year's top six students at the final assembly, this young man held his breath tightly, and his heart almost leapt out of his throat. He prayed and prayed, 'Bless me! Last one for me! Bless me! Last one for me!' Suddenly he heard:

'Our second prize-winner is – Guo Jinren . . .'

He just couldn't help it, he burst into tears and couldn't even go up to accept his prize. Just one place down – his whole year's hard work had been for nothing. His dream was dashed. His Austin car had vanished!

Then came the final announcement:

'Our first prize-winner is – Ling Yuxin!'

He couldn't even look at her. He now hated her entirely.

Before the university holiday, the principal invited all the top students to a formal dinner reception. All the young men had to wear dinner suits, and the young women had to wear an evening dress. The British & America mission, the local mayors, the Guanchou city mayor, the university's sponsors, and all the well-known personages, were all to attend the reception. The invitations to the students had two different colours – red and gold. The majority of the students received a red envelope. Only a few received the gold, which meant that they would be seated amongst those important personages.

All the young men looked extremely handsome, and all the young women were richly dressed and beautiful indeed! But for Yuxin, her best clothes were her school uniform. The officials thought she must have walked into the wrong place, and they tried to stop her and ask for her invitation. In the end, they had to conduct her to sit at the master table, beside the chancellor. Next to the chancellor was a young man. The man who hated her entirely!

Nobody could have imagined that this reception would turn this young man's hate to love, and change his life at once, and forever.

Afterwards, Yuxin returned to Wei-Zo for her summer holiday. But Jinren just couldn't get her rich beauty out of his mind, nor her reticent smile, her simple and modest appearance. That the whole year's hard work had been for nothing, and he had lost his Austin car, now no longer interested him at all. He spent most of his time closeted in his room, writing letters to Yuxin.

Yuxin was so shocked by receiving those love letters like a waterfall, that she really didn't know what to do. Her quandary was noticed by Song Lao-Shi.

He said to her, 'Yuxin, I want you to do me a favour, and reply to this young fellow as soon as possible. A top student of Chong-Sa is a good fellow for you! In this world, nobody can do without love. Understand? Child, love is our destiny's conqueror! A human's one inalienable right and sacred bounden duty is to receive and give love.'

Respecting a father's dignity, she wrote to Jinren, saying, 'I am sorry, I am not interested in love, as it's far too early for me. But if you would like to delve into Eastern Literature with me, which is my current study subject, it would be most welcome.'

How was this poor Economics student, my father, who had no interest in Eastern Literature and knew hardly anything about it, going to win Yuxin's heart? Surely, this overserious young woman needed a good shaking . . .

Yei-Yei and Nana knew their son very well. If there was something he was dying for, he would never give up. But why had he grown so suddenly quiet about the Austin car? Since the university reception he had hardly been out with his friends all holidays. He seemed very busy in his room all the time. Was he writing? Studying? Whatever it was he was extremely quiet! They began to worry that he must be deeply hurt by their hard control. Yei-Yei then decided that he was going to have serious words with him.

This is how they found out that he had somebody special in his heart. It was most exciting news for both of them. They decided that they were going to throw him a big birthday party. He could invite as many friends as he wished, and certainly the one who had his heart would be the first on the list!

How marvellous! How exciting! How fascinating! Yei-Yei and Nana couldn't wait to meet her. Nana believed strongly that a girl who was Chong-Sa's top student must come from a very decent family, just like them. What else could they expect? It was a 'Men Dang Hu Dui' (the appropriate door fits the frame of the correct house) match. In other words – a perfect match!

My father's birthday was on October 2, just one month after the new university year started. In China, the beginning of October marks the end of summer and the beginning of autumn, before the cold winter sets in. In Guanchou, the majority of families would spring-clean twice a year, around the month of May (before the start of summer) and October (at the end). But that year, Nana's spring-cleaning could not possibly wait until October – midway through September, she had already started! Three women came in to help. Such scrubbing and polishing of the floors; such brushing of walls and ceilings; such washing and cleaning of windows; such shifting out and moving back in of furniture; such taking down and putting back up of curtains; such polishing of furniture and leather chairs; such wiping and polishing of ornaments . . . Nana was thrown into ecstasies by the birthday party preparations and the prospect of her 'Men Dang Hu Dui' future daughter-in-law's first visit.

Finally, the big day arrived. All the preparations had been completed. The whole house was richly decorated and brilliantly illuminated. Nana had her hair beautifully done and all coiled up. Her gentle pale round face was still well preserved. Waiting to meet the guests, she presented a very erect, slight figure in her black and blue-grey patterned silk dress; her silver-grey scarf of rich foreign lace; her pearl ornaments; her hand-embroidered silk handkerchief; her high-heeled shoes and her subtle French perfume. Indeed, she was the most handsome, proud, but arrogant hostess in the world!

They say a person born on October 2 possesses a sweet and kindly disposition, is well liked and admired, and has many friends and no enemies. This was so true of my father, who was a general favourite among the young men and women of his own age. And so, he had invited almost 30 friends, plus their partners – in total 50 guests – to his birthday party. Because of the school he attended, and the area in which he lived, the majority of his friends came from either well-known or well-to-do families. That night all the most expensive cars, such as

Rolls Royces, Mercedes Benzes and so on, pulled up along Yei-Yei and Nana's street. The doorbell rang nonstop, with one good-looking young visitor after the next; and to our Nana, this fascinating moment was far beyond expression! She thought all the young men were extremely handsome – obviously they all wore the correct attire, which suited her taste perfectly. The richly-dressed young ladies were so brilliant, elegant and accomplished; they were the most beautiful ladies in the world, a treat for Nana to meet. She stood by the side of her darling son, waiting for him to introduce all his friends one by one: such as the child of . . . an ambassador; a financial magnate; an oil baron; a steel mogul; a well-known politician; a local mayor . . . Nana was completely intoxicated!

Nevertheless, Nana was eagerly waiting for her son's heart, her future 'Men Dang Hu Dui' daughter-in-law to arrive; she was more convinced than ever that this young lady would be the belle of the ball! Once more, the doorbell rang. This time Nana could no longer control her excitement – not even waiting for the servants to open the door, she rushed to answer it herself. There was a university-uniformed female student in front of her; she thought this girl must have pushed the wrong doorbell. And so, leaving the door open, she walked away without a word, and tried to find some help to get rid of this strange shabby being as soon as possible.

'Mama, this is my best friend, Yuxin,' my father introduced her to his arrogant mother proudly.

'Yeeessss,' Nana drawled, almost numbed. She bit her lip and swept her eye over Yuxin from top to toe. Then, with no expression, no greeting, she left, and disappeared for the rest of the evening.

Early the next morning, Nana woke my father up. 'Yuxin – what a stupid, uneducated name!' she fumed. 'Man or woman? The name made me nervous!' she said, trembling. She stopped and tightened her hand-embroidered silk dressing gown, then continued, 'Tell your mother, Jinren. You didn't say to your mother last night that she is your best friend, did you?' Then she walked out. She had not even noticed that some of her son's friends had stayed the night in the same room!

The next university year went so quickly, and soon the summer arrived, and the holiday began again and they would have to be apart for another long summer break.

Using a needle to prick the blood from her right-hand finger and his left-hand finger, they made their first oath of true love. Then they had their first kiss, and went their separate ways, to bear this long summer holiday's merciless parting.

When she arrived home in Wei-Zo, Song Lao-Shi was in bed and suffering great pain in his left leg. He had lost a great deal of weight as well. A week later, the doctor examined him and found that he had advanced bone cancer.

For Yuxin, this shocking moment was far beyond expression. Song Lao-Shi was now her only family, her most respectable beloved father. By the end of the school holiday, Song Lao-Shi could hardly walk, but he still wanted her to return to Guanchou for her new university year. A week before she was due back she sat beside his bed and watched him sleep, and the realisation that she might actually lose him – after all that he had done for her – cut through her heart.

She decided to stay, to fulfil a daughter's responsibility to look after him, to repay his affections. She then wrote to the university principal and asked for permission to suspend her schooling and retain her scholarship for half a year, so that she could nurse him till the end of the year. Sadly, 10 days before Chinese New Year, Song Lao-Shi passed away.

It was the greatest sorrow and loss for this young life so far. After Song Lao-Shi's funeral, all his relatives, who Yuxin had never met before, came to his house. They found his will in his desk drawer. It said: '. . . all my assets are for my goddaughter Yuxin to keep . . . If any of you could kindly help me to take care of her till she marries, it would be very much appreciated . . .' One of his relatives jumped up, slapped her in the face and cursed, 'Bloody fuckin' whore! You must have forced him to write it for you! Get out of here! Now! Now!' then tore the will into pieces and threw all her belongings out the window.

In tears, this girl walked into Song Lao-Shi's room, picked up one of his photos (which had hung on the wall for many, many years) and his last-used walking stick, and gathering up her belongings from the ground outside, begged some train ticket money and left for Guanchou.

The train arrived back in Guanchou on the afternoon of the following day, one day before the Chinese New Year's Eve. She walked to her hostel, but the door was locked and all the people had gone home for the celebrations. As the dusk closed in mercilessly around her, she sat on the ground in front of the hostel and began to sob. 'Song Lao-Shi, wake up and tell me – am I a cheater? Am I a whore? Do I deserve to be slapped in the face, driven out, expelled from my home? Song Lao-Shi, wake up and tell me – where should I go? Where is my home now . . .?'

Suddenly, she heard Song Lao-Shi's voice in her mind: 'Yuxin, I want you to do me a favour, and reply to this young fellow as soon as possible. A top student of Chong-Sa is a good fellow for you! In this world, nobody can do without love. Understand? Child, love is our destiny's conqueror! A human's one inalienable right and sacred bounden duty is to receive and give love . . .' Now Yuxin knew where to turn.

When Dad brought Yuxin home Nana was so busy organising the New Year's preparations she did not even notice that she was there. Dad was far too scared to tell his mother, so he took Yuxin into his own room straight away, and then left the rest to fate.

After the loss, the sorrow, the harshness and the long journey, Yuxin was exhausted. As soon as she rested her head, she immediately fell into a deep sleep.

Next thing she knew, it was around eleven o'clock in the evening. The door opened and Nana walked in, calling, 'Jinren! Jinren –' She switched on the light, took one look, and marched out.

'Jinren! How dare you! How dare you at not even 20 yet, sneak a female home to your room!' Nana yelled at him.

'Sorry Mum, let me explain to you,' my father replied quietly.

'No explanations! Take her out! Now!' Nana commanded.

'Calm down,' Yei-Yei ordered her. Then he continued, 'Jinren, come and sit here and tell us what is happening.'

After Dad explained everything, Nana asked in a trembling voice, 'Jinren, is all this true? Do you believe her? How well do you know her? And . . . are you ready to keep her?'

Dad didn't answer, so Nana continued, 'Jinren, you are far too young, too naive to understand all this! Your mother can tell you that what you've seen in her isn't really her. What you've heard of her isn't really her either. This girl must have a very complicated background. How could she afford to study at such an expensive school all these years – especially as she has got her own single room. How could such a small-town, poor schoolteacher afford all this? I don't think her parents are really dead. At least one must still be living. And I believe her birth parents won't be like your mother and father are, with respectable lives. You see, she has got a very pretty face, her mother must be an illustrious prostitute, or an illustrious dance-hostess, or songstress – lots of wealthy men make a mistake with those kinds of cheap but good-looking women, have a child, and then are too ashamed to tell, and abandon them.' She stopped.

Again my father didn't reply, so she continued, 'You see, our bloods are so different, how could we let this kind of dirty blood flow into and mix with ours? You are far too young to understand. But one day you will know. Once the blood is tainted, you can never clean it! You see, if the father is a thief, the son becomes a thief as well; if the father is a hooligan, then the son turns out a hooligan too. It doesn't mean that those sons really want to be bad, they just have no control over it. It's something in their blood –'

'If so, I believe she has excellent blood and both of her parents must be very good people. How could the daughter of an illustrious prostitute, or an illustrious dance-hostess or songstress, turn out to be a top student at Chong-Sa and even better than any of us?' Dad interrupted in a very low voice.

'Oh! How dare you say that to your mother,' spluttered Nana. 'If they were such good parents, why did they abandon their own child? Would your parents do something like that?' yelled Nana angrily.

'The abandoning wasn't her fault.' Again, Dad spoke in a very low voice.

'Jinren, you have never spoken against your mother in this way before! You see, you have only been mixing with her for a very short time, and you've changed already. If people know you are mixing with this kind of low, poor-quality person, how will your family survive in this society? You are our only son, how can this family rely on you to carry on?' Nana began to cry.

This time Dad didn't answer.

'After tomorrow, we shall have so many visitors. If they see her, what shall I say? How shameful! You aren't married but you have this low, cheap kind of girl hiding at home. Please move her out! Please do it for our family's dignity, and move her out now!' pleaded Nana.

'No. Let her stay tonight.' said Yei-Yei. 'It's nearly two

205

o'clock in the morning. Where could she go? She has no home. Jinren, you can stay in the spare room tonight. Let's talk about it tomorrow.'

'But we aren't a charity! We can't let our family, our son's life contribute to charitable social services!' Again, Nana cried.

'Mum, Mum, please understand – it's not pity, it's not mercy, it's *love*! I love her!' Dad insisted vehemently.

'What? You love her? How dare you say so to your mother! You are far too young to understand what the real meaning of love is. Anyone you want to choose to love has to meet your mother's approval first!' Nana screamed until she was almost out of breath.

'Please stop! We've had enough. Jinren, go to bed!' Yei-Yei shouted loudly and walked out.

Meanwhile, Yuxin had heard every single ugly word. Early the next morning, around seven, she packed her belongings and left a thank-you note on the bed. Nana was sitting in the hallway, already waiting for her. There was no morning greeting, no eye contact, just a brief and distant conversation.

'Are you ready to go?' Nana asked.

'Yes, thank you, Mrs Guo.' Yuxin replied.

'Here is some money and a list of places you can go,' said Nana coldly, pointing to a place called Women's Refuge. 'They are very good places and nice people indeed,' she continued. 'They help and look after all sorts of people. Very nice free accommodation, very nice free food, clothing and everything you could possibly want . . . and, you never know, you might meet some nice people there, who will take you home, love you, and make you part of their family – "Every cloud has a silver lining!" Good luck!'

When Yuxin offered no reply, Nana added, 'You see my son is only 19, not even 20 yet. He is very kind, but far too young, too naive. He doesn't even know how to look after himself, so how could he look after you? He is interested in studying economics, not social services! Therefore, my girl, in the future, if you have any kind of problem, or need any kind of assistance, please go to them instead of my son,' Nana finished sourly.

Yuxin then replied with dignity, 'Thank you, Mrs Guo for all your valuable time. I know these places very well, maybe better than you think. I know what to do, where to go, and I have enough money.' And she left.

On her way out, she was followed by a burst of arguing.

'Mum! Please let her stay! She has nowhere to go!'

'How dare you!' Nana shouted back.

Then, 'Be kind. It's New Year's Eve!' came Yei-Yei's deep voice.

This then, was the tale of my mother's early life . . .

Eight

晴天霹靂

Dream and Nightmare

After that night at my parents' Yee Bing's adorable smile disappeared, he grew extremely quiet, and he knitted his brows like an old man. He no longer mentioned the ninth of the ninth, and so my birthday came and went unmentioned. But Yee Bing developed a very cordial dislike towards my mother . . .

Shortly after my birthday, Yee Bing began getting ready to host his cousin from Yue-Qiu, with his wife and their five-year-old son, at his home for two weeks of the summer holidays. Early one morning, Yee Bing rang me to say that his cousin and his wife were very keen to meet me, so we met at Yee Bing's – our so-called new home – that same day.

His cousin was very much like Yee Bing – very northern Chinese-looking, rather tall, handsome, and a very confident speaker. He worked for the Yue-Qiu Municipal Government Propaganda Department as a political editor. His wife, a young physician, worked at Yue-Qiu's Du-Yang People's Hospital. From the moment we met, I felt as if I had known them all my life. We had a long enjoyable chat, which lasted almost six hours. They seemed to know everything about me – such as my career, my family, my current situation, and how our marriage plans were blocked.

At one point, Yee Bing's cousin said, 'Why don't you two come up to live in Yue-Qiu and get away from that batch of old idiots?' referring to our parents. 'I could find you both a dream job with my eyes closed!'

Yee Bing looked at him then turned to me, the old light in his eyes, and nodded – 'Not a bad idea, eh?'

Then his wife said to me with a big smile, 'Yes! Come up! You must come up and keep me company. I don't know why I married this man.' She pointed to her husband, then continued, 'Life with them is so boring! All they talk about is politics, Party policy, and that sort of garbage. I can't relate to it at all. My Mum and Dad are medical doctors – intellectuals like yours. We are all "Chou Lao Juo" (a saying from the Cultural Revolution, meaning all intellectuals are stinking, disgusting and bad). I have no brothers or sisters, so we of the same kind should stick together!'

Then she giggled and asked her husband, 'Am I right?'

'Oh, yes!' he agreed. 'Of course! You are right as always.' Her husband giggled too.

After they left Guanchou for Yue-Qiu, Yee Bing and I began to contemplate our future plans very seriously.

Yee Bing loved his cousin's idea. He was from northern China originally and he much preferred the northern Chinese lifestyle to Guanchou. Yue-Qiu was also one of the biggest cities in China and he had many relatives, friends and high-ranking Party contacts there. That meant that he could obtain great opportunities, more than if he lived in Guanchou. Also, he found that now that he had grown up, there was less in common between his parents and himself. In his own words: 'They are brainwashed by the hyperbole of Marxism, Leninism and Mao's thoughts, and it's far too hard to break that. All their thoughts are focused on one thing – power!'

I agreed too – it was not a bad idea. At this stage, my life overwhelmed me. My job was still suspended pending the outcome of the investigation, my studies had been badly disrupted, my 'health' problem was still an issue, and then there were our family difficulties. I strongly desired to go, to leave everything behind and start afresh. Mainly, we were both craving to begin our life together. But when I discussed it with Dad and Da-Bo, they were extremely uneasy.

Dad said, 'If you feel 100 per cent sure and comfortable to go, Dad won't stop you. But if you don't feel quite sure and want to solicit Dad's opinion, Dad says, "I don't think it's a good idea." You see, for Yee Bing, moving to Yue-Qiu is just like returning home. The place and the lifestyle are both in his favour. Even the air will suit him perfectly well. He knows many people there, but you know none and would be completely alone. Of course, Dad believes you are mature enough to take full responsibility for yourself, and that Yee Bing will look after you as well. But if things go wrong, like this time, who will be with you? You mustn't underestimate the value and importance of family support. In fact, Dad can see very clearly that you two are trying to evade the problem by walking away from where it exists. You both have to understand that problems aren't solved by walking away from them – you must rely on yourselves to resolve them!' He stopped and frowned at me anxiously.

Then Da-Bo spoke. 'Why don't you two ignore what your stubborn mother says, stay here, and do whatever you've been planning. You have the flat already and I will give any financial support you need to help set up your new life. I know that your job worries you the most. But I believe we can get this sorted out for you. Then your life will get back to normal and you will be secure and can relax again. So why take this kind of risk?'

Dad was looking at Da-Bo and nodding. He added, 'You see, our family has stuck with this innocent, heart-saddened nation through so many difficulties. We have suffered, we have struggled, but we have learned to survive. Now the tide has ebbed again and we are finally able to settle down and relax, but –' Dad suddenly stopped and struggled to control his emotions.

Da-Bo looked at me and said, 'Listen to your Dad! Don't make this move. It will do you great harm! Stay where you are. But if you have already made up your mind, you must promise to talk to your mother, otherwise you will put your Dad and I in a very difficult position,' he finished desperately, looking towards Dad for support.

Dad nodded in agreement, then repeated, 'Yes, you *must*!'

I understood that Da-Bo and Dad were both deeply concerned about my future safety, and the loss of family support. Making me promise to talk to my mother was really their last card.

About a week or two later, Yee Bing received a phone call from his cousin, saying that he had two job offers and I had one. Yee Bing's first offer was to the position of Assistant Political Reporter for the Ding-Fen News Agency, one of the most powerful propaganda machines in China. To Yee Bing, brought up in a Loyal Proletariat Revolutionary family and with his passion for politics, this truly was a golden opportunity. But the job title 'Political Reporter' really made me nervous for my political security and safety. The history of the country since 1949 had taught me that any kind of political movement begins by making an example of someone and punishing them through propaganda first, to warn off others. The innocent victims of propaganda always stand in the gap and bear the brunt.

Yee Bing was also offered a job as Assistant Financial Advisor for the Du-Yang Bureau of the Yue-Qiu municipal government. This was similar work to what my father did in Guanchou, but it was a very much more powerful position. However, although the job related to his field of study, the role was too senior, the shoe too big for him to fit at this stage. He did not have the necessary experience, and felt rather intimidated by the thought of taking the position. However, for the sake of our future political safety, I felt I should encourage him to choose this kind of career. I have always believed, in this world, if other people can pick up, learn, and grow competent at a new task, then *we* should be able to as well! So, why not him?

I was offered a job as Assistant Chief Director of Finance for the Yue-Qiu Art & Craft Company, which was the head office of the hand-embroidery industry to which my own company belonged. This was the kind of place in which I had dreamed of working ever since I'd started in the finance department of our company. It was a large and powerful state organisation, and a great opportunity indeed! I was delighted. I could almost smell the privilege of power and I could picture my future there. Such as Chief Director of this! Chief Director of that! I could almost hear the respect, the high esteem – 'Yes, Chief!'

Nevertheless, since the discussion I had had with Dad and Da-Bo, I could not entirely get rid of a niggling feeling of uncertainty and doubt, and Dad's words came to mind: 'Listen to Dad, sometimes our intuition is trying to tell us something – if you are not quite sure, it always means that there must be something wrong.' Were Yee Bing and I really making the right decision for our future life? Was this truly our best chance of being successful in our future careers? I decided to have a serious discussion with him.

First of all, I told Yee Bing, if he really wanted me to go with him, my political security and safety had to be guaranteed. Thus, I disagreed with his decision to take the Assistant Political

Reporter's job — it was far too risky. He would be better to extend himself by taking on the finance job. Secondly, I wanted our acceptance to be on a conditional and temporary basis — for a half-year trial only. That meant that I would stay employed by the Guanchou company. Consequently, our Guanchou residencies had to be kept until we made our final decision. Because China's population was so swollen and inflated at this time, the government had very tough rules regulating movement in and out of the large cities. If we gave up my residency in Guanchou now, but found later that Yue-Qiu did not agree with us, or that the jobs were not right, or our relationship didn't work out, then I would have great difficulty in returning to my home.

Surprisingly, Yee Bing accepted all my conditions without argument and we replied to Yue-Qiu immediately. That meant I now had to have a heart-to-heart talk with Mum, Dad and Da-Bo straight away.

When I told them that Yee Bing and I had accepted job offers from Yue-Qiu, for a six-month trial only, they were utterly stunned.

After a long silence, Mum opened the conversation. 'Tell us from the bottom of your heart, Sheng, do you feel that you have made this decision purely for love, or for your career ambitions, or merely to escape your current situation?'

'For all of them,' I replied quietly.

'Right! Right! Right! For all of them! It's purely jumping from the hot pan into the fire! It's suicide! What's the difference between temporary trial or permanent shift, if you have promised to go with somebody else already?' Mum questioned sharply.

I had no answer.

'Have you ever thought about the duality of power?' she continued in a trembling voice. 'It seduces you with a great favour like this offer! But it can just as easily injure you and destroy you completely! Haven't you learned anything? To risk your life for love –!'

I stared at her numbly.

'Answer me! Answer me! Why don't you answer me?' shouted Mum. 'Are you all deaf? Are you all dumb?' Mum stabbed her finger at Dad, Da-Bo and me in turn, as she completely lost her temper.

I dared not reply.

'Okay!' she continued, barely controlling her voice. 'Very simple. Now listen very carefully, all of you. This dreadful decision must be reversed at once. This relationship must be terminated immediately – these bloods cannot possibly mix! It's totally, totally, totally wrong! If you go with him I will have nothing to do with you from this moment on. Full stop! Understand? We will be finished! We will no longer be mother and daughter! This door will no longer be open for you and I will not want to hear anything about you! This family has endured far, far, far too much, and we long for peace!'

And that was it. From that very moment all communication between my mother and myself was completely extinguished.

Now Yee Bing no longer cared about what either of our parents thought. All he wanted to do was leave Guanchou as soon as possible. He believed that he had hammered enough nails, and now it was time to seek some peace of mind. So he immediately began to organise our departure. He made long lists of the things he wanted to sort out before we left, such as contacting Yue-Qiu to make sure our Guanchou residence would stay open for at least a year; our new jobs' commencing date; the travel arrangements; our accommodation in Yue-Qiu; returning the current flat to the Housing Corporation, and so on. Lastly, I was reminded that my medical certificate needed to be updated and extended, but only if I felt it necessary.

Three days before our departure, after Yee Bing had picked up our tickets from the booking office and returned home, an unexpected phone call came from the Housing Corporation. The new tenants wanted him to remove all his belongings from the flat as soon as possible as they wanted to move in early the next morning. He rang to ask me whether I could give him a hand and we agreed to meet there.

When we met, he looked extremely tired. He sat down on the edge of the bed and said, 'I'm exhausted, let's sit for a few minutes,' putting his arm round my shoulders.

I was looking around the flat, and blurted out on an impulse, 'What a pity. I really like this flat, Yee Bing.'

'Yes, so do I,' he said, 'But –'

Before Yee Bing could complete his answer there came a loud banging on the door. We held our breaths and listened carefully for a while, then there was a fit of shouting: 'Open the door! Xiao Bing, open the door!' It was Yee Bing's mother! He stood up, said, 'Don't move! Stay here,' and walked out. I listened anxiously to their conversation.

'Xiao Bing! Tell us! What are those tickets for?' It was his father.

'Sorry, Dad. I haven't had time to tell you – Sheng and I have accepted job offers from Yue-Qiu,' Yee Bing replied.

'Humph! More likely you have fallen under the influence of a devil and turned blind, deaf and dumb! Listen to me, Xiao Bing! Without our permission you are not allowed to go anywhere with this psychotic!' his father shouted.

'Sorry, Dad! Everything has been arranged,' Yee Bing answered angrily.

'No! You listen to me! Your jobs have already been with-drawn. This flat was taken over by the new tenant yesterday. Those tickets were cancelled half an hour ago! Now, I order you to go home with us!' his father commanded him loudly.

'How come? How come such an important job for a psychotic?' his father continued his tirade, when Yee Bing didn't respond.

'No! She is not a psychotic!' his mother interrupted loudly. 'She is Anti-Communist party, Anti-Communist China! A Counter-Revolutionary devil! She should be locked up!' she screamed.

'Stop it, Mum! She is not a Counter-Revolutionary devil. She was never Anti-Communist Party, Anti-Communist China. She was ill!' Yee Bing desperately tried to defend me.

'What is the illness?' his mother screamed back. 'How come a psychotic is able to go to Yue-Qiu to take over such an important position? It's purely a political manoeuvre. Stop playing tricks with us Xiao Bing. She is using her evil intentions to lead you astray! Where is she?' she charged in, still screaming.

When she saw me, she ran towards me, seized my hair and began vigorously slapping my face. Then, exerting all her energy, she started banging my head against the wall and swearing, 'Bloody fuckin' whore! Bloody fuckin' devil! Do you want to use your evil intentions to lead our son astray, to wrest away our son's soul, and to destroy his life? Bloody fuckin' dirty Counter-Revolutionary! Bloody fuckin' stinking night-soil! Do you want to sneak into our Red Revolution Family and pollute our pureness? Bloody fuckin' whore! Fuckin' devil! Do you want to take our son away from us, break up and destroy our family forever? Okay, fuckin' devil! Let me tell you, your conspiracy won't triumph, fuckin' devil! We're sending you to jail and locking you up forever – till you die! Do you hear? Till you die!'

'Mum – stop!' Yee Bing ran towards his mother and grabbed both her wrists to stop her. I was shocked to tears and too numb to move.

216

And then his father started shouting again. 'Guo Sheng! I order you to get out of here immediately!' he pointed to the door.

After I walked out of the flat, I couldn't think which way to go. My legs were trembling, my ears were roaring, and my head was pounding. I stood there, leaning against the wall for a moment, and heard:

'Out! Get out of here! You violently hitting her, accusing her, and insulting her, is equal to violently hitting me! Accusing me! Insulting me! This has nothing at all to do with "sneaking into", "destroying", "taking away from" or "breaking up" the Yees! This is love! Do you understand? Do you understand the meaning of love? I love her and I want to unite my life with her. If you send her to jail and lock her up forever, I shall have nothing to do with you! You will no longer be my mother and father and you may as well forget that I am your son. We will sever relations at one stroke and go our separate ways,' Yee Bing bellowed.

And still Yee Bing kept shouting. 'Out! Get out of here! You make me ashamed! You make me sick! You are unworthy to be my parents! Finished! We are finished! Get out now! Now!'

Suddenly the lift came up, and an unfamiliar woman held open the door and called, 'Hey! Do you want to come in? Quick! Come in.' And I made an effort and stumbled in. When the lift reached the ground, my legs were still trembling, and I could hardly stand, let alone walk. Then my head rose, and to my horror, there was our company's Human Resource Manager, flanked by three strongly-built uniformed policemen. I collapsed to the ground.

'See! Zhuo Zai Xing Xu (a thief has a guilty conscience)!' the Human Resource Manager shouted out triumphantly.

'Fuckin' stand up! Fuckin' feign death!' one of the policemen yelled out and kicked me. Then four pairs of rough hands were immediately laid upon me and I was thrown into a windowless jeep . . .

Next thing I remember, I was lying on a narrow wooden bed, about 60 centimetres in width, inside a small, dim, damp room. The room was about three square metres and windowless, with only one poor ceiling light. The odour from the toilet was so overpowering I could scarcely breathe.

I was totally disoriented. Where was I? In Yue-Qiu? In my new office? In our new home? But where was Yee Bing? Was I awake or asleep? Was this a nightmare . . .?

Suddenly, light poured in as the door opened. To my horror, I saw it was made of thick iron! A formidable-looking man moved slowly towards me.

'Sit up! Sit up! It's meal time,' he growled, like a wild animal.

What? What was the meal for? Our farewell party? Our welcoming party? But where was Yee Bing? Where was he . . .?

'Here's your afternoon meal,' the gruff tone continued. 'It's twice daily, 8 am and 4 pm. The toilet is in the corner beside the bed. Here's the pen and paper, so you can confess!' He slammed the meal bowl onto the ground and threw the writing material towards my face.

I picked them up, hurled them back at him and screamed, 'Confess for what? Let me out!'

'Fuckin' bitch! How dare you!' he roared, and seized my hair with one fat hand, slapped my face with the other, and threw me to the ground.

They say, 'A dead pig is not frightened of the boiling water.' Indeed! When my head dashed against the concrete floor by the meal bowl, I picked the bowl up and flung it at his head.

'Fuck! Fuckin' bitch!' he screamed, as the burning hot meal splashed all over his face and blood began streaming from his forehead.

About five or six hulking policemen rushed in with their electric sticks. 'Fuckin' psychotic! You've only just come off the EST (Electric Shock Treatment), and you're already violent again! Fuckin' bitch – send her back!' they yelled. The punches, kicks and electric sticks hit me like a barrage of shellfire and I was knocked into unconsciousness . . .

When I came to, my wrists were handcuffed together and attached to the bedhead. A soft hand was gently stroking my forehead and saying, 'Guo Sheng, can you hear me? Nod to say "Yes" . . . Guo Sheng can you hear me? Open your eyes to say "Yes" . . .'

I struggled to wake up and heard the voice cry, 'Yes! She is reviving! Yes! Oh, thank you! Thank you our Chairman Mao! Thank you our Communist Party! Thank you our Great Leader Chairman Mao! Thank you! Thank you!' the woman cried in her excitement, thanking Mao and the Party over and over as though she had completely forgotten that Mao had died ages ago.

When I finally managed to open my eyes, I saw a middle-aged female army doctor, together with two young army nurses, standing beside my bed. 'Guo Sheng, can you hear me?' the doctor asked, with that same soft voice. 'Please! Don't pull the needles out again! You've been unconscious for almost 40 hours – I'm going to ask them to take the handcuffs off you. Your palms are as swollen as pumpkins, your fingers are like carrots! Your wrists are badly bruised and bleeding. You could end up losing both your arms! Please, Guo Sheng, open your eyes and blink "No" . . . Please, Guo Sheng, nod and say "No, I won't" . . .'

Then I heard a fierce argument:

'This isn't a police station, it's a hospital! I am the doctor! I am in charge! I have requested you to remove her handcuffs six times in the last 39 hours. Each time you have refused. Now

I'm telling you for the last time – her blood pressure is extremely low, her circulation is cut off. She could die at any minute!'

'No, woman! I have no authority to take them off. Understand? She's fuckin' violent! She deserves to be dead!' was the gruff response.

'Okay! You win,' replied the doctor. 'But don't forget to tell that to Commander Yee and his wife. Don't forget that I have been sent here to give her emergency treatment at Commander Yee's orders: "Do not allow her to die!" Now she could die at any moment.'

After a short silence the gruff voice resumed. 'Fuckin' violent psychotic! I'm taking your cuffs off now! If you break my mate's skull again I'll use them to chain you to death! Fuckin' psychotic! Do you hear me?'

Soon the soft voice called me again. 'Guo Sheng, we're going to clean your wrists. If it feels sore, scream out, it's good for you . . . Afterwards we'll bandage them for you, then you won't get an infection. Can you hear me Guo Sheng?'

'Doctor Yu, shall we move the needle down a bit in case she pulls it out again?' asked one of the nurses in a very low voice.

'No,' replied the same soft voice, 'I don't think that will be necessary. You see, when we arrived here her arms were handcuffed already – who knows if she really pulled the needle out herself or even if she was violent?'

'How long have they had her like this?' interrupted the other nurse. 'From the look of her injuries I think it would be at least a week.'

'I really don't think we have to worry in the meantime,' the doctor reflected soberly. 'She won't be able to move her arms for at least a day or two.'

Then I heard her whisper to the nurses, 'She seems to have

220

come right now. We must report to Commander Yee. I will leave you two here for a while. I want you to make sure you observe her very closely. If anything abnormal happens call me immediately!'

'Yes, Doctor Yu.' both nurses answered simultaneously.

After Doctor Yu had left I heard the nurses holding the following whispered conversation:

'Do you think she really is a violent psychotic?'

'No, I don't!'

'But why did she have the ESTs so close together? I mean — two times within three days. Rather unusual, and very dangerous too! It could have killed her!'

'I know, it's very dangerous indeed. That's probably why it took her so long to revive. It's lucky for her she's so strong!'

'Yes, she really is lucky. If Commander Yee's son hadn't committed suicide, Commander Yee and his wife wouldn't have sent Doctor Yu here and perhaps she would be dead already.'

'What? What's Commander Yee's son got to do with all this? Why did he commit suicide? Tell me!'

'Sorry, I can't. If Commander Yee found out I'd be shot!'

'Please tell me! I promise I won't tell! If I tell, I'll be shot too! I cross my heart! I swear with my life!'

'Promise?'

'Yes! I promise!'

'Cross your heart?'

'Yes! I cross my heart!'

'Swear with your life?'

'Yes! I swear with my life!'

'Well, this girl is Commander Yee's son's girlfriend — some say his fiancée. Commander Yee and his wife, however, never approved of this relationship, as she comes from a very problematic Counter-Revolutionary family. Her grandparents were Japanese war criminals, secret spies with heavy blood debts. Her parents were also Counter-Revolutionaries, sentenced to forced labour for many years. And now, she too has turned against our Party. Poor Commander Yee's son was hoodwinked by her evil intentions, and could no longer distinguish between good and evil, Revolution and Counter-Revolution. This evil girl brainwashed him then made him take her side, turned him against his parents and even persuaded him to live with her secretly! How shameful! How disgusting! He used to be very close to his parents and loyal to our Party – but now everything is turned upside down, his bright future is ruined, the family's happiness is destroyed, and all by this devil! So you see, how could Commander Yee and his wife possibly allow such bilge water, such stinking night-soil, to pollute their Pure and Red Revolution Family?'

'Oh, no! Is this true?'

'I don't know. When I look at her, it is hard to believe it. But we can't judge a book by its cover, can we? Besides, this is directly from Commander Yee's wife and her company's Human Resource Manager, so it must be 100 per cent true!'

'But you still didn't tell me what happened with Commander Yee's son. Why did he commit suicide?'

'Well, you see, there's another shocking thing. Initially she was violent towards Commander Yee and his wife, and they had no choice but to call the police. And then she was violent towards the policemen and they had no alternative but to send her here. Anyway, then her parents put extensive pressure on Commander Yee's son to find their daughter. Of course, he couldn't find her. Severely depressed, he came to see Doctor Yu. He didn't mention anything, just said that he was both mentally and physically exhausted by his heavy study load. He said he wasn't sleeping well, and asked for some sleeping tablets. Then he went back to his flat and took the whole bottle at once. Luckily, that day, just after he left, Doctor Yu attended a Party Committee meeting that was run by his mother. She mentioned to her that her son had just been to see her. His mother realised immediately that there must be something wrong and she rushed to his flat. Nobody answered the door. Then her driver broke the lock, opened the door, and found him already unconscious. Lying beside him was a note to his parents saying, "Presumably you are happy now! You have locked her up to die and now I will die too." '

'Oh, no! Did he die?'

'Shhh! Be quiet!'

'Sorry. But please, tell me quickly. Did he die?'

'No, I mean, I don't know. I guess not, but I'm not sure. You see, if he was already dead why would Commander Yee and his wife send us here? Commander Yee's command was – "Do not allow her to die!" – right?'

'But, but . . . what was the meaning of his note to his parents – "You have locked her up to die and now I will die too"? Who is locking her up to die?'

'Nobody! Commander Yee's wife said that it was all a misunderstanding. Because of her violence towards the policemen they had no alternative. They had sent her to hospital and her son misinterpreted.'

'But why would Commander Yee and his wife save her life? What a shocking devil! If she destroyed people's lives and people's families then she deserves to die.'

'Yes, indeed! But that's our Commander, with his high morality. He is so kind, so unselfish, so broad-minded. After the nightmare she put Commander Yee and his family through, he still tried to save her life. He really is worthy of our respect and admiration.'

My ears were roaring, my body was trembling, I felt as though I was suffocating . . .

I woke up again feeling as though I had just had a frightful nightmare. Through blurred vision I saw a squad of uniformed male and female policemen in front of me.

'Guo Sheng! Sit up! Get ready to go home,' I was commanded.

Home? But where am I? Who are they? What am I doing here? What's the matter with me? Why does my body hardly move?

Somebody was speaking on the phone: 'Are Guo Sheng's parents there? . . . I'm ringing from the police station. I want you to come here and pick your daughter up now. What? Her father isn't home? . . . What about you? . . . Are you her mother? . . . Are you –?'

'Hey – she just hung up the fuckin' phone! She's mad!'

'No problem! We'll leave her here – the mother can collect her ashes later,' interjected the gruff voice.

'No, we can't,' a woman interrupted. 'Remember? We were told that she had to be home today! We have to get hold of her father.'

'What? Her fuckin' father? What if her fuckin' father's mad too, what are we going to do then?' said the first man. 'Let her go back home by herself!'

'No!' insisted the woman loudly. 'We were told that we weren't allowed to let her go home by herself, and we need her parents' signature. Otherwise she isn't permitted to leave here.'

I had to wait there for another 35 long hours before Dad finally appeared in front of me. He looked extremely tired and pale; his hair had turned silver and he had lost a great deal of weight in the 11 days since my disappearance. When he saw me he was shocked into tears.

'Oh, no! Sheng! Are you okay?'

I nodded, then we walked together out of the police station.

After we had been home an hour or so, the doorbell rang. Yee Bing had arrived with a big bunch of roses.

Yee Bing? Was he truly alive? Was I dreaming again? After what I had overheard from the nurses, I could not believe my eyes.

When he saw me, he stiffly lifted a hand to push his glasses upwards and then just stood there staring at me for an age until he blurted out, 'No! It can't be! No! It can't be!' The flowers fell to the floor as he sped towards me, grabbed me in his arms and began crying, 'Sorry! I owe you too much! Sorry! I owe you far too much!' I don't think he even realised that he was in my home and that my family were all sitting in the same room.

When Mum saw him she could not control her anger. She picked the flowers up off the floor, threw them into the rubbish bin in front of him and said, 'Finished! The play is over! If you truly love her, please leave here immediately and never darken this door again! Her life is now in great danger and entirely in your hands.' Then she walked towards the door, opened it, and added, 'Please, finish off this relationship completely and leave her alone at once!'

Dad jumped up from the sofa and said softly to Mum, 'Dear, you're exhausted. Please close the door and go to your room for a rest.' Then he took one of Mum's arms and gently walked her to her room, closing the door behind her. Then he turned to Yee Bing and said, 'Sorry Yee Bing, Guo Mama is overtired. I hope you understand a mother's feelings.' Dad suddenly stopped and struggled to control his own emotions. Then he asked Yee Bing to sit down.

'Yee Bing, we really need an explanation.' Dad began. 'After disappearing for 11 days, Sheng suddenly turns up at the police station with a badly swollen face, hands, and wrists, and covered in bruises. Clearly, she has been badly beaten and tortured! But by who? Why? The afternoon she left here, she went to give you a hand. How come she suddenly disappears then turns up at the police station without explanation? Why are the police demanding my signature for her release? What has happened?' Now Dad was at the root of the matter, his brows knitted and his pleading eyes desperately fixed upon Yee Bing.

Yee Bing just stared at Dad dumbly.

'I'm sorry, Yee Bing! Is this too difficult for you to answer?' continued Dad. 'If so, can you suggest somewhere we can go to find out? Or any person we can contact? Like you, we love Sheng dearly and we cannot bear to see her tortured like this!'

'I am so terribly sorry Guo Bo-Bo!' Yee Bing finally blurted out. 'I owe you and your family an apology, especially Sheng. Please believe me – I truly don't know what's happened. I promise you that I won't come here to see you or Sheng again until I do. This is the most shameful, dirty and ugliest event that I have ever experienced in my life –' He suddenly stopped. The colour had drained from his face and sweat had broken out on his forehead. His body began to shake and he said, with a trembling voice, 'Sorry! May I excuse myself – I must leave now,' and he stood up, frowning at me sorrowfully. I could see the words almost visible on his quivering lips. But he simply said nothing and went.

I watched him leaving and I still didn't know if I was asleep or awake . . .

Nine

撞擊

Crash

After my ordeal Dong Mama and Dong Bo-Bo suggested that I spend some time recuperating with them. Dong Mama was a very warm, gentle and caring woman. Because neither Dong Mama nor my mother had brothers or sisters they became best friends from the moment they met, and indeed were like a pair of blood sisters. Both she and Dong Bo-Bo were very fond of children, but because Dong Bo-Bo had suffered testicular cancer as a teenager they were never able to have their own. However, they were happy and enjoyed sharing their friends' children and, as our godparents, had watched us grow and loved us as if we were their own son and daughters.

During the time I stayed with them, I was run-down both mentally and physically. I felt like my chest had been hit by a hammer and totally smashed. My body seemed to have lost its power to move; my wrists were extremely swollen, sore and continuously bleeding; and my face was so bruised and battered that I was too ashamed to venture out in public – in fact, I could barely even look at myself in the mirror, let alone be face to face with Dong Mama and Dong Bo-Bo. I confined myself to the bedroom all day long, and became increasingly withdrawn. My dreams had been annihilated, my courage was sunk and I began contemplating a journey to Yei-Yei and Nana's . . .

However, Dong Mama's warm heart never grew cold. She always strived to cheer me up and make me happy. Every day, she cleaned and disinfected the wounds around my wrists and put new dressings on them. Whilst she was tending my injuries, she would tell stories of their life and their marriage, and of the considerable hardship and unhappiness that they had endured over the past few decades, and their fight to survive. 'Child, cheer up!' she said to me. 'Be strong! Remember – life is just like sea waves, up and down. Today's low tide is gone tomorrow. We have to learn to accept whatever comes to us today, prepare for the worst but do the best for tomorrow, and always fight to survive! We must appreciate the opportunity we have been given to live. One day you will understand what I mean.'

But right from the beginning, Dong Mama irritated me. All I wanted was to be left alone, so I kept shouting at her: 'Be quiet!' Looking back on it now, I cannot believe how rude I was to her. But Dong Mama would just smile gently and say: 'Alright, alright – "Sue lao gen duo, ren lao hua duo" (an old Chinese saying that means "an old tree has many roots, and old people have lots to talk about")' – then she would leave with: 'Okay, okay, let's talk some other time, perhaps tomorrow, yes? Smile! Come on, smile! Say yes, and make Dong Mama happy!'

At the end of the day, Dong Bo-Bo would always come home from work with a big smile and a cheerful greeting – 'How are we today?' – and would often say: 'Child, arise! Kick away the obstacle, get your willpower back and be yourself again!'

Dad and Da-Bo also came to see me every single day. Da-Bo would knock on the door, then call out loudly: 'Open the door! Open the door for Da-Bo, "My Pride"!' Lao-Zhu and his wife came to see me very often too, and all my sisters and my brother came back specially to Guanchou to see me also.

Dad and Da-Bo then suggested that we make a visit to Li-Shan, a small mountain area very near Guanchou. So one morning we made the effort and got out of bed very early, around 3 am, to see the sunrise. It was so dark that we couldn't even see our outstretched fingertips, let alone each other. Dad was walking by my side and asked, 'Now do you understand the real meaning of the "darkness before dawn"? Don't be too despondent and always remember – "the night is always darkest before dawn, but following the dawn is morning!"' His words have remained sharply engraved on my mind ever since. Whenever my life is in difficulty, I always remember that morning, and what Dad said to me.

The day before my siblings were due to return to their homes, they said to me, 'Be strong and remember – we are "Tong Bao Shou Zhuo" (blood sisters and brother). We will never, ever, let you be alone! We will always be with you. Whenever you need us, we are always there for you. You are always our most special, proud sister! We all love you and forever.'

It was my family and my family's closest friends who turned this piece of tragic experience into one of loving memories. They made me feel so special, not just to myself, but to them all. I was deeply touched by their care for me during this most difficult and despondent time in my life. They made me comprehend the real value of flesh and blood, and friendship. Thanks to them, within a month or two, I largely recovered from both my mental and physical exhaustion. I regained the desire to fight back!

Dad then suggested that I should use this opportunity to catch up with my studies. It was just a few weeks into the university's new academic year and two weeks before the previous year's make-up examinations. Unfortunately, the university was resistant. They had no authority to let me return to class, and they had also been advised by the Guanchou police that they had to suspend my studies from 21 June 1983 and wait for a decision as well. It was suggested to Dad by an old friend at the university, Professor Tong, that I should transfer to another university 'through the back door'. We knew it was a bit risky, and that if they found out, my hard work could end up being for nothing. However, both Professor Tong and Dad agreed that even if it failed, at the least I would have learned something and I wouldn't have wasted any time. Professor Tong organised everything. I obtained entrance to the new university and they granted me permission to participate in the make-up examinations as well. Finally, Dad said to me, 'Now, everything is ready for you. Dad wants you to set your goal and be determined to achieve it. Believe in yourself and always remember that you've got more power to your elbow and you will win in the end!'

Sadly, after I completed all my studies several years later, my unorthodox transfer was discovered and adjudged an 'unhealthy tendency', and I was not able to obtain my degree. Therefore, I was only allowed to obtain a certificate from my previous university for the papers I had completed before 21 June 1983. But when Mao's China came under Deng's power everything changed dramatically. Professor Tong suddenly realised that he had not completed doing something for my late father and he requested a review of my case under the new system, and finally, I rightfully obtained my degree.

However, that first half of the academic year went by quickly. It was very challenging, and I was far too engrossed with my heavy study load to keep remembering yesterday's tragedy. My mind was fully occupied by preparing for the previous academic year's make-up examinations, and by taking in this year's study as well. That made me forget everything and, surprisingly, I thoroughly enjoyed it in the end.

Early one morning, only a few days after the Chinese New Year's festival, Lao-Zhu unexpectedly rang me from his office and whispered urgently, so low that I could hardly hear him, 'Stay where you are. Don't move. I mean, stay put! Don't go out. I'll be there as soon as I can.'

When I opened the door, he looked extremely panicked and confused. He quickly led me into the living room, and said, 'Close the door! Quick! I have to tell you something. Gooosh. I just can't believe it. Gooosh!'

'What's it about?' I asked impatiently.

'Did you know?' he kept asking repeatedly.

'Did I know what? Come on, spit it out!' I urged.

'Did you know that Da Bei (the company Human Resource Manager) was arrested by the police this morning! But the news hasn't been broken to the staff members yet, only the executives,' he replied breathlessly, with a shocked expression.

I was shocked too – I couldn't believe what I had just heard. 'What?' I asked incredulously. 'Please say that again – and slowly and clearly.'

'Da Bei was arrested by the Guanchou police at his home early this morning,' he repeated.

'Why?'

After a pause he replied, shaking his head, 'Truly, I don't know . . . nobody in the company knows anyway.' At this point he fixed his gaze on me sharply and I could see a realisation slowly dawning in his eyes as a chill of dread ran down my spine . . .

A week or two later, early one morning, I received an unexpected phone call. It was the Chairman of the Communist Party Committee of the company, Lao Lee, the previous

Director of Finance. He asked whether it was convenient for him to pay a visit to wish me a very happy New Year. It seemed that the news was about to be officially broken . . .

When he arrived he said, 'We have recently been advised by the Guanchou Police that Da Bei has been arrested for stealing top-secret papers. Special investigators were sent into our company's head office to conduct a further probe. Several very serious cases of misconduct were uncovered, and we believe that you were one of these cases. Thus, the urgent circular note that he sent out on behalf of the company Party Committee on the 21st of June last year has now been withdrawn.' Here he stopped, and stared at me intently for a while.

I didn't know what to say.

'Anyway,' he carried on, 'your name has now been cleared – both internally and externally. Da Bei has been thoroughly disloyal and dishonest in his leadership of our company Party Committee, and we are extremely ashamed of his actions against you.'

Again I didn't know what to say, so he continued, 'Today I have come on behalf of the Party Committee of the company to make a most sincere apology to you and your family. You are highly respected by all our staff members, team leaders, executives, and both the Party members and non-Party members of the company, and it is acknowledged unanimously that you have displayed integrity beyond question. Our staff needs you, our company needs you, and our Party's Revolutionary cause needs you. We sincerely wish that you get well soon and we look forward to seeing you back in your post when you are fully recovered.'

And with that, he went. Meanwhile, I remained fixed on my seat and spent the rest of the morning thinking I must have dreamed it!

The same afternoon, I got another unexpected phone call.

It was our company's Director, Lao Chen. He urged me to allow him to see me as soon as it was conveniently possible.

When we met, he was unable to give me any proper greeting. All he could do was jabber, 'Ridiculous! What else can I say? I am terribly sorry to hear what a dreadful time you have gone through! Ridiculous!' Then he added, with his hands open widely, 'But what else can we do when there are two chains of command at the top of the company? It's absolutely impossible to accomplish anything, but more than simple enough to spoil everything!'

Lao Chen was of course referring to the Communist Party Committee and the Administrative Executive of the company. This was the way Communist China ran all state enterprises, with two groups of people controlling the same company. However, the majority of the Party people knew next to nothing about management or administration – in fact, some of them didn't even know how to write their own names! Their major responsibility was for the company's political affairs, and as political affairs were paramount in Communist China's management system, it was these ignoramuses who held the balance of power. The administrative officers, on the other hand, were not necessarily members of the Communist Party. The majority of them were educated people, but before any decision was made they had to consult with the Party people first. Thus, they were always struggling, frustrated, and always got the blame!

'We are the firefighters, they are the bureaucrats!' he continued. 'They hold their "Red Passports" (slang for identifying a Communist Party member – sitting on their "Red Chairs", waving their "Red Batons", and blowing their "Red Whistles", were similar expressions), and if we do well, it's *their* brilliant leadership! But if anything goes wrong, it's contrary to our Party Revolutionary cause and has been intended to disrupt and destroy our Party, our nation, and our country! Oh goodness me! How can we win . . .?'

'Listen, Stubborner (as he always called me), I am much older than you and know far more than you do. Please listen to me and make sure you keep your mouth shut and never try to fight with them politically – you will never win! Listen to me, and don't be too stubborn! Be cautious and remember – in this society, self-defense is everything. None of us can afford to be framed politically. It's suicide!' He suddenly stopped and stared at me sorrowfully.

I just sat there numbly, staring back at him, and still wondering whether I was awake or not.

Once again he continued, 'Actually, today I came to beg you to come back to work urgently as the fire is singeing the eyebrow! As you know very well, our company's expense-to-income ratio has always been as good as that of our leading competitors and certainly up there with the best. But, for some unknown reason, this year we've slipped to last. The Inland Revenue even cut off our staff's annual bonus payment as a result of the company's losses, and this morning an urgent report arrived on my desk advising me that our staff's salaries were dishonoured yesterday for insufficient funds! The new Head of Accounts didn't even know there weren't sufficient funds and let the salaries be dishonoured! What can I say? Should I cry or laugh? It's bloody ridiculous!'

I was shocked too. 'Who is this new replacement?' I asked. 'Is he an accountant?'

'I was told he was a knowledgeable accountant, a financial expert. Oh yes, and he is a loyal member of the Party for sure! And this morning somebody told me that he is Da Bei's wife's brother. Goodness me!' Lao Chen almost screamed.

He frowned at me for a while, then said, 'I know it's probably far too much for you to absorb in one day. What about we make an appointment? Then you could have some time to sit down and have a good look at all the monthly financial reports he's produced and see exactly what the problem is; then we could discuss it afterwards.'

To be totally honest, I really didn't know what response to make to Lao Chen. I was utterly dumbfounded.

'Sorry, I shouldn't be pushing you so hard!' he apologised. 'I fully understand your current situation and I really should let you have a think first . . . Why don't we talk it over some other time?'

And I walked him to the door without a word.

Lao Chen was a very sincere, reasonable and straightforward Director, and a general favourite in the company. I had worked very closely with him from the time I was appointed his Director of Finance. He was always willing to foster the young members of his staff and I thoroughly relished being a member of his executive team. But at this state it seemed far too rushed, too risky, to start back at work straight away. Especially under the current circumstances, when nobody knew exactly what had happened. The mystery of Da Bei's arrest – all rather dramatic and dreadful – filled me with fear, anxiety and apprehension. Thus I obtained another medical certificate, which enabled me to have a further three months off work. Then I began to work some mornings, took lots of work back home, until eventually I was back working 12–16 hours a day.

At the first meeting Lao Chen called with the executives and the new Head of Accounts, I spotted the problem at a single glance over the financial reports. Almost 40 million yau, at the time worth US$24 million, now worth only US$6 million, of our merchandise inventory was buried in our annual account balance sheet – this was almost three times higher than usual. To my knowledge, the average monthly merchandise inventory should have been round 10 million. The executives were aghast, while all the Head of Accounts could offer was – 'Really? Unbelievable!'

But it was not a joking matter! Because of this fundamental neglect, after their whole year's hard work our blameless staff members ended up losing their 13th income payment (in other words, their annual bonus payment) from the Inland Revenue, which all employees are entitled to receive unless the company is broke. The 13th payment is usually the biggest portion of an employee's annual income, accounting for around 25–35 per cent of their salary, and possibly more. It's purely dependent on the company's current expense-to-income ratio and the turnover tax paid to the Inland Revenue.

After that meeting I felt that, as Director of Finance, it was my duty to give a clear answer to my Director, to our executive team, and to all of our company staff members. And so I set to work. I visited our branches, our buyer (the State Trade Department), and even our competitors. I found that each of our branches had thousands of yau worth of raw materials and products stockpiled in their warehouses. The main reason was that our product's popularity had been dramatically reduced by a shift in buyer focus from quality to price. As Guanchou's living standard was much higher than that of other cities and the countryside, the cost of labour was impacting on our competitiveness as well. A further problem was that our branches all operated independently from our head office and had tried to come up with their own remedies to the downturn. Thus, some of them had changed the product's raw material from high-grade to lower-grade silk to reduce the manufacturing costs, and other branches had imitated them – except they changed the raw material completely and used a cotton and polyester blend instead of pure silk to further reduce the costs in order to beat the others. Finally, the undercutting upset the rest of the branches, so they decided to simply buy the goods from other manufacturers instead of manufacturing themselves, to reduce the cost still further and beat them all!

In other words, one ship steered east, another steered west, and the fleet lost direction completely while gaining extra competitors – ourselves! This civil war had exhausted all our branches, until finally, the bargainer – the State Trade Department – threw out their last dirty card: they coerced our branches into further reducing their prices and then turned around and purchased from our competitors, allowing all our goods to sit there and wait to perish!

In my belief, there are always ways to transform a situation from disadvantage to advantage. In our current situation, a new administrative system was imperative – the branches' marketing needed to be centralised under the command of our head office. Then, under this new system, we had to put our focus into seeking opportunities to establish cooperative hand-embroidery processing factories in the countryside to reduce the cost of labour.

After the massive task of researching and investigating the problem, dissecting and analysing it, I finally produced a report of recommendations and suggestions to rectify the situation. Although my plan met with initial resistance from the majority of our executives and branch managers, and even our buyers, nevertheless, it was backed up by our Director and the minority executives. We were also surprised to see our company's Communist Party Committee Chairman, Lao Lee (the previous Director of Finance), strong in his support. Then Lao Chen decided that I should make a presentation of it to all the company's executives, branch managers, heads of department and staff members. We also put on a special one for our Yue-Qiu head office, Inland Revenue and the State Trade Department. After these few presentations, the majority of the executives and our branches changed their minds and agreed that my solution was the best one to help U-turn the company's fortunes. We also received endorsement from our Yue-Qiu head office and Inland Revenue, so then our buyers had to follow and accept our new system. My suggestions were put into effect immediately and in their entirety.

In June 1984, after my last three months' medical leave had expired, I was appointed as Marketing Manager to the Director of the company. Publicly, I responded very enthusiastically; inwardly, I had come to the decision that being a career woman was probably the best, and the only, solution for my life. However, since my inhuman detention, and especially after I found out that Yee Bing had made an attempt on his life because of his parents' cruelty towards me, I found my love for him had grown even deeper than before. I wanted to be with him always and I was certain that he felt the same way.

But ever since the day Yee Bing walked out our door he never returned to my parents' house. Either he felt he could no longer accept my mother's rudeness and was too humiliated to see the rest of my family and friends, or else he felt that my mother was merely worrying that she was going to lose her baby daughter. My mother always said to her friends, even in front of Yee Bing, that I was her only loving child. Later, I found that Yee Bing had written to me almost every single day during that period. Sadly, I never received a single letter. I don't know why and frankly I don't want to.

Because Yee Bing could no longer accept his parents' coldness and cruelty either, it was impossible for him to live under the same roof as them. He found himself another flat and lived separately from that time on. However, I worried that he might not be taking care of himself properly. I had so much feeling for him, as the only child of the family and as someone who had never lived alone. It seemed far too hard for him to both take care of himself and look after the household affairs. So I asked my best girlfriend A-Ba-Du and her fiancé to help me look after him while I accustomed myself with my new job.

I had known A-Ba-Du since we came back from Ku-Shan in 1973 – she was A-Yee Nana's neighbour's child. She was the eighth child in her family, so she was simply called A-Ba-Du, which means number eight. She was also the baby, and the only daughter of the family. She had seven brothers, all rather tall and big, who were the absolute overlords of that neighbour-hood. When we first arrived, the neighbours were always bullying us – until A-Ba-Du asked her brothers to help out. We had been very good friends ever since.

Not long after my new appointment, Yee Bing's cousin and his wife made a special trip from Yue-Qiu to Guanchou to see us, on behalf of Yee Bing's parents. They said that they felt terribly sorry about all that had happened to us and they wished that both Yee Bing and I could make an effort to forgive and forget. They told us that Yee Bing's parents were unwell, especially his mother, as they much regretted the big mistake they had made. They claimed that they did not do it on purpose and were purely used by others. However, they wanted to make a formal apology to both of us, if we wished. They hoped Yee Bing could forgive them and return to them immediately. It was as clear as crystal to me that in fact this so-called apology was not to the both of us, but to their son only!

Yee Bing then replied to his cousin and wife: 'If you two come to see us, you are most welcome. If you two come to see us on behalf of them, I will say to you – "Out, Cousin! We never want to see you again!" Please understand, this is no trifling matter – you cannot so wilfully make a mistake one day and withdraw it the next! Everybody has only one chance to live. How many of their mistakes can we afford? We have had enough! From now on, Sheng and I have no wish to hear a single word from that pair of cold-bloods! We are finished with them completely!'

And indeed, their relationship was finished completely, and has been ever since.

My new job's primary responsibility was to seek out opportunities to establish hand-embroidery processing factories in the countryside. Because I had the strong support of the Director, I was quickly able to recruit 21 staff to join me. I then divided them into three groups. One focused mainly on the northeast, one on the northwest, and the third on the southwest provinces. I assigned competent managerial and technical support staff to each group. We spent exactly one month together deliberating and discussing, drawing up our plans, and formulating our policies. We worked very closely and extremely hard – 12 to 16 hours a day, seven days a week. Once our drafts were approved and implemented by the company's Communist Party Committee, the Administrative Executives and Inland Revenue, we swiftly established 46 new cooperative processing factories in only 14 months. In no time at all our company's costs were almost cut in half and its annual output was double what it was before. By the end of the first financial year, our company's loss had turned into a gain. The following financial year, its profit and tax turnover was right back up to the top among the hand-craft industries. Telephone calls and letters of congratulation flooded into our offices from our branches, Yue-Qiu head office, the State Trade Department, Inland Revenue, and even our competitors! My ideas had saved the company. Yesterday's dismissed traitor, today's hero! During those two and a half years, I continuously won high praise for my performance – both within and outside the company. In November 1986, I was promoted to Deputy Director in charge of marketing and financial matters. Three months later, I was promoted to Chief Director of Marketing to the Chairman of Yue-Qiu head office. But I declined. Privately, I had already made other plans for my future.

During those two and a half years, I still had my studies to attend to, so I worked extremely long hours and all weekends; I worked, worked and worked until I dropped to sleep. Very often, I didn't even bother to go home; I stayed at my office overnight and then carried on the next day. Sometimes Dad would ask me to make an effort, to have an early night and to come home for dinner with them. But when I did go, Mum seemed like a stranger at our dinner table and we always ended up eating in dead silence.

Yee Bing and I hardly saw each other throughout this time. Occasionally he would ring me at work, but often while we talked over the phone, I would fall asleep. My life during those years was overloaded and exhausting, but Yee Bing's own existence was rather empty and aimless. After he finished his Masters degree in 1984 he had absolutely no motivation to start working. Instead, he decided to undertake another two years' studies towards his PhD. But two and a half years slipped past and he still struggled to complete his first half-year's papers!

At the end of January 1986, just before Chinese New Year, I had to attend an annual conference and prize-giving ceremony on behalf of our company in Yue-Qiu head office. I was also specially invited to give a speech on how we made our U-turn – titled 'Turning Loss into Gain' – at the conference.

The day Yee Bing saw me off at Guanchou airport, he begged me with tears in his eyes, 'Sheng, please change your job quickly! Please! I can no longer bear living without you. Please, do understand that I want no other person but you in my life! I need you, not others! I need your love, I need your support

. . .' He held me tightly and whispered in my ear, 'Say yes, it's our last separation. Please say yes! Yes? Yes . . .?'

I was speechless, and rushed off, not knowing what to say.

The conference lasted only one day. However, I had decided to take the opportunity to stay with Dong Mama and Dong Bo-Bo at their new home in Yue-Qiu for a further three days. At the end of 1984, Dong Bo-Bo had been promoted to head of a Yue-Qiu psychiatric institution, and I had not seen them since their move and missed them both very much – especially as communication between Mum and I was almost dead. But with Dong Mama I could still have the kind of mother and daughter talks that Mum and I had lost. Mum was too much an authority figure – always the Paramount Commander.

After my speech at the conference, many people came up to congratulate me. The Chairman of the Yue-Qiu head office had especially arranged my transportation to Dong Mama's and came to see me off in person. However, to my great dismay, he placed his lips on mine and kissed me softly, saying, 'What a beautiful, brilliant, bright, capable young woman. I want you to stay in Yue-Qiu alongside me for ever! I want you to be mine – my assistant, to assist my career, and my –' He suddenly stopped and seized me tightly, like a wild animal! I was shocked into tears, but he was undeterred. My painful realisation of the vulnerability of being a single career woman was far beyond expression. My need for Yee Bing's support was greater than ever.

When I walked into Dong Mama and Dong Bo-Bo's after the conference, still shaken by my encounter with the Chairman, both of them hugged me wildly and kissed me with joy. Dong Bo-Bo took me by the hand and said, 'Sit down! Sit down! Sit down! Our Big Hero, please do sit down and tell us everything! Everything! And everything!'

'Yes, child. Everything! We must be told every, every,

everything!' Dong Mama joined in excitedly, reaching out to grasp my other hand.

'Child, tell us how life has been treating you since we left? We think of you all the time. We miss you so much! Obviously you have won back your career – we heard this from your Dad already. Now we want you to tell us about your personal life. How is your Yee Bing? Has he finished his studies? Does he still love you? Do you still love him? Do you still love each other? Are you still loyal to each other? Are you still frightened to be together? Do you still avoid mentioning your marriage?' Dong Bo-Bo asked, almost running out of breath.

This sense of family warmth touched me, as something I had missed badly in recent years. I assured them that Yee Bing and I still loved each other, and were loyal as always. I explained that there was no significance in the fact that we had not married yet – that I had simply not had the time because of my demanding workload. I told them that Yee Bing begged me to change my job as he could no longer bear to live without me. That he'd said he wanted me in his life, but not the others, and he needed my love and support badly. I also told them that I felt rather guilty that I had decided to spend these three days with them instead of him, but I believed that he would understand. Finally, I told them about the conference and the Chairman of the Yue-Qiu head office, and again we shared some tears . . .

After I had told them about my unwelcome experience after the conference, Dong Bo-Bo stared at me in silence. Then Dong Mama blurted out anxiously, 'Was the Chairman wanting you to marry him? Has your Yee Bing got somebody else in his life?'

'Yes, he was. But Yee Bing doesn't,' I assured her quickly. 'He would never do that kind of thing to me, nor I to him. I've known him almost eight years now. He really is someone on whom I can totally rely and trust – and beyond question! There is no need to worry, Dong Mama,' I comforted her.

'But what does he mean by saying he can no longer bear to live without you and he wants you in his life "but not the others"?' Dong Mama queried anxiously.

'Oh, no! It means nothing at all, Dong Mama! He is very lonely and he misses me, that's all.' Again I answered quickly and with utmost confidence.

Both Dong Mama and Dong Bo-Bo looked at me and nodded solemnly before we silently went in for dinner.

The next morning, Dong Mama came into my room and gently woke me up. She sat on the edge of my bed and said, 'Child, Dong Bo-Bo and I could hardly get any sleep last night. We think you and Yee Bing should get married as soon as possible as we believe you are both living in a state of self-torture! Do you understand? Self-torture!' she said repeatedly, and her tears gushed out.

After breakfast, Dong Bo-Bo called me into the living room and said, 'Child, do sit down. Today your Dong Mama and I want to have a serious talk with you.' And Dong Mama chimed in, 'Yes, child, we do.'

Dong Mama opened the conversation. 'Child, listen to Dong Mama. Your Yee Bing is right that you should change your job immediately and enjoy a normal family life. You cannot live your life forever working 12 to 16 hours a day, seven days a week. You see, not just your Yee Bing, but also your father hardly sees you at the dinner table. He is really worried about you! You cannot let your career completely take over your life! You will burn yourself out. I mean, everybody needs to be cuddled, to be loved, to be cared for, to be secure! Why not you two? Why?'

'You must wake up and stop this.' Dong Bo-Bo said sternly. 'Let's have this long sentence cut short, child. Today we want you to do two things for us, for your Yee Bing and for yourself. And you must do them now!' he insisted adamantly.

'Firstly, we want you to write a resignation from your

current job and apply for a new job. And secondly, we want you to share these three days with your Yee Bing, so you must change your ticket and return to Guanchou by tomorrow morning and get married straight away! Under the circumstances, we believe it is best that you do not solicit your stubborn mother any more. But your father is looking forward to this marriage and so are we. Now, all you have to do is get married in the way that you planned three years ago, and Dong Mama and I will ring your Dad and Da-Bo to let them know what you have decided.'

'Will you do that for us all?' Dong Mama asked anxiously.

I was struck dumb.

'Child, you must say yes! You have to do it! It's your whole life, your future! Please listen to Dong Mama. Life is so short – if you cannot catch up you will be lost for ever.'

'Child,' Dong Bo-Bo continued, 'you can analyse a business situation precisely and save a company with an idea. Why not do the same thing with your own life? I agree with your Dong Mama – you cannot let your career take over your whole life! What if Yee Bing was working in exactly the same way as you are now? How would you feel about your life? Full? Or empty? What's really missing in between?'

'Yes? Yes? Yes! She *will* do it for all of us, for her Yee Bing and herself,' Dong Mama said, her hands reaching out for mine.

Looking at them I thought: Yes, this is really what I want. Suddenly I felt as meek as a lamb. I nodded, agreeing mutely with everything they had suggested.

Dong Mama jumped up from her chair, hugged me and cried, 'Yes, child, Dong Mama knew you would do it! Yes, child!'

Dong Bo-Bo then said solemnly, 'Let us pray for Sheng and Yee Bing's tomorrow.' Then he continued, 'This afternoon, Dong Mama will take you to Hei-Fen-Jei (the main commercial centre in Yue-Qiu city) and she will organise your dowry.' Dong Bo-Bo suddenly stopped here and looked at me with a big smile, then added, 'Come here, come here, child. Let Dong Bo-Bo give you a big hug,' taking me in a tender fatherly embrace.

'Actually, that is all nonsense!' Dong Bobo resumed. 'No need! A real dowry is true love. But your Dong Mama wants to do it for your mother. So let her do it and let her feel happy. We believe that one day your mother will be happy about it too. In fact, neither your mother or Dong Mama had a mother at their own weddings.' He broke off here and his eyes misted over with sadness.

Dong Mama's father had been an illustrious personage, a well-known landlord in South China. In 1945, aged 24, after her graduation from DaXin University in Guanchou (a well-known Catholic university), she became engaged to her classmate – the son of a humble owner of a small grocery store – Dong Bo-Bo. Her parents were shocked by her 'horror engagement', which was extremely contrary to 'Men Dang Hu Dui'. It involved a great loss of face and was most shameful for her family's dignity, and especially for her father's social station and reputation. Thus, Dong Mama's parents announced in the newspaper that they were breaking off their relationship with their daughter and disinheriting her. Five years later, in 1950, the Land Reform Movement was launched and her entire family was judged guilty of the most heinous crime of being the biggest landlords in Zhenxi and the country. Her father was sentenced to death straight away and her mother committed suicide. Her three brothers were sent to forced labour and they died one after the other, in less than two years. Dong Mama was the sole survivor.

Dong Bo-Bo paused as he recalled their history, then continued, 'You see, when Dong Mama and I were married, all she got was a piece of public notice. Yesterday she was a daughter of the rich and famous, today a daughter-in-law of the poor. At first, we had to share a room with my family and sleep on the floor. In those days, women were not encouraged to work, but Dong Mama found work as an office junior, with extremely poor pay, to support my studies. Later we found ourselves our first cozy home – only six square metres, which was all we could afford. We squeezed ourselves into a narrow single bed for almost six long years, until I finished my medical studies. During those six years I had no money to buy myself textbooks, so Dong Mama sold her jewellery to buy them for me. We had no table for my studies, so Dong Mama's back was my table, while she slept. We had no rice bowls, so we ate from the pots. We had no money to buy Chinese New Year's presents for people, so we simply did not go out to celebrate. However, we had the purest love in our hearts. We struggled together; we fought together; we survived together; and eventually we achieved today's happiness together. I love Dong Mama as my flesh and Dong Mama loves me as her blood. Forty years after our marriage, we know that it was the best thing we have ever done in our lives!'

That afternoon, Dong Mama took me to Hei-Fen-Jei and bought Yee Bing and I a feather duvet, a couple of duvet covers, pillows, pillowcases, sheets and a woollen blanket. Then she said to me, 'These are for beginning your new life. Dong Bo-Bo and I had nothing like this when we got married. And I've missed this in my life. One day you will understand what I mean. It is a mother's love. In this world every girl is supposed to have it, so why shouldn't you?' She stopped suddenly and tried to control her emotions, then kissed me softly.

'But don't be too upset' she added. 'One day your mother may change her mind and redo it for you. Then you shall be the luckiest girl in the world – you will have received two dowries!'

By the time we arrived home it was dark already. When we opened the door, a warm, soft candlelight spilled out. The dinner table was well set and the wine glasses were full. Not waiting until we had closed the door, Dong Bobo greeted us cheerfully, 'Ah! Here they are! My dearest girls, let's have a celebration!'

I stood in front of a pair of glowing red candles and looked into their flames avidly. In my mind, I could see thousands and thousands of people dancing, waving, clapping hands and cheering. They were shouting with joy and congratulating Yee Bing and I – it was a dream come true! I knelt down in front of them and invoked God's blessing in a special prayer. I was happy for both Yee Bing and myself. Finally God had given his consent and our dream was coming true! My heart was pounding, my blood was boiling, and I wanted to share my joy with the whole world!

Both Dong Mama and Dong Bo-Bo agreed that I should not ring Yee Bing up that night. As it was a very special thing in both our lives, we must discuss it in person. But I called all my sisters and my brother. They were so glad and also grateful for the wonderful encouragement Dong Bo-Bo and Dong Mama had given me. They all congratulated me for making such a great positive decision and assured me that, once the news had broken, they would all come back to Guanchou to share a big celebration with Yee Bing and I, as they blew kisses to me down the phone.

That night was the longest night that I ever spent in my life. I could not close my eyes a single minute! I counted the time, wished for the morning to come, and cried with all the overwhelming emotions. What a time I had been through since Yee Bing's birthday in 1983. Dream, nightmare, and now dream again! However, I was not frightened to dream once more, as my confidence in our true and faithful love had grown ever deeper through the years.

Early the next morning, Dong Bo-Bo helped with my packing. Then Dong Mama gave me a big hamper of dumplings and roast duck (which she knew both Yee Bing and I loved), a bottle of MaoTai wine and a pair of red candles, and said, 'Child, they are for your celebration dinner. God bless you!'

Then Dong Bo-Bo passed me a red envelope and said, 'Child, here is something from us for you two to set up your new lives with. Good luck! And God bless you always!'

I looked at them gratefully and truly did not know what to say. In the end I simply said, 'Dong Mama, Dong Bo-Bo, I will remember you always.' Sadly, it was the last time that I saw Dong Bo-Bo. Six months later he died from a heart attack. A year later Dong Mama passed away from the loneliness of being without him.

It was Sunday 2 February 1986. The plane departed on time, at 7 o'clock in the morning. It took about three hours to get to Guanchou. But those three hours seemed longer than three years!

Yee Bing was a real night owl. He read and studied during the evenings and slept in the mornings. When I arrived, at 9.45 am, I was sure that he would still be in bed and fast asleep. I wanted to sneak into his bed, lie down beside him, hold him, kiss him, then say: 'Yes, Yee Bing, I will marry you and be your wife – now, and for ever!'

Before I unlocked his door, I took my shoes off and tried to make no noise. Walking on tiptoes, I slowly, quietly, crept towards his bedroom. My heart was pounding, my breath was short. Within just another few seconds, his blood would flow into my blood vessels, and mine would flow into his; he would be mine, I would be his, and we would never be parted again!

'Oh God! My God . . .' I cried inwardly.

Yee Bing lay naked on the bed, his arms clasped behind his

head, eyes wide open and fixed upon the ceiling. Beside him lay the bare body of A-Ba-Du, her arms wrapped tight around him, in a deep sleep.

My ears roared; my head pounded; my heart smashed; my body froze; my hope quenched; my dreams burnt down and I longed for death . . .

Ten

一個失敗者的自白

A Failure's Confession

That afternoon, I aimlessly went back to work. When I walked in the gate, there were huge streamers hanging across the company yard: 'Welcome back Guo Sheng!' 'Welcome back our model worker! 'Welcome back our pacesetter!' 'Welcome back our advanced worker!' I stared at them numbly, tears streaming down my face. Was this my reward?

When I walked into my office, there was a letter sitting on my desk. It was from the disgraced Human Resource Manager, Da Bei. It said:

Comrade Guo Sheng,

Congratulations to you and me!

My miscarriage of justice has been clarified and reversed and I shall be back at my post in two weeks' time (after the New Year). I thought you might be interested to know and looking forward to it. I am sorry I left your mystery case unsolved for such a long period, almost three

years! I promise you, this time I will make an all-out effort to clarify
the situation, as it matters to both of our political lives!

Da Bei

2 February 1986.

The memories of his dreadful shouting flooded back over
me:

'You fuckin' bloody Counter-Revolutionary! You insult our
Great, Glorious, Right Communist Party of China! Remember
your words! You'll pay for them! Our Party has an account to
settle with you! Our Party won't let you go!'

Then visions of his insidious and treacherous face welled up;
the uniformed stretcher-bearers; the ambulance; the
policemen; the windowless police jeep; the narrow wooden
bed; the small, dim, damp, stinking room; the thick iron door;
the formidable guard; the meal bowl; the pen and paper; the
blood; the electric sticks; the blows; the kicks; the hospital; the
army doctor; the nurses; the big drip bottle; the handcuffs; the
throng of uniformed police officers . . . A chill ran through me
and my whole body began to shake as I realised the letter was a
signal – Da Bei's battle was about to recommence!

'What am I to do? What am I to do?' I asked myself
repeatedly. Then the answer came clearly to me – *Leave! Leave
China at once!*

And true to my predictions, as soon as Da Bei was returned
to power he targeted me as his enemy instantly. I was accused
of using Yee Bing's parents' power to concoct the 'miscarriage
of justice' that had made him suffer for three long years. With
unremitting hatred, he continually challenged and attacked me
politically, putting my life in ever increasing danger.

After that New Year I attended a business conference in Beijing, where by providence I met a kind-hearted New Zealand couple who became my sponsors and helped me obtain a three-month visa to learn the English language.

However, it took me more than a year to get out of the country. The most difficult task was to obtain my passport from the Guanchou police, as this had to be approved by the company where I worked. Fortunately, Lao Lee, the previous Director of Finance and now Chairman of the company's Communist Party Committee, lent his personal assistance. Then there was the matter of the legal document establishing a relationship to the sponsors, who had to be my relatives. Here I was helped by a contact of Da-Bo's, who forged a document which said that the sponsors were my godparents. After that, in case the police read my correspondence, I had to address them as godparents and sign myself as their goddaughter. Looking back, I think they must have been quite perplexed by this form of address.

Finally, in 1988, I quietly abandoned the only life I'd known and moved to an English-speaking country – New Zealand – without a word of the language. Upon my arrival, I immediately wrote three letters. The first was to my parents. I told my mother that I would never marry Yee Bing, that I would never return home, and that I never wanted to see her again. I said to my father that I was terribly sorry to hurt him, but that I hoped he would understand and accept my decision in time. My second was to Yee Bing. I told him that I had married and wished him to get married if he desired. The third was a letter of resignation to my company director.

And so I cut my ties with China altogether and embarked on my new journey in New Zealand.

Two years later, in November 1990, I suddenly heard from my sister that Dad had lung cancer. I didn't know what to do. I was horrified at the prospect of returning and felt that I could not possibly face it. But I also knew clearly that a fight with cancer is generally fatal. I missed him badly. I rang him almost every day and dreamed of him every single night.

One day, Dad said to me over the phone, 'Don't worry, Dad is now getting peace. You take care of yourself and take care of your mother for Dad. Dad believes that one day you will understand your mother completely. Please listen to Dad – get married, have a safe home and let Dad relax.'

The next night, I dreamed that Dad had died at 10 o'clock in the morning. When I awoke, my tears were still pouring down and my pillow was soaking wet. Alarmed by this ill omen, I went to a fortune-teller, who told me that a close relative was now departing. With ringing ears and a sinking heart I left and called home immediately. I couldn't believe the mournful news – Dad had passed away at 10 o'clock that morning! Dad had lived only 80 days from the time his illness was diagnosed. My heart was broken . . .

After the loss of my father, I developed severe stomach discomfort. I could hardly eat anything, and my weight slipped down from 54 to 36 kilos. I was worried I might have cancer too. But after a thorough examination, my doctor couldn't find anything wrong with my health. In the end, he asked me what it was that I really wanted to do. I replied that I wanted to have a stable job and a secure life in New Zealand. He prescribed me a three-month supply of painkillers and sleeping pills, which I could take as required, and also advised me to try and find employment, as stress could be the cause of my present symptoms. We would then see how I was getting on in a few months.

I did try, and it worked. I found a job and my weight increased dramatically. Just like the time we came back from Fei-Yn, I had to sew myself a new skirt almost every day.

Then, at the end of September 1993, more bad news came

from home. My mother had had a heart attack. She was critically ill and in hospital. Sensing Dad's will, I hurried back to China. One of my sisters met me at the airport and took me to see Mum straight away. When I got there she was half unconscious. Her face was extremely swollen and covered with an oxygen-mask, and she was on an intravenous drip. I stood beside her bed, my tears streaming down. I wanted to say 'Sorry Mum!' but she wasn't able to hear me.

That night, after she took me back to Mum's flat, my sister had to rush off to catch the train back to her husband and daughter.

Mum no longer had the flat to herself, as after Dad's death she had been compelled to take in neighbours. She only had one room and had to share the kitchen facilities. Our living room had become the common hallway and was piled up with furniture and junk. Dust and filth covered everything. The flat was now nothing like when I was at home.

Six months after my father's death, Mum had received an unexpected letter from the Guanchou Conglomerate of Industrial Enterprises informing her:

... The flat you currently occupy is the local Conglomerate of Industrial Enterprises department staff hostel, for staff members only. Previously, it was for the convenience of your late husband, certainly not for his family, and especially nowadays, as local government has great difficulties with housing matters, we believe you will understand and cooperate with us. We will therefore arrange for you to move into a new flat in another part of the city. You must vacate your flat by xx date.

The new place was a single-room flat located many miles away from where we lived, and there was no shopping centre, no hospital or transportation whatsoever. Mum was shocked.

She wrote back, saying that in her understanding our flat had been provided in compensation for our old house. The Conglomerate of Industrial Enterprises replied:

. . . We have no time to carry on this argument. It is a matter of conscience. If you cannot help our Party government solve the great housing shortage problems then, according to the housing policy, you are only entitled to one room, not a whole flat. You must empty the rest of the rooms by xx date.

When the time arrived, the authorities sent three very rough men, claiming they were there to help with the shifting. My mother asked to see their boss first, but of course, it was impossible! In this society, there was no law but rule! The rough shifting damaged many of her possessions and she couldn't bear it. She collapsed and became very ill.

After my sister left, I stood alone in the middle of Mum's room and looked at Dad's photo hanging on the wall. I stared numbly at his smiling face and just couldn't believe that I would never see him again. Dad had been gone for two years, and now Mum was dying I felt so desolate and alone. It was far too hard for me to stay there.

Fortunately, Da-Bo was on the staff of the hospital. So the next day he discussed it with the administration, and the nurses put in a spare bed beside my mother's. I stayed there with her for another six days until I had to return to New Zealand for my job. That departure was the hardest in my life. I thought I would never see Mum again and I would never have a home to return to.

Before I left, Da-Bo arranged an urgent meeting with our family. He told us that Mum didn't have any serious health problems, but that it was purely an emotional breakdown, brought about by the upheaval and the callous treatment she had received at the hands of the authorities.

A few months after I returned to New Zealand, I was surprised to hear from my sister that Mum was making a speedy recovery. I then arranged for her to come to New Zealand for a special holiday. Nine months later, at the beginning of 1995, Mum arrived. She looked so much better, and I was happy beyond belief to see her again. When I met her at the airport, I cried and couldn't stop saying, 'Mum, I'm so sorry!'

Mum stayed with me in New Zealand for six months, and during that time I was surprised to discover that she was no longer as I remembered her – an authority figure, lacking in warmth and understanding. She really was a thoughtful, caring and deeply loving mother.

When we were children, our love for our grandparents was far deeper than that for our parents, especially our mother. Mum hardly gave us a hug, or a kiss, or spent any time with us. We lived in the same house, but we hardly heard her voice or saw her each day. She never bathed us; she never dressed us; she never combed our hair; she never took us to school or picked us up afterwards; she never helped us with our homework; she never lay on our beds and read us a story before we went to sleep. I remember vividly, asking Mum to go with me to the school end-of-year ceremony when I knew I would be receiving a prize. She just said, 'No – either grandma or grandpa will go with you.' I was extremely disappointed and cried, but she simply walked away. After that ceremony, my schoolmates would sometimes taunt me that I had no mother. It was the most painful memory of my childhood and I could never understand why my mother didn't love us. It took me more than 40 years to find out . . .

The day my mother was compelled to leave Nana's house was New Year's Eve. Mum didn't know where to go – in fact, she had nowhere to go. She walked aimlessly from street to street until she exhausted herself. Eventually she found a quiet street corner, put down her belongings, sank to the ground and began to sob, desperately missing Song Lao-Shi's comforting words of advice. Suddenly she felt something pushing against her back. She turned and realised she was leaning on a door and that the people inside couldn't get out. She stood up quickly and said, 'Sorry,' as an old couple came out. They stared at her for a while, then asked, 'Who are you looking for?'

'Sorry, I'm not looking for anybody. I thought it was a wall,' she replied, and tried to slip away as soon as possible. But they followed her, and she overheard their whispering.

'This is very strange, this young girl must be very rich – look at her uniform, it's Chong-Sa's,' said the woman.

'Yes, I know. Very few can go there,' the man replied.

'But why is she crying at this early hour of the morning? She sounds like she is in despair,' the woman said.

'I don't know! But what can we do?' asked the man.

'Perhaps we should find out if she needs any help,' the woman said.

'Alright, then,' the man replied.

And so they walked up to Mum.

'Excuse me miss, that's our shop over there. Would you like to rest inside for a while?' the old woman asked her.

It was a tiny fruit shop, with several tables and chairs inside the window. She sat down at one and stared out at the street through the glass in a dead silence.

The old couple sat down opposite her and said, 'It's too early for anybody to be coming in yet, particularly today. It's New Year Eve. We're going to have breakfast. Do you want some?'

Mum just sat there staring at them for a while, then said, 'No thank you, I haven't got any money.'

'Oh, we don't sell breakfast here, this is just for ourselves,' the man replied.

So they set some plain rice porridge and pickled vegetables on the table and the old woman said, 'You don't mind these kinds of things for breakfast, do you? We are very poor, and we cannot afford to have milk and bread for our breakfast like you rich people.'

Then the old man passed the rice bowl to her and said, 'Please help yourself.'

Mum wolfed her porridge down at once and helped herself to a second, third, and even fourth bowl. Poor thing, she hadn't eaten since the day she left Song Lao-Shi's, almost three days before! As she ate her breakfast, her tears streamed down. Afterwards, she thanked them, and then asked whether they had any jobs for her to do.

'Are you serious?' asked the old man in surprise. 'What about your study? Would your parents allow you to work here? It's very dirty and hard physical work! Every day you have to lift and carry box after box of fruit in and throw box after box of rubbish out; during the winter you have to wash box after box of fruit in freezing cold water; during the summer you have to peel off sugarcane skin with a big knife one after another; you have to work from very early morning till midnight; you have to work seven days a week, 366 days a year – if there is an extra day in the year,' the old man blurted out in a single breath.

'Where are you from? You don't have a Guanchou accent. Where is your home? Where are your parents? Are you a Chong-Sa student?' asked his wife.

Mum burst into tears and said, 'Yes, I was. But I can no longer go there.'

'Why not?'

'My father has just died.'

'Where is your mother?'

'She died a long time ago.'

'Where are your grandparents and siblings?'

'I have none.'

'Where is your home?'

'In Wei-Zo. But not any more.'

'But your father must have been a very rich man and left you plenty of money?'

'No, none.'

'Where are you living in Guanchou?'

'I was in a hostel.'

'No – last night?'

'I've just got off the train.'

The two old people stared at her in bewilderment for a long time, then the man said, 'If you like, you can stay here. There will always be plenty for you to do. But we cannot afford to employ someone.'

'No, no, you don't have to pay me, I only need a place to stay,' said Mum quickly.

The old couple had seven children, all daughters, all married, and none of them living in Guanchou any longer. They were very hard workers indeed, and very kind too. They worked all day long, and ate in the shop and lived in a very small room about two or three minutes' walk away. They had no spare bed, but they joined some wooden fruit boxes together to make a single bed and kept her in the same room as themselves. They treated Mum just like their own granddaughter.

After the new school year began, every day Mum saw her classmates passing the shop. She would rush and hide out the back until they had gone by. Winter passed, spring came and went, and summer arrived. The weather was getting hotter, and the shop grew busier. Lots of customers stopped in for fruit and cold drinks, and to get out of the strong sun for a while. The shop was packed with customers each lunchtime. One day, when she was flat out serving customers, she looked up and there was Dad standing right in front of her. She burst into tears and ran out the back.

At long last, Dad had found her! There were no school holidays to separate them now; no tears seeing her off; no impatient wait for her mail to arrive; no long wait for her to return. He could see her every single day! And she could see him. And so their surreptitious love resumed.

When the weather grew cooler and the shop was not so busy, Dad brought her all the course textbooks and she began to study again. But one day, after he had promised to take her to the movies, he did not turn up. She was terribly disappointed, and could hardly believe he would do that to her. But the next day he still did not come. Or the next. Or the next. She started to grow worried. She asked the old couple if she could ring him at home, but there was no reply. Mum was in despair.

A week later, Dad suddenly reappeared and said, 'I'm sorry I broke my promise to you but –' He stopped and tears streamed down his face.

'What happened?' asked Mum anxiously.

'My sister accidentally died.'

'You mean she was killed in an accident?'

'No, I mean she accidentally became pregnant, and when she gave birth she died from a severe womb haemorrhage.'

Not waiting for him to tell the whole story, Mum asked in her penetrating way, 'Where is this child?'

'Still there.'

'There? Where is there?'

'In Quan-Sa – the place she and her boyfriend chose to have this secret birth.'

'What? Still there? Alone?' Mum's voice shook. 'Is this your rich family's rich blood? Rich hearts? Rich minds?'

Dad was silent.

She then added with tears, 'At least I had a mother for three years. But this child has none!'

'Yes, I know. I want to do something. But —' Dad suddenly stopped.

'But what?' asked Mum impatiently.

'I need your help,' Dad finished.

'Of course! If there is anything I can do for this child, I will!' Mum answered firmly.

'Could we get married now and keep this child with us?' asked Dad, staring at her beseechingly.

Marriage? She was stunned into silence.

That night Mum just couldn't close her eyes for a second. She knew what life without a mother was like. She felt she could not possibly bear to see any child become a shadow of her own life. Next day, she offered Dad her help.

Nana had just lost her daughter, so Dad was now even more important to her than before, but she couldn't let her son rush into marriage for this particular reason and ruin his bright future. Mainly however, she still couldn't allow her precious son's blood to mix with such low, cheap and poor-quality blood!

But to Yei-Yei, this new life was part of his blood, and he could not bear to abandon the child. He also felt he could see the richness of his future daughter-in-law's inner world and even the richness of her blood! He agreed with and supported Dad's idea and then arranged a meeting with Mum in person.

He said, 'Child, marriage is a serious issue. You can't get married because of pity for this child. You must get married because you truly love each other. I am so proud of my son's rich heart. And now, the richness of yours. I feel so ashamed of ourselves. Our pockets might be fuller than yours, yet our minds are far emptier!'

Now that the father and son were in unity, Nana had to

compromise. So she said, 'But I have to consult the fortune-teller first.'

She then asked Dad for Mum's birthday. Dad told her that he didn't know the date of Mum's birth, but he knew she was about three years older than him. This was too much for Nana, and she burst into tears and cried, 'No! This marriage can't go forward! She is three years older than you. Once she has walked into this house, this house will have another disaster. We have had enough! We can't afford any more. No! Full stop and finished!'

An old Chinese saying goes – 'Man older than woman by three years, the family will prosper and boom; woman three years older than man, the family will have disasters and death.' But in fact, Mum never knew her exact age and date of birth.

To help them, Yei-Yei decided to make up Mum's date of birth and managed to convince Nana that Mum was actually three years younger than their son. And, according to the fortune-teller: 'Such a life shows a remarkable talent. The free, uncaged bird will shake the world!'

Nana was compelled into silence and convinced to condone the marriage. Mum and Dad then brought the baby Da-Jei home and she became their first child, and Yei-Yei and Nana's first granddaughter. In order to cover up the story however, Nana insisted on moving to a new house.

Now, because Nana had just lost her only daughter, Mum grew very important to her. She wanted to train her to be a real lady – 'a real Guos lady' – like her daughter! So, after their marriage, Dad still carried on with his studies, but Mum stayed at home. However, when she asked whether she could do anything to help with the baby, the answer from Nana was: 'No! You have no need to learn that, it is far too early. I want you to learn how to dress yourself properly first!'

Then, whenever

she sat, Nana would say, 'Please learn to sit properly — Straight!';
she walked, Nana would say, 'Please learn to walk properly —
Slowly!';
she talked, Nana would say, 'Please learn to talk properly —
Quietly!';
she laughed, Nana would say, 'Please learn to laugh properly —
Don't show your teeth!'

Mum was shocked into submission. She had never had a mother before, and never knew what a mother was really like. She was brought up in the boarding school — what kind of food she was served, she ate; what kind of clothes she was given, she wore; and now, what kind of life befell her, she accepted!

Nana sent her to a special school to learn how to put on make-up, how to dress, how to walk, how to smile, how to laugh, how to shop, how to meet people, how to respect people, how to respect her husband, how to respect her parents-in-law, and how to, and how to, and how to . . . be 'a real Guos lady'!

A year later, when Mum gave birth to her first child — a daughter — Nana found a wet-nurse for the baby before Mum was even out of hospital. In Nana's opinion, because Mum was brought up in a boarding school, she had never had proper foods and her milk wouldn't be strong enough to nourish her grandchild. Besides, Nana couldn't possibly imagine how my mother could manage with a baby. So the baby had to sleep in the wet-nurse's room, and be supervised by herself. When Mum went and bought some new clothes for her daughter, Nana sniffed and said, 'Oh, no, these are not for my granddaughter! Go, quickly, take them to a charity for me please!'

And so it was with her second granddaughter. However, after the arrival of her third granddaughter — myself — Nana grew impatient. She craved a grandson. So, for the first couple of days, whenever I cried, Nana simply shut her door and did not even want to hear.

This was a very exciting moment for Mum and she began to learn to nurse me. Then, one day when Mum was bathing me Nana came in to watch. Suddenly she gave a shout of excitement — 'Look at her little face! Look at her little body! Look at her little arms! Look at her little legs! Look at her little feet! Look at her little hands! Look at her little fingernails! Look! Just like Jinren!' Then she quickly helped Mum dry me and carried me off to her room. She called the photographer to come and take a photo of me, and then put my father's and her own baby photos together beside mine, and nobody could tell the difference between them. As Nana believed strongly that if a girl takes after her father, next would come a brother, she kept me with her until I had almost turned four. And, indeed, four and a half years later, Mum gave birth to her fourth child – a son. A grandson for Nana! But Mum had had enough. She gave up as a mother, left the household and became a voluntary civilization propagandist of the Neighbourhood Committee till 1966, when the Cultural Revolution was launched.

While Mum was with me in New Zealand, I decided to obtain some formal qualifications in my new country. Both Mum and the manager of the company where I worked encouraged me in this goal. So, in March 1996, I resigned and began attending a Diploma in Accounting towards ACA studies.

From the moment I started my course, I thoroughly enjoyed it. I received an 'A' for my first assignment and all my old 'can do' confidence came back. This was the one goal I'd been dying to achieve ever since my arrival in New Zealand.

Then one night an unexpected phone call came from China. It was my previous managing director from the Guanchou hand-embroidery company. He said that the company was in crisis once more, but seeking to reverse its fortunes by extending into the Australian market. They were looking for a liaison person, with the job title – Senior Assistant to the Managing Director for the Chinese side. The successful applicant had to be able to speak both English and Chinese and have a knowledge of the hand-embroidery industry. This position would be based 50 per cent in Australia, 50 per cent in China. The starting salary was AU$65,000 per annum (equal to NZ$75,000), plus transportation in Australia and a three-bedroom flat in Guanchou. The cost of transfer would be covered by the company as well. The director considered me the best candidate for the position.

I was utterly stunned by the offer. The day I had abandoned my life in China and landed in an English-speaking country without a word of the language I had awoken to the realisation that language is power. I had felt like I was blind, deaf and dumb and my whole life had turned upside down. Yesterday's deputy director in charge of marketing and finance, today's cleaner and housekeeper. It was one of the most upsetting experiences of my life so far.

Before I quit my job to attend university I was a fund administrator, earning only NZ$28,000 per year; a new university graduate had a starting salary of around NZ$35,000. This job opportunity meant I would receive an income which would secure both my mother and myself a comfortable life as well as my future retirement. Furthermore, I dreamed of getting my career back – I was a typical career woman! It was my lifeblood! I couldn't pass the opportunity up. I decided to go. I was convinced that the dawn had finally broken on my life's darkness, and that a bright morning was now beckoning me on.

So, in May 1996, I gave up my studies, farewelled all my New Zealand friends and shipped my furniture to Sydney to commence my new position. But I found, to my horror, that the Chinese authorities had refused to approve my appointment, as I was now a New Zealand citizen. The job offer depended on me reverting to Chinese citizenship. I was not prepared to do so, and abandoned the job offer and returned to New Zealand at once. Because I had abandoned it voluntarily I had to cover all the expenses myself.

When I returned I didn't even have money for my new flat's bond. I had to rush into a job straight away. A few months later, when I had gathered some savings, I decided to resume my studies. Sadly, the diploma course no longer existed – it had become part of the four-year degree. The only option left for me was to take on the MBA (Master of Business Administration) course. It took two full-time years to complete at a cost of around NZ$20,000–$25,000, which was far beyond my financial capacity. Once again, my dreaming had turned into nightmare . . .

I became unwell once more. Initially I suffered from sleeplessness, and then it was discovered that I had cervical polyps. I had a small operation but they returned. Then I developed severe and constant abdominal pain. My doctor warned me that it wasn't a good sign, and later recommended a hysterectomy. That meant that I would never be able to have a family. I just couldn't face it!

Which way was I to choose? To take the risk of having a family in due course? Or to have the operation and regain good health and quality of life? I decided the latter, and my operation took place shortly afterwards.

Unfortunately, at the time of the operation my doctor found some endometriosis cysts between my intestine and bladder which he was unable to remove – to do so would have endangered my life. Consequently, the physical pain continued and still impacts on me, both physically and emotionally. Sometimes I can't even walk, the discomfort is so extreme.

I went back to my GP and consulted several other specialists. The answer was always the same – there was nothing the doctors could do about it. They told me that things might improve when I went through the menopause, around the age of 50, and the endometriosis cysts would gradually disappear by themselves. But at this stage I was only 44 – I had to suffer for another six long years, maybe even longer! Once again, my heart was broken!

The day after I came back from my doctor for the last time, I lay on my bed staring at the ceiling and asked myself where I had gone wrong. Why did I always suffer? Why must I keep on suffering? And why did I linger on here? If the Yang world's (earth's) abandoned orphan is the Yin world's (heaven's) darling pet, why was I lingering in this Yang world?

It was a cold winter's night. I lay on my bed, recalling the past 44 years. I felt the weather was cold; the air was cold; the people were cold; the world was cold; my heart was cold; and my blood and body were ready to be cold. It was time for peace! I was dying to bury my head into my Yei-Yei, Nana's and Dad's chests, to pour it all out . . .

And then the telephone rang. With empty heart and a darkened mind, I was slipping away already, but the soft voice on the other end of the line fought to recapture me and bring me back. It reached my heart and reawoke me.

'I want to have a good cry,' I told her. And I did.

Later, the same soft voice called me again. She was deeply concerned about me.

' . . . I've been thinking – there are a few things I would like to suggest for you to do. One is yoga, it's a very good exercise for your current health condition. And the other thing I remember is that you are very good at sewing, right?'

Not even waiting until she finished I blurted out, 'How about writing?'

'Writing? Wonderful!' she enthused, 'In fact, I know a bit about writing, and I am more than happy to help you with it! You can start at once, and send it to me as you go, and I will correct your English and send it back to you the same day . . .'

And so that one unexpected contact blew the thick clouds away and brought the sunshine back into my life! Without it, I would never have been able to give birth to this tale from my heart's core – a labour which has kept me busy, filled my empty heart, helped me recall, enriched my soul, and completely transformed my life ever since.

At the beginning of 2001, another bundle of bad news came from my Er-Jei (second sister), that my San-Jei (third sister) had advanced ovary cancer. Di-Di also had diabetes and kidney failure. They were all in hospital. And Da-Jei had had a stroke a half year before. My heart sank.

My family, my sisters and brother are the most important thing in my life. I was desperate to see them. However, at this stage, our company was restructuring and I was faced with redundancy. Therefore, finances worried me the most. Since my father's death I had voluntarily taken on full financial responsibility for my mother. The financial tightness really held me back. I was at a loss to know what to do.

Again, the same voice aksed: 'What is the meaning of life?' It woke me up. I made my decision, set my feet, and one month later I returned home. Di-Di was getting better. But my San-Jei was critically ill. All her hair was falling out, she was suffering, struggling and fighting with the chemotherapy.

One day, as I sat beside her, I asked, 'When Dad was ill, did he suffer like you are now?'

San-Jei's tears streamed down, and she replied, 'No, Dad's suffering was far, far worse than mine! When the doctor found that Dad had cancer, it was spreading all over his body and into his brain. Before he passed away, his eyes protruded out and he lost his sight. He could hardly hear anything. His neck swelled so much that he could not even breathe, let alone eat or talk. One morning he suddenly got his hearing and voice back, and was able to sit up and talk. When you rang, it was the last time he heard or spoke. His final conversation was with you.'

After a brief rest, she continued, 'After Yee Bing received your letter he went to Dad's office, threw it on his desk and said, 'If you want to help yourself you had better get your daughter back to me as soon as possible!' And he turned and went.

According to San-Jei, a month later Yee Bing found himself a managerial position in the Guanchou Conglomerate of Industrial Enterprises – the head office of the thermos factory – and he became Dad's boss. Three months after Yee Bing's posting, Dad's line-manager passed a letter to him from the thermos factory addressed to the General Manager's Office. It said the company was verging on a financial crisis and they needed an expert to save the factory. It urged Dad's immediate return to the factory to help out in the emergency. After Dad's return they gave him an office and named it the Finance Management Office. Dad was the only manager and staff member. In fact, the factory's management was in perfect order – Dad had absolutely nothing to do! Eventually, Dad realised that he had lost his job, and at whose instigation. He was shattered. His job was the only thing that had kept him going after the sufferings of the Cultural Revolution.

San-Jei had to stop and struggle with her emotions before she could tell me the rest of the story.

'Dad didn't want you to find out and we all had to promise him that we weren't going to tell you. He didn't want to discuss it with the family or close friends either, not even with Mum. In fact, he hardly talked to anybody from then on. Every day he took two or three packs of cigarettes to work with him. After dinner Mum would go to bed, and Dad would sit there with another pack of cigarettes. In the morning Mum would find mountains of cigarette butts piled up on the coffee table. Mum wrote to us, begging us to come back home. We sat in front of him in tears, pleading with him to stop. Dad wouldn't reply.

'About a year later, Dad started to dry cough. Mum made several appointments for him to see the doctor, but he refused them all. Half a year later, in the middle of November, Dad's cough got worse. Each time he coughed, there was lots of blood. Once more, Mum made an appointment for him to see the doctor, but he refused this too. Then she urged all of us back home again and we forced him to go to the hospital, but it was far too late. The doctor found that he had advanced lung cancer, and 80 days later he passed away. Our hearts were broken!' Again, San-Jei stopped and struggled with her feelings.

'I'm sorry! I'm so terribly sorry to tell you that!' she continued. 'Oh, Dad! I'm sorry Dad! I've broken my promise to you before your coma . . .'

I was utterly devastated by her account!

The next day I went straight to Yee Bing's. Wu-Ma answered the door. She was so surprised to see me. Recognising me at once, she said, 'You haven't changed a bit! How long has it been since I last saw you?'

'More than thirteen years,' I replied, and followed her in.

She called out excitedly, 'Xiao Bing, guess who's here?' However, when she reached the living room door, she stopped suddenly, looked inside, and then looked at me with her head shaking and a dull expression in her eyes and simply walked away.

Yee Bing was leaning back on a sofa, his feet propped on the coffee table. Wine bottles and glasses were piled up all around him. A teenage girl with a very tight, low-cut and almost see-through top, was sitting on his knee sharing a cigarette. The room was filled with smoke.

When Yee Bing saw me he was shocked. He jumped up at once and said, in a trembling voice, 'You? Is it really you? Is it real? Is it true? Am I awake or daydreaming?'

Naturally his young lover wasn't very happy about my interruption, so we arranged to meet at a hotel the following day.

When we met he ordered a bottle of whisky, then just sat there, his head drooped, as drink followed drink in a dead silence. I sat opposite him watching, not touching a drop.

Eventually I opened the conversation in a shaking voice. 'So . . . So . . . What have you to say for yourself?'

His head snapped up. He set his lips and stared at me, still silent.

'Answer me! What have you to say for yourself? What did you do to my father's job? What have you done to my mother's flat? What have you done to my family over the last thirteen years? Answer me! Answer me at once!' I began to lose my temper.

'What? Don't you remember? Have you forgotten everything they put us through? They distorted our life! What I have to say is this —*What I have done, they deserve!*' He was shouting at me and thumping his fist on the table.

But he didn't stop there. 'No! I'm too soft! I'm far too soft! The old bitch is still living! She should be dead too! She deserves to die! You tell her to just wait!'

I was totally appalled by his outburst. I had never realised he was such a cold-blooded being!

He scowled at me and continued, 'I love you! I still love you! Do you understand? You walked out without a word! Later you wrote to me that you were married and shocked me into

272

rushing marriage myself. A month later, I found I was mistaken. She wasn't the person I dreamed of and it was too late. The whore was already pregnant. Five months later, she gave birth to our son. A month later, we divorced, and she remarried straight away. She left the baby with me and never returned. Five years later, I heard that you had returned home and I discovered that you had never been married at all! My heart was wrenched! I tried to find you, but it was too late. You had left the country already. I then set up a plan for you, found you an interesting job, a flat to redeem the past, and tried to get you back. But you were cold as stone, and refused it all. You –'

At this point I interrupted him, yelling, 'Right! Right! You love me! You still love me! Because you still love me, my father deserved to die? Because you still love me, my mother deserves to die as well? Because you still love me, my whole family deserves to suffer? Can the past be redeemed by an interesting job and a flat? Where is my father's job? Where is my mother's flat? Where is my family's security and safety? Where is my family's happiness? Can my broken heart be redeemed by this dirty trick – an interesting job and a flat! You! You couldn't bear your parents' cruelty but you did exactly the same thing to my parents. Like father, like son!' I was almost breathless with rage.

I paused, and continued more coldly, 'Have you ever thought who the person who destroyed our relationship really was? Who the person who drove you into your marriage really was? Who the person who made your wife remarry straight away and leave the baby child with you really was? Can't you remember what your parents did to me? Can't you remember the morning you shocked my heart into numbness? Can't you understand that *YOU* are the person who destroyed our relationship? Can't you understand that it's you and your parents who destroyed my life and drove me out of the country?'

273

Yee Bing sat there in silence, tipping back the whisky and growing steadily more drunk.

Eventually he slurred, 'Oh, honey, let's forget about the past . . . Don't you know I miss you baby? Don't you know I love you honey? Let's get married and have a family straight away,' he leered, then put his arm round my shoulders and tried to kiss me.

'Get away from me! Don't touch me! I don't want your dirty hands touching me ever again!' I screamed in disgust.

Yee Bing casually withdrew his arm and laughed as loud as he could. Then he raised his glass, took a big mouthful of whisky and spat it all over my face!

'Bloody fuckin' whore! You thought you were the purest woman in the world! Bloody fuckin' idiot! You don't even know how to appreciate my favour! I've got power! Have you got any? I've got money! Have you got any? I've got a child! Have you got any? I've got dozens and dozens and dozens of young girls who love me! Do you have anybody? You bloody fuckin' old bitch! Don't overrate yourself! My current honey, my current baby is only 18, and she loves me dearly! Bloody fuckin' idiot! You never knew how to appreciate my favour, my money, my power! Bloody fuckin' whore!'

Then Yee Bing tottered to his feet, calling and waving to a young waitress. When she came over he put one arm round her shoulders, reached his other hand into her blouse, kissed her and said, 'Aren't you beautiful? Baby, let's go and get married and have a family straight away . . .' The horrified waitress screamed and struggled out of his drunken embrace.

The hotel manager rushed up and said, 'Excuse me, ma'am, you must take him out of here immediately!'

Shocked into tears, I hurriedly asked a waiter to call a taxi and help put him into it. Then I tried to quickly slip away. But it was too late. The taxi driver said, 'Excuse me, ma'am, if you aren't getting in too, I won't take him home!'

Again, Wu-Ma answered the door. She shook her head angrily and yelled at him, 'Shame! Shame! Shame! Xiao Bing you're drunk again! Your poor mother is dying, and you drink all the time and never go to see her! You dally with young girls in front of your 13-year-old son! He now refuses to study and plays on the game machines in the recreation centre all day long! You drink all the time and take no responsibility! I am getting old, I shall die one day. Who is going to take responsibility for this child then? If your father knew he would jump out of his coffin and slap your face! Xiao Bing, Xiao Bing! Shame! Shame!'

I simply said goodbye to Wu-Ma and walked away, but I couldn't block Yee Bing's cruel words ringing in my ears.

I've got power! Have you got any?
I've got money! Have you got any?
I've got a son! Have you got any?
I've got dozens of young girls who love me! Do you have anybody?

No! I had none!

They say that when wine is in, truth is out. Yee Bing's drunken taunts had left me feeling like a total failure. That night, after I got home, I fainted no sooner had I got in the door. My overwrought emotions could take no more . . .

The following day, I made a special trip to Hei-Zi – Nana's native place, where Yei-Yei, Nana and Dad's graves are – to visit Dad's grave. I knelt in front of it and sobbed my heart out. 'Dad, I'm sorry! I let you down. I let the whole family down. I made Mum suffer and struggle in her twilight years. I made the whole family suffer. Dad, I'm so sorry! It was me! It was me who

275

shortened your life! It was me who killed you! Dad, I owe you! I owe the whole family! I deserve to be punished . . .'

In the middle of May, I brought Mum with me and returned to New Zealand. A friend had organised her friend to meet us at the airport with a warm welcome, a bunch of flowers and a basketful of food for our supper and took us home. When we opened the door, there was another bunch of flowers on my desk, with a most touching note – 'Welcome home, Sheng!' Beside them was a delicious home-baked cake, all from my kind-hearted landlord. The flat's air was freshened, the hot water was on, and the mail had been collected and neatly stacked, all courtesy of a warm-hearted neighbour. I was deeply touched and felt a real sense of belonging in New Zealand for the first time since I left China.

That night I just couldn't close my eyes. I recalled those past 22 years, since I met Yee Bing in 1979 – my 22-year-long dream. I recalled all the things that had happened to me – what Yee Bing's parents had done to me, and what I had gone through. And later, what he had done to my father's life, my mother's life, and my family. I just couldn't stop my tears.

Early the next morning, the phone rang. A soft, warm voice greeted me from the other end: 'Welcome home, Sheng!' It was my friend. I didn't know what to say, or where to start, and could only manage to get out – 'He has changed, he has totally changed!'

'Has he really changed, or was he like that all along?' she asked.

Her question stirred my deepest thoughts . . .

Will water turn to stone?
Will the sun rise in the west?
Will the earth orbit the moon?
Will the lamb turn upon the wolf?

Will a kind-hearted man turn to cruelty and persecute people to death?

Sadly, it took me 22 long years to understand the heart of such a person. Twenty two long years to wake from my delusion . . .

Epilogue

My tale draws to its close. One word respecting my experience of my life in China, and one brief glance at the deep feelings I still hold towards my homeland and then I will be done.

By now, almost half a century of my life has passed, and as a human, facing the failure, I have regrets. The greatest mistake I have made is not just that I have wasted such a long period of my own life, but that I have also injured my entire family – both physically and emotionally. Despite their understanding and forgiveness, my profound guilt and self-blame will remain with me for ever. The depth of this feeling is beyond expression. However, I have learned to live this life – even if it is the hard way. They say, 'failure is the mother of success', and I have always believed –

You get let down, you learn;
You get frustrated, you learn;
You get lost, you learn;
You struggle, you learn;
You fall, you learn;
You are brokenhearted, you learn;
You grieve, you learn;
You scream, you learn;
If you are alive, you always learn until your breath ceases!

Compared to China, life in New Zealand has helped me realise how fortunate people are to live in an egalitarian, democratically free country. In other words, after Deng's Economic Reforms, the Chinese economy is unquestionably prospering and booming, yet some of the high-ranking Party officials are still abusing their power, are corrupt, and give and take bribes. Before Deng's Economic Reforms:

> They've got the power, they've got the rights;
> They've got the power, they've got the law;
> They've got the power, they've got the rule;
> They've got the power, they've got the key to grow it into their
>   own power!

Now:
> They've got the power, they've got the right to grow money!
> They've got the power, they've got the law to grow money!
> They've got the power, they've got the rule to grow money!
> They've got the power, they've got the key to grow it into their
>   own money and lord it over others!

The past is forever with me and I remember it all. Some of these tragic memories are more than 30 years old, yet I still remember them vividly. I have been in New Zealand for almost 13 years. This country has become my second homeland and I am so proud of being a New Zealand citizen; partaking of this country's equality, freedom, democracy, rights, security and safety. However, I am still a Chinese descendant. My veins still flow with Chinese blood. Despite everything, I still love my people, I still love my motherland, and I still love to sing this song:

My Chinese Heart

Homeland is in my dreams,
Many years away from my Motherland.
Yet, they can't change
My Chinese heart.

Western clothes are on me,
But my heart is always a Chinese heart.
As my forefather stamped me with
The Chinese brand.

Yang-Zhi River, Great Wall,
Yellow Mountain, Yellow River,
Are important to my heart.
And anytime, anywhere
Is the same love in my heart.

Blood flows into my heart,
It surges Chinese sound.
Despite me living in a foreign land,
It can't change my Chinese heart.

. . .

Western clothes are on me,
Homeland is in my dreams . . .

And now my dream is that, one day, all my people can be like me and the four million other New Zealanders who fully enjoy the equality, freedom, democracy, rights, security and safety to which they are entitled . . .

Farewell

Farewell my dearest reader. Some of these memories were hidden inside me for many, many years. As painful as it has been to relive them, you have enabled me to pour out my heart. I thank you for sharing my tale. I sincerely wish you well and I look forward to meeting you in the near future.

Guo Sheng
Auckland
9 September 2002

Acknowledgements

Now my book is completed I have to acknowledge my special debt to Penguin Books (NZ) Ltd for having made *Tears of the Moon* possible. They have brought to the task an extraordinary wealth of knowledge and a profound understanding of the cultural and emotional needs of others. I feel privileged to have been associated with such people as Geoff Walker, editors Mike Wagg and Rebecca Lal, marketing manager Penny Hartill and cover designer Dexter Fry. I am also thankful to other staff members who have worked on the book in its various stages.

To my initial editor Mandy Hager and reviewer Adrienne Jansen, I owe a very special gratitude for their skills and comments. The invaluable friendship they have given has deeply touched me.

I would also like to extend my deepest gratitude to Creative New Zealand. I feel fortunate to have met their convivial, thoughtful and helpful Rosemary Wildblood. The strong support, encouragement and advice she has given are very much appreciated, they gave a focus to improve my work and travel the path to completion and publication.

I would also like to take this opportunity to express my heartfelt gratitude to a kind-hearted New Zealand couple (my sponsors) and to many friends I subsequently made here – for their effort in bringing me to this country and in helping me adjust to a new homeland. Their warmth, kindness, generosity and friendship have been unique and invaluable. Without them, I would never have had the freedom and courage to pour my heart out.

Lastly, I must acknowledge that there was no possibility of giving birth to this book without *'that cold winter night's call, and the caller'*, my special Jewish friend. With sincerity and consideration she helped and encouraged me all the way through; she read all my early drafts and shared my bitterness and sadness. I therefore do hope that my deepest appreciation is sufficiently expressed to her in our shared chapter of the book, for which I owe her a debt of gratitude that is unpayable.

Furthermore, there was no possibility of giving birth to this book without my family's entire love. Without that, this book, *Tears of the Moon*, means nothing.

Guo Sheng
Auckland, 2003